Know Thyself

Collected Readings on Identity

D1239662

Edited by
David Cernic
and Linda Longmire

PAULIST PRESS
New York♦Mahwah

DEDICATION

To Buddy
(In Memoriam),

To our parents,

*and to all others whose love
has helped us to know ourselves—
Pat, Louise, Erica, Clara, Eileen, Betty,
Joanie, Janice, Marisa, Connie, Reuben,
George, Carrie, Chris, Carol, Tim, David,
Marjorie, Ray, Barbie, Margaret*

Library of Congress Cataloging-in-Publication Data

Know thyself.

    1. Self (Philosophy) I. Cernic, David,
1941–   . II. Longmire, Linda, 1949–
BD450.K628   1987   126   87–2521
ISBN 0–8091–2872–1 (pbk.)

Published by Paulist Press
997 Macarthur Boulevard
Mahwah, New Jersey 07430

Printed and bound in the
United States of America

Contents

Preface

“**K**now thyself.” With these words Socrates started a revolution in philosophy. Instead of looking outward, man began looking inward. He found an entirely new universe. Sometimes it frightened him to enter it. Often he had difficulty in unlocking its secrets. When he did gain access, however, he discovered an incredibly rich and varied world.

Plato's introspections, for example, uncovered a collection of “forms” forgotten from some previous existence. Augustine found within himself a light from God. Kierkegaard's self-awareness unearthed a hidden spring of love. Some discoveries were not as positive. Descartes, despite finding absolute certainty within himself, had difficulty finding his way back to the outer world. Jean-Paul Sartre found only an empty consciousness, a kind of “nothingness” which needed to borrow all its being in order “to be.” Given such diversity, one must wonder what is really there within the self.

Man noticed other differences as well. Thoughts and feelings both swarm in every attempt at self-awareness, confusing the self about its primary identity. Some philosophers sided with reason. The Stoics and Aristotle, for example, cultivated objective, dispassionate thinking, believing that rational behavior, not feeling, secures happiness and peace of mind. Other philosophers sided with feeling. Freud saw pleasure as the ability of the self to express its feelings, and realize its desires and dreams in the world. Reason merely served to facilitate that fulfillment. Still other philosophers, like Nietzsche and Dostoyevsky, reveled in the conflict and contradiction that the head and the heart produce. Tension and anxiety were seen as the hallmarks of mature consciousness. Again, one has to wonder which dimension most truly characterizes the self.

Man also notices that his inner life changes. No matter how many times he considers it, it is always different. Bergson and Hesse likened the self to a stream. Flowing continuously the self never stands still. In the course of its movement, it presents a thousand faces, yet none of them occurs twice. So novel is the self at each moment, one wonders with William James if there is really one single self, or if there is only a succession of many disparate selves. But if one cannot discover the same self even once, what holds all these selves together in the same

3

succession? What provides their continuity? Is there a deeper, more authentic self hidden beneath the surface appearances linking them together into a unified whole? Is there a stable, constant, substantial self resistant to all movement? Why then is it never found? Why then am I never the same? Maybe this deeper self is itself an illusion? Capturing the self as it changes is like stopping a stream with a nail and hammer.

Man also realizes that his inner life is not wholly his own. As a social being much of who he is has been derived from others—parents, family, and friends. The boundaries between the self and others are never clearly drawn or consistently maintained. In solitude, then, he is not wholly alone; in company he does not fully relate. For one part of himself resists absorption into others, while another part resists isolation from others. The need to be an individual, someone unique and different, is as strong a desire as the need to belong, to share, and to communicate with others. Solitude and dialogue are cherished and complementary companions. Like Siamese twins they need each other in order to be.

Man notes that the present is not big enough to capture all that he is. The self is not only rooted in the past, it also is blossoming toward a future. In a very real sense, it lies behind and ahead of itself. Memory and expectation both grip the present self. The present experiences the tension of origins and ideals. The self thus appears as a project of working free from the given without disregarding it, and working toward the ideal without consuming it.

Man discovers that his life is both full and empty. It has purpose and meaning (thus full), but never absolute purpose or meaning (thus empty). There is always a sense of incompleteness or lack in whatever one does. Commitments sincerely made are often broken; purposes clearly established often dim; projects begun often remain unfinished. Seldom does one fall into absolute futility, but seldom does one wholly maintain course. Simultaneously a triumph and a failure, the self must wonder who it is.

Given the changes, the diversity, the countervailing tendencies, the often conflicting views, the triumphs and failures, it is difficult to imagine a more elusive being than oneself. The self appears to be like nothing else in this world; indeed it appears to be a world of its own. Surely it is unique. That is why philosophers since Plato have disputed its rightful place. Some, like Heidegger, recognize this uniqueness of the self, but are reluctant to allow the self to lose its "in-the-world-ness." Others, like Scheler and Berdyaev, see the self beyond the world as a transcendence, freedom, and creativity independent of all worldly concerns.

It would appear, then, that the self is a mystery—a mystery not in the sense that it cannot be known, but rather a mystery in the sense that knowing it only adds to its depth and elusiveness. The more one seeks to know himself, the more his contents change, his moods and feelings shift, his conflicts and contradictions surface. Each new awareness thus disturbs his identity, and requires a new configuration. The paradox is that instead of dispelling the mystery by exploring himself, he enhances and deepens it. The fact that he can therefore never know himself completely is not cause to lament but cause to celebrate.

The aim of this work, then, is to explore the mystery of the self. The text considers some of the more important facets of this mystery, seeking to display the self in some of its complexity and depth. It begins with what we have just been doing—searching.

The Searching Self (Chapter I) is the principal theme of this work. Searching is the primary way of beginning to know oneself. Thus in each chapter the searching self is present (indeed all selves are present in every chapter) stirring the waters of identity, and, in the process, becoming one of its faces.

Searching, however, would not even begin without the light and activity of consciousness (including unconsciousness). Consciousness (Chapter II) is the center in which objects and influences are first illuminated, sorted and synthesized.

But the self is more than a luminosity or a center of awareness. Alone, consciousness lacks the rich existential (Chapter III) texture of a real self. Choosing, willing, believing, loving, rebelling, etc. are other modes of self-creative activity which, though founded upon consciousness, add substance to its otherwise hollow nature.

Yet even the existential self is not fully mature, for existence without ideals has no orientation. Ideals (Chapter IV) allow the self to rise and expand by giving it direction and purpose, thus inducing the self to grow.

Ideals, however, are abstract and intangible. A self, therefore, even with ideals, would still not be fully mature. Needed is the concrete dimension of a person—a center which transcends (Chapter V) simple luminosity or agency. The personal self is unique and individual. It holds the ideal to itself, but at the same time imprints its specificity upon it. Searching is universal or common to all selves, yet it is absolutely singular in each of them.

However magnificent a personal self may be, consciously and existentially pursuing its ideals, it is nonetheless incomplete. For the self is still inextricably connected to and embedded in a world. Its origins are still material, its development still physical. This cosmic self (Chapter VI) realizes that it is grounded and at home in this world.

One of the principal forms of being-in-the-world, however, is with others. The self is interpersonal (Chapter VII) in nature. Other persons challenge the self and nurture its development through dialogue and communication. All searching, therefore, is co-searching; it springs from shared experience. For the best part of each self—the caring, giving, loving, understanding—belongs to others; the self is only its trustee.

Even all of the above, however, do not capture the self in its totality. As a synthesis the self seeks a consummation and effulgence that only infinite relatedness could satisfy. Indeed, the search for self is a search for God (Chapter VIII).

Ultimate self-knowledge, then, happens only when awareness reaches the level of the ineffable, and the self is awed by this encounter with its authentic being. As each synthesis progressively clarifies the self, its mystery paradoxically deepens. To know oneself is to be stunned by the depth and sublimity of one's own nature. In the exhilaration of being fully open to boundless power and freedom, the self celebrates its true humanity.

Self-knowledge, however, cannot be taught or given from without. It can only be evoked or awakened from within. Unless something begins to stir and come to life in each of us, no genuine understanding of the self will be possible. This work, then, is only a tool for such awakening. The text is self-explanatory, but it must be read in its entirety. Like the various selves, each chapter is one facet of a larger whole. Only at the end is the mystery revealed in all its complexity and depth.

I

THE
SEARCHING
SELF

A. Who Is Man?

Abraham Heschel

TO THINK OF MAN IN HUMAN TERMS

To ask a question is an act of the intellect; to face a problem is a situation involving the whole person. A question is the result of thirst for knowledge; a problem reflects a state of perplexity, or even distress. A question calls for an answer, a problem calls for a solution (from the Latin *solvere,* to loosen, to dissolve).

No genuine problem comes into being out of sheer inquisitiveness. A problem is the outcome of a situation. It comes to pass in moments of being in straits, of intellectual embarrassment, in experiencing tension, conflict, contradiction.

To understand the meaning of the problem and to appreciate its urgency, we must keep alive in our reflection the situation of stress and strain in which it comes to pass, genesis and birth pangs, motivation, the face of perplexity, the varieties of experiencing it, the necessity of confronting and being preoccupied with it.

To clarify, to study, and to communicate a problem we must put it into words, for without translating the moments of wondering into logical terms there would be no possibility of testing the trans-subjective validity of what is thought in these moments, nor the possibility of its intersubjective communication.

Yet the act of verbalization extracts the problem from the situation in which it arises. The question verbalized, however, must not be equated with the problem confronting us. The danger always exists of those moments becoming distorted and even lost in the process of translation from situation to conceptualization. Too often speculation becomes analysis-by-long-distance of sounds transmitted over a poor connection. We formulate and debate the issues while oblivious to, and alienated from, the experiences or the insights which account for our raising the issues.

The predicament of much of contemporary philosophy is partly due to the fact that ongoing conceptualizations have so far outdistanced the situations which engender philosophizing that their conclusions seem to be unrelated to the original problems. After all, philosophy was made for man rather than man for philosophy.

A question is due to knowing too little, to a desire to know more; a problem is often due to knowing too much, to a conflict between opposing claims of knowledge. A question is the product of curiosity, a problem reflects an embarrassment of knowledge.

The impulse to reflect about the humanity of man comes from the conscience as well as from intellectual curiosity. It is motivated by anxiety, and not simply by a desire to add to the sum of information about a member of the class of mammals.

We are concerned with the problem of man because he is a being afflicted with contradictions and perplexities, because he is not completely a part of his environment. A good horse, properly cared for, lives as part of his habitat and is unencumbered by problems. In sharp contrast, man is a problem intrinsically and under all circumstances. To be human is to be a problem, and the problem expresses itself in anguish, in the mental suffering of man. Every human being has at least a vague notion, image, or dream of what humanity ought to be, of how human nature ought to act. The problem of man is occasioned by our coming upon a conflict or contradiction between existence and expectation, between what man is and what is expected of him. It is in anguish that man becomes a problem to himself. What he has long disregarded suddenly erupts in painful awareness.

In our reflection we shall consider what man means to himself as well as what man means to his fellow man. The animality of man we can grasp with a fair degree of clarity. The perplexity begins when we attempt to make clear what is meant by the *humanity* of man.

What we aim at is not an analysis of a word as a semantic problem, but rather the investigation of a reality or a situation. Being human is not just a phrase referring to a concept within the mind, but a situation, a set of conditions, sensibilities, or prerequisites of man's special mode of being.

We can attain adequate understanding of man only if we think of man in human terms, *more humano,* and abstain from employing categories developed in the investigation of lower forms of life. The struggle for survival, for example, is not the same for human beings as it is for animals.

Sir Arthur Keith, a strong Darwinian, told his Aberdeen students in 1931: "Nature keeps her human orchard healthy by pruning. War is her pruning hook." According to a German general, "War is a biological necessity of the first importance, a regulative element in the life of mankind which cannot be dispensed with. . . . But it is not only a biological law but a moral obligation and, as such, an indispensable factor in civilization." "God will see to it," says Treitschke, "that war always occurs as a drastic medicine for the human race."

We are concerned with the totality of man's existence, not only or primarily with some of its aspects. Vast scientific efforts are devoted to the exploration of various aspects of human life—for example, anthropology, economics, linguistics, medicine, physiology, political science, psychology, sociology. Yet any specialized study of man treating each function and drive in isolation tends to look upon the totality of the person from the point of view of a particular function or drive. Such procedures have, indeed, resulted in an increasing atomization of our knowledge of man, in the fragmentation of the personality, in metonymical misunderstandings, in mistaking the part for the whole. Is it possible to comprehend one impulse separately, disregarding the interdependence of all impulses within the wholeness of the person?

DO WE LIVE WHAT WE ARE?

What is it that we seek to know? What does the knowledge of man aim at? What knowledge or object of knowledge do we question when we raise the question about him? What does the question about man hope to accomplish?

Man is not a *tabula rasa*. Unlike other objects, the desire to know himself is part of his being. To know himself he must first question himself, and that means questioning his self-knowing, disturbing what may be a narcissistic relationship of the self to its conceits, ingrown thinking. To raise such questions is more than to seek an approach to an answer; it is a breakthrough.

The task of a philosophy of man cannot be properly defined as a description of the nature of human being. It is critique as well as description, disclosure of possibilities as well as exposition of actualities of human being. The trend of our thinking leads us not only to form questions about human being but also to question human being. We question what we are in the light of an intuitive expectation or a vision of what man ought to be.

Something is meant by human being which involves more than just being; something is at stake in human being which is obscured, suppressed, disregarded, or distorted. How to penetrate the shell of his adjustments and to inquire whether adjustment is his ultimate vocation? We study human behavior; we must not disregard human bewilderment. We analyze expression, we must not disregard the inability to express what we sense. We know more about man's possessions than about his moods. We describe deeds; we must not fail to explore how one relates inwardly to what one does.

Do we live what we are or do we live what we have, or by what we have? Our difficulty is that we know so little about the humanity of man. We know what he makes, but we do not know what he is. In the characterizations of man, for example, as a tool-making or thinking animal, reference is made to the functions, not to the being, of man. Is it not conceivable that our entire civilization is built upon a misinterpretation of man? Or that the tragedy of modern man is due to the fact that he is a being who forgot the question: Who is man? The failure to identify himself, to know what is authentic human existence, leads him to assume a false identity, to pretend to be what he is unable to be or to fail to accept what is at the very root of his being. Ignorance about man is not lack of knowledge but false knowledge.

SELF-KNOWLEDGE IS PART OF OUR BEING

Man is not free to choose whether or not he wants to attain knowledge about himself. He necessarily and under all circumstances possesses a degree of such knowledge, preconceptions, and standards of self-interpretation. The paradox is that man is an obscure text to himself. He knows that something is meant by what he is, by what he does, but he remains perplexed when called upon to interpret his own being. It is not enough to read the syllables of a text written in a language which one does not understand, to observe and to recount man's external behavior, important and necessary as such an enterprise is. Man must also interpret them in terms larger than his inner life.

What is the right method of exegesis of human existence?

The philosopher's primary task is not merely to describe and to judge the modes and facts of man's actual behavior, but also to examine and to understand the meaning of describing and judging the modes and facts of his behavior. We obviously judge the behavior of man by standards which we do not apply to the hippopotamus. Is it not possible that our standards are unfair? Is it not conceivable that we expect too much or too little of man? Man was, is, and will always remain a beast, and nothing beastly is alien to him. And yet such an epigram, though rationally plausible, is intuitively repulsive. Is that repulsiveness intrinsic to our existence as human being? Or is our acceptance of nonbeastly standards a stratagem designed to protect our beastly instincts?

In asking about man we ask of man what he knows about himself as a human being. This self-knowledge is part of his being. Thus, knowing oneself and being a self are not to be kept apart.

Like all concrete beings, man occupies a place in physical space. However, unlike other beings, his authentic existence goes on in an inner space. Geography determines his physical position; his thoughts are his personal position. The thought we think is where we are, partly or entirely. The thought we think is the space of the inner life, comprehending it. A person is in his thoughts, particularly in the way in which he knows or understands his own self. His thoughts are his situation. His nature includes what he thinks he is.

Unlike a theory of things which seeks merely to know its subject, a theory of man shapes and affects its subject. Statements about man magnetize the inner space of man. We not only describe the "nature" of man, we fashion it. We become what we think of ourselves.

We use the term "nature" in contrast to culture, natural in contrast to artificial, to denote that which has not been changed and affected by human action, free from calculations and conscious design, completely artless, abiding in the state in which it has come into being. In this sense the natural man is a myth and a contradiction in terms, because man has become man by acts of culture, by changing his natural state.

Human nature in its pristine, uncorrupted state is not given to us. Man as we encounter him is already stamped by an image, an artifact. Human being in distinction from all other beings is endowed with consciousness of its own being, not only with awareness of the presence of other beings. Consciousness-of implies awareness of one's special position in relation to other beings. Any conception as to what I am going to do with myself presupposes my having an image of myself

It is questionable whether man's nature can be treated as "a substance" in isolation. Behavior is determined not only by processes inside such a substance, but also by forces and standards that prevail in society, by heterogeneous pressures from the outside. What is given is a complexity. The decisions, norms, preferences affecting both action and motivation are not simply part of human nature; they are determined by the image of man we are committed to, by the ultimate context to which we seek to relate ourselves. Man is endowed with an amazing degree of receptivity, conformity, and gullibility. He is never finished, never immutable. Humanity is not something he comes upon in the recesses of the self. He always looks for a model or an example to follow. What determines one's being human is the image one adopts.

Thus the truth of a theory about man is either creative or irrelevant, but never merely descriptive. A theory about the stars never becomes a part of the being of the stars. A theory about man enters his consciousness, determines his self-understanding, and modifies his very existence. The image of man affects the nature of man. Any attempt to derive an image from human nature can only result in extracting an image originally injected in it.

THE IMPLICATIONS OF BEING HUMAN

There is no substitute for the work done by the various sciences dealing with man. Yet there is an urgent need for an approach seeking to identify what is unique about the humanity of man, a task beyond the scope of the sciences mentioned above.

Behavioral sciences have enriched our knowledge of psychological, biological, and sociological facts and patterns of behavior by observation and description. However, we must not forget that in contrast to animals man is a being who not only behaves but also reflects about how he behaves. Sensitivity to one's own behavior, the ability to question it, to regard it as a problem rather than as a structure consisting exclusively of irreducible, immutable, and ultimate facts, is an essential quality of being human. The fact that to the mind of man his behavior is a problem instead of an unquestioned immutable fact is as important a datum of inner activity as the facts of external behavior.

Empirical intemperance, the desire to be exact, to attend to "hard" facts which are subject to measurement, may defeat its own end. It makes us blind to the fact behind the facts—that what makes a human being human is not just mechanical, biological, and psychological functioning, but the ability to make decisions constantly. Facts exhibited in life, cut off from antecedent decisions and determinations, from simultaneous attitudes as well as from subsequent reactions and reflections, cannot be exactly described.

It is an intellectually stifling assumption to regard a behavior pattern as a matter of fact pure and simple, just because it can submit itself to exact methods of inquiry. Is it not a fallacy to regard a behavior pattern as if it were a ghost city, an agglomeration of buildings with no living soul dwelling therein? A human behavior pattern is not a monument to a life that is gone, but a drama full of life. It is a system as well as a groping, a wavering, a striking forth; solidity as well as outburst, deviation, inconsistency; not a final order but a process, conditioned, manipulated, questioned, challenged, and guided by a variety of factors.

The more refined and accessible the avenues to the study of behavioral facts become, the greater the scarcity of intellectual audacity in probing what is imponderable about human being.

Our understanding of man is dangerously incomplete if we dwell exclusively on the facts of human being and disregard what is at stake in human being. The facts, man's actual behavior, are explicit; what is at stake is implied. Since behavior patterns may be easily observed and described with a degree of statistical precision, we are inclined to reduce all of man to what is explicit, manifest, observable.

It is a mistake, however, to equate man's essence with his manifestations. The power and secret of his being reside as much in the unsaid and unproclaimed, in the tacit and ineffable, in the acts of awareness that defy expression as in the vessels man creates for his expression.

Physical things can be defined in terms of objective properties; man can be understood only in terms of his total situation, in terms of the demands he is called upon to answer. The chief problem of man is not his nature, but what he does with his nature.

Human being, therefore, must not be reduced to human nature. Human being is a fact as well as a desideratum, a given constellation as well as an opportunity. It can be understood only in relation to a challenge. It includes both the process and the structure of the facts of his being as well as the surprise and the events that come to pass in his existence.

THE SELF AS A PROBLEM

Our intention, therefore, is not to engage in a purely descriptive exploration of the total scope and pattern of human behavior, but to ascertain ends and directions, asking questions and raising issues which are implied in description. The task of our inquiry is to explore modes of being which characterize the uniqueness of being human. What constitutes human existence? What situations and sensibilities belong necessarily to the make-up of being human?

Man is never neutral or indifferent in relation to his own self. Love and knowledge, value judgment and factual description cannot be kept apart in establishing self-knowledge. Self-knowledge embodies either acceptance or rejection. One's relationship to the self is inconceivable without the possession of certain standards or preferences of value.

The notion of the strict contrast between descriptive and normative, analysis and evaluation, observation and interpretation, loses its relevance in the process of man seeking to establish his being human.

Facts of personal existence are not merely given. They are given through self-comprehension, and self-comprehension is an interpretation, since every act of self-comprehension involves the application of value judgments, norms, and decisions, and is the result of a selective attentiveness, reflecting a particular perspective. Thus even the facts of my existence are disclosed to me by way of interpretation, the terms of which determine the mode of my living and self-understanding.

Self-understanding can hardly be kept strictly within the limits of description of facts, since the self itself is a compound of facts and norms, of what *is* as well as of a consciousness of what *ought* to be. The essence of being human is value, value involved in human being.

As said above, the problem of man is occasioned by our coming upon a conflict or contradiction between existence and expectation. Thus the root of self-understanding is in the awareness of the self as a problem; it operates as critical reflection. Displacement of complacency, questioning the self, its acts and traits, is the primary motivation of self-understanding.

Self-understanding is entirely dependent upon self-judgment, and must not be equated with observation or self-observation. Mere description, simple dogmatic acceptance of the self, amounts to the deproblematizing of the man and is really the cessation of self-understanding. In short, if being human continues to be a problem, we must realize that the method of description, used exclusively, can at best offer us self-observation but is incapable of dealing with the problem.

CARE FOR MAN

Wondering is a mode of human being. But wondering may just be sheer wandering, moving aimlessly, roaming, rambling. Channeling our wondering into the form of a question is the imposition of a pattern and a procedure upon the mind.

There is more than one question that can be asked. The choice of question determines the trend of the inquiry. In other words, each question is a preconceived pattern, and there is more than one pattern. A pattern orders the inchoate wondering and determines in advance the process of thinking about its theme.

To know that a question is an answer in disguise is a minimum of wisdom. This is the thought that comes to all men, to every man in the form of question: What am I here for? What is at stake in my existence? This question is not derived from premises. It is given with existence. Man, a problem to himself, does not take his existence for granted.

We must always start from the beginning. The most vital problems cannot be settled vicariously. No solution is established once and for all. We must all ponder the same question and wonder at the same puzzle. Just as I had to go through childhood, adolescence, and maturity, so must I go through the crises, embarrassments, heartaches, and wrestlings with this basic issue.

In asking the question about man, I have in mind not only a question about the essence but also a question about the concrete situation in which we find ourselves, a situation that puts the problem of man in a new light. The issue is old, yet the perspective is one of emergency. New in this age is an unparalleled awareness of the terrifying seriousness of the human situation. Questions we seriously ask today would have seemed utterly absurd twenty years ago, such as, for example: Are we the last generation? Is this the very last hour for Western civilization?

Philosophy cannot be the same after Auschwitz and Hiroshima. Certain assumptions about humanity have proved to be specious, have been smashed. What has long been regarded as commonplace has proved to be utopianism.

Philosophy, to be relevant, must offer us a wisdom to live by— relevant not only in the isolation of our study rooms but also in moments of facing staggering cruelty and the threat of disaster. The question of man must be pondered not only in the halls of learning but also in the presence of inmates in extermination camps, and in the sight of the mushroom of a nuclear explosion.

What is happening in the life of man, and how are we to grasp it? We ask in order to know how to live.

The nature of our inquiry stands in marked contrast to other inquiries. Other issues we explore out of curiosity; the issue of man we explore out of personal involvement. In other issues inquirer and theme are apart: I know the Rocky Mountains, but I am not the Rocky Mountains. Yet in regard to knowledge of myself I am what I seek to know; being and knowing, subject and object, are one. We have seen that we cannot reflect about the humanity of man and retain a relationship of complete detachment, since all understanding of man is derived from self-understanding, and one can never remain aloof from one's own self.

The most valuable insights into the human situation have been gained not through patient introspection or systematic scrutiny, but rather through surprise and shock of dramatic failures. Indeed, it is usually in the wake of frustration, in moments of crisis and self-disillusionment, and rarely out of astonishment at man's glorious achievements, that radical reflection comes to pass.

This is an age in which it is impossible to think about the human situation without shame, anguish, and disgust, in which it is impossible to experience enjoyment without grief and unending heartache, to observe personal triumphs without pangs of embarrassment.

Why do we ask the question about man? Because the knowledge about man which we had accepted as self-evident has proved to be a mass of bubbles bursting at the slightest increase in temperature. Some of us live in dismay caused by what man has revealed about himself.

The sickness of our age is the failure of conscience rather than the failure of nerve. Our conscience is not the same. Stultified by its own bankruptcy, staggered by the immense complexity of the challenge, it becomes subject to automation. Pride in our immediate past would be callousness, just as optimism about the immediate future would be stupidity. In the period of Enlightenment a major concern of philosophy was to emancipate man from the clutches of the past. Today our concern seems to be to protect ourselves against the abyss of the future.

One cannot study the condition of man without being touched by the plight of man. Though biologically intact, man is essentially afflicted with a sense of helplessness, discontent, inferiority, fear. Outwardly Homo sapiens may pretend to be satisfied and strong; inwardly he is poor, needy, vulnerable, always on the verge of misery, prone to suffer mentally and physically. Scratch his skin and you come upon bereavement, affliction, uncertainty, fear, and pain. Disparity between his appearance and reality is a condition of social integration. Suppressions are the price he pays for being accepted in society. Adjustment involves assenting to odd auspices, concessions of conscience, inevitable hypocrisies. It is, indeed, often "a life of quiet desperation."

B. The Enneads

Plotinus

Therefore we must ascend again towards the Good, the desired of every Soul. Anyone that has seen This, knows what I intend when I say that it is beautiful. Even the desire of it is to be desired as a Good. To attain it is for those that will take the upward path, who will set all their forces towards it, who will divest themselves of all that we have put on in our descent; so, to those that approach the Holy Celebrations of the Mysteries, there are appointed purifications and the laying aside of the garments worn before, and the entry in nakedness—until, passing, on the upward way, all that is other than the God, each in the solitude of himself shall behold that solitary-dwelling Existence, the Apart, the Unmingled, the Pure, that from Which all things depend, for Which all look and live and act and know, the Source of Life and of Intellection and of Being.

And one that shall know this vision—with what passion of love shall he not be seized, with what pang of desire, what longing to be molten into one with This, what wondering delight! If he that has never seen this Being must hunger for It as for all his welfare, he that has known must love and reverence It as the very Beauty; he will be flooded with awe and gladness, stricken by a salutary terror; he loves with a veritable love, with sharp desire; all other loves than this he must despise, and disdain all that once seemed fair.

This, indeed, is the mood even of those who, having witnessed the manifestation of Gods or Supernals, can never again feel the old delight in the comeliness of material forms: what then are we to think of one that contemplates Absolute Beauty in Its essential integrity, no accumulation of flesh and matter, no dweller on earth or in the heavens—so perfect Its purity—far above all such things in that they are non-essential, composite, not primal but descending from This?

Beholding this Being—the Choragus of all Existence, the Self-Intent that ever gives forth and never takes—resting, rapt, in the vision and possession of so lofty a loveliness, growing to Its likeness, what Beauty can the Soul yet lack? For This, the Beauty supreme, the absolute, and the primal, fashions Its lovers to Beauty and makes them also worthy of love.

And for This, the sternest and the uttermost combat is set before the Souls; all our labour is for This, lest we be left without part in this noblest vision, which to attain is to be blessed in the blissful sight, which to fail of is to fail utterly.

For not he that has failed of the joy that is in colour or in visible forms, not he that has failed of power or of honours or of kingdom has failed, but only he that has failed of only This, for Whose winning he should renounce kingdoms and command over earth and ocean and sky, if only, spurning the world of sense from beneath his feet, and straining to This, he may see.

But what must we do? How lies the path? How come to vision of the inaccessible Beauty, dwelling as if in consecrated precincts, apart from the common ways where all may see, even the profane?

He that has the strength, let him arise and withdraw into himself, foregoing all that is known by the eyes, turning away for ever from the material beauty that once made his joy. When he perceives those shapes of grace that show in body, let him not pursue: he must know them for copies, vestiges, shadows, and hasten away towards That they tell of. For if anyone follow what is like a beautiful shape playing over water—is there not a myth telling in symbol of such a dupe, how he sank into the depths of the current and was swept away to nothingness? So too, one that is held by material beauty and will not break free shall be precipitated, not in body but in Soul, down to the dark depths loathed of the Intellective-Being, where, blind even in the Lower-World, he shall have commerce only with shadows, there as here.

"Let us flee then to the beloved Fatherland": this is the soundest counsel. But what is this flight? How are we to gain the open sea? For Odysseus is surely a parable to us when he commands the flight from the sorceries of Circe or Calypso—not content to linger for all the pleasure offered to his eyes and all the delight of sense filling his days.

The Fatherland to us is There whence we have come, and There is The Father.

What then is our course, what the manner of our flight? This is not a journey for the feet; the feet bring us only from land to land; nor need you think of coach or ship to carry you away; all this order of things you must set aside and refuse to see: you must close the eyes and call instead upon another vision which is to be waked within you, a vision, the birth-right of all, which few turn to use.

And this inner vision, what is its operation?

Newly awakened it is all too feeble to bear the ultimate splendour. Therefore the Soul must be trained—to the habit of remarking, first, all noble pursuits, then the works of beauty produced not by the labour of the arts but by the virtue of men known for their goodness: lastly, you must search the souls of those that have shaped these beautiful forms.

But how are you to see into a virtuous Soul and know its loveliness?

Withdraw into yourself and look. And if you do not find yourself beautiful yet, act as does the creator of a statue that is to be made beautiful: he cuts away here, he smoothes there, he makes this line lighter, this other purer, until a lovely face has grown upon his work. So do you also: cut away all that is excessive, straighten all that is crooked, bring light to all that is overcast, labour to make all one glow of beauty and never cease chiselling your statue, until there shall shine out on you from it the godlike splendour of virtue, until you shall see the perfect goodness surely established in the stainless shrine.

When you know that you have become this perfect work, when you are self-gathered in the purity of your being, nothing now remaining that can shatter that inner unity, nothing from without clinging to the authentic man, when you find yourself wholly true to your essential nature, wholly that only veritable Light which is not measured by space, not narrowed to any circumscribed form nor again diffused as a thing void of term, but ever unmeasurable as something greater than all measure and more than all quantity—when you perceive that you have grown to this, you are now become very vision: now call up all your confidence, strike forward yet a step—you need a guide no longer—strain, and see.

This is the only eye that sees the mighty Beauty. If the eye that adventures the vision be dimmed by vice, impure, or weak, and unable in its cowardly blenching to see the uttermost brightness, then it sees nothing even though another point to what lies plain to sight before it. To any vision must be brought an eye adapted to what is to be seen, and having some likeness to it. Never did eye see the sun unless it had first become sunlike, and never can the Soul have vision of the First Beauty unless itself be beautiful.

Therefore, first let each become godlike and each beautiful who cares to see God and Beauty. So, mounting, the Soul will come first to the Intellectual-Principle and survey all the beautiful Ideas in the Supreme and will avow that this is Beauty, that the Ideas are Beauty. For by their efficacy comes all Beauty else, by the offspring and essence of the Intellectual-Being. What is beyond the Intellectual-Principle we affirm to be the nature of Good radiating Beauty before it. So that, treating the Intellectual-Cosmos as one, the first is the Beautiful: if we make distinction there, the Realm of Ideas constitutes the Beauty of the Intellectual Sphere; and The Good, which lies beyond, is the Fountain at once and Principle of Beauty: the Primal Good and the Primal Beauty have the one dwelling-place and, thus, always, Beauty's seat is There.

C. On the Improvement of the Understanding

Spinoza

After experience had taught me that all the usual surroundings of social life are vain and futile; seeing that none of the objects of my fears contained in themselves anything either good or bad, except in so far as the mind is affected by them, I finally resolved to inquire whether there might be some real good having power to communicate itself, which would affect the mind singly, to the exclusion of all else: whether, in fact, there might be anything of which the discovery and attainment would enable me to enjoy continuous, supreme, and unending happiness. I say "I *finally* resolved," for at first sight it seemed unwise willingly to lose hold on what was sure for the sake of something then uncertain. I could see the benefits which are acquired through fame and riches, and that I should be obliged to abandon the quest of such objects, if I seriously devoted myself to the search for something different and new. I perceived that if true happiness chanced to be placed in the former I should necessarily miss it; while if, on the other hand, it were not so placed, and I gave them my whole attention, I should equally fail.

I therefore debated whether it would not be possible to arrive at the new principle, or at any rate at a certainty concerning its existence, without changing the conduct and usual plan of my life; with this end in view I made many efforts, but in vain. For the ordinary surroundings of life which are esteemed by men (as their actions testify) to be the highest good, may be classed under the three heads—Riches, Fame, and the Pleasures of Sense: with these three the mind is so absorbed that it has little power to reflect on any different good. By sensual pleasure the mind is enthralled to the extent of quiescence, as if the supreme good were actually attained, so that it is quite incapable of thinking of any other object; when such pleasure has been gratified it is followed by extreme melancholy, whereby the mind, though not enthralled, is disturbed and dulled.

The pursuit of honours and riches is likewise very absorbing, especially if such objects be sought simply for their own sake, inasmuch as they are then supposed to constitute the highest good. In the case of fame the mind is still more absorbed, for fame is conceived as always good for its own sake, and as the ultimate end to which all actions are directed. Further, the attainment of riches and fame is not followed as in the case of sensual pleasures by repentance, but, the more we acquire, the greater is our delight, and, consequently, the more are we incited to increase both the one and the other; on the other hand, if our hopes happen to be frustrated we are plunged into the deepest sadness. Fame has the further drawback that it compels its votaries to order their lives according to the opinions of their fellow-men, shunning what they usually shun, and seeking what they usually seek.

When I saw that all these ordinary objects of desire would be obstacles in the way of a search for something different and new—nay, that they were so opposed thereto, that either they or it would have to be abandoned, I was forced to inquire which would prove the most useful to me: for, as I say, I seemed to be willingly losing hold on a sure good for the sake of something uncertain. However, after I had reflected on the matter, I came in the first place to the conclusion that by abandoning the ordinary objects of pursuit, and betaking myself to a new quest, I should be leaving a good, uncertain by reason of its own nature, as may be gathered from what has been said, for the sake of a good not uncertain in its nature (for I sought for a fixed good), but only in the possibility of its attainment.

Further reflection convinced me, that if I could really get to the root of the matter I should be leaving certain evils for a certain good. I thus perceived that I was in a state of great peril, and I compelled myself to seek with all my strength for a remedy, however uncertain it might be; as a sick man struggling with a deadly disease, when he sees that death will surely be upon him unless a remedy be found, is compelled to seek such a remedy with all his strength, inasmuch as his whole hope lies therein. All the objects pursued by the multitude not only bring no remedy that tends to preserve our being, but even act as hindrances, causing the death not seldom of those who possess them, and always of those who are possessed by them. There are many examples of men who have suffered persecution even to death for the sake of their riches, and of men who in pursuit of wealth have exposed themselves to so many dangers, that they have paid away their life as a penalty for their folly. Examples are no less numerous of men, who have endured the utmost wretchedness for the sake of gaining or preserving their reputation. Lastly, there are innumerable cases of men, who have hastened their death through over-indulgence in sensual pleasure. All these evils seem to have arisen from the fact, that happiness or unhappiness is made wholly to depend on the quality of the object which we love. When a thing is not loved, no quarrels will arise concerning it—no sadness will be felt if it perishes—no envy if it is possessed by another—no fear, no hatred, in short no disturbances of the mind. All these arise from the love of what is perishable, such as the objects already mentioned. But love towards a thing eternal and infinite feeds the mind wholly with joy, and is itself unmingled with any sadness, wherefore it is greatly to be desired and sought for with all our strength. Yet it was not at random that I used the words, "If I could go to the root of the matter," for, though what I have urged was perfectly clear to my mind, I could not forthwith lay aside all love of riches, sensual enjoyment, and fame. One thing was evident, namely, that while my mind was employed with these thoughts it turned away from its former objects of desire, and seriously considered the search for a new principle; this state of things was a great comfort to me, for I perceived that the evils were not such as to resist all remedies. Although these intervals were at first rare, and of very short duration, yet afterwards, as the true good became more and more discernible to me, they became more frequent and more lasting; especially after I had recognized that the acquisition of wealth, sensual pleasure, or fame, is only a hindrance, so long as they are sought as ends not as means; if they be sought as means, they will be under restraint, and, far from being hindrances, will further not a little the end for which they are sought, as I will show in due time.

I will here only briefly state what I mean by true good, and also what is the nature of the highest good. In order that this may be rightly understood, we must bear in mind that the terms good and evil are only applied relatively, so that the same thing may be called both good and bad, according to the relations in view, in the same way as it may be called perfect or imperfect. Nothing regarded in its own nature can be called perfect or imperfect; especially when we are aware that all things which come to pass, come to pass according to the eternal order and fixed laws of nature. However, human weakness cannot attain to this order in its own thoughts, but meanwhile man conceives a human character much more stable than his own, and sees that there is no reason why he should not himself acquire such a character. Thus he is led to seek for means which will bring him to this pitch of perfection, and calls everything which will serve as such means a true good. The chief good is that he should arrive, together with other individuals if possible, at the possession of the aforesaid character. What that character is we shall show in due time, namely, that it is the knowledge of the union existing between the mind and the whole of nature. This, then, is the end for which I strive, to attain to such a character myself, and to endeavour that many should attain to it with me. In other words, it is part of my happiness to lend a helping hand, that many others may understand even as I do, so that their understanding and desire may entirely agree with my own. In order to bring this about, it is necessary to understand as much of nature as will enable us to attain to the aforesaid character, and also to form a social order such as is most conducive to the attainment of this character by the greatest number with the least difficulty and danger. We must seek the assistance of Moral Philosophy and the Theory of Education; further, as health is no insignificant means for attaining our end, we must also include the whole science of Medicine, and, as many difficult things are by contrivance rendered easy, and we can in this way gain much time and convenience, the science of Mechanics must in no way be despised. But, before all things, a means must be devised for improving the understanding and purifying it, as far as may be at the outset, so that it may apprehend things without error, and in the best possible way.

Thus it is apparent to everyone that I wish to direct all sciences to one end and aim, so that we may attain to the supreme human perfection which we have named; and, therefore, whatsoever in the sciences does not serve to promote our object will have to be rejected as useless. To sum up the matter in a word, all our actions and thoughts must be directed to this one end. Yet, as it is necessary that while we are endeavouring to attain our purpose, and bring the understanding into the right path, we should carry on our life, we are compelled first of all to lay down certain rules of life as provisionally good, to wit the following:—

I. To speak in a manner intelligible to the multitude, and to comply with every general custom that does not hinder the attainment of our purpose. For we can gain from the multitude no small advantages, provided that we strive to accommodate ourselves to its understanding as far as possible: moreover, we shall in this way gain a friendly audience for the reception of the truth.

II. To indulge ourselves with pleasures only in so far as they are necessary for preserving health.

III. Lastly, to endeavour to obtain only sufficient money or other commodities to enable us to preserve our life and health, and to follow such general customs as are consistent with our purpose.

D. The Way to Wisdom

Karl Jaspers

The history of philosophy as methodical thinking began twenty-five hundred years ago, but as mythical thought much earlier.

The beginning however is something quite different from the source. The beginning is historical and provides those who follow with a mounting accumulation of insights. But it is always from the source that the impulsion to philosophize springs. The source alone lends meaning to present philosophy and through it alone is past philosophy understood.

This source is of many kinds. Wonderment gives rise to question and insight; man's doubt in the knowledge he has attained gives rise to critical examination and clear certainty; his awe and sense of forsakenness lead him to inquire into himself. And now let us examine these three drives.

First: Plato said that the source of philosophy was wonder. Our eyes gave us "the sight of the stars, the sun and the firmament." This "impelled us to examine the universe, whence grew philosophy, the greatest good conferred upon mortals by the gods." And Aristotle: "For it is owing to their wonder that men both now begin and at first began to philosophize: they wondered originally at the obvious difficulties, then advanced little by little and stated difficulties about the greater matters, e.g., about the phenomena of the moon, and those of the sun, and of the stars, and about the genesis of the universe."

Wonder impels man to seek knowledge. In my wonderment I become aware of my lack of knowledge. I seek knowledge, but for its own sake and not "to satisfy any common need."

In philosophical thought man awakens from his bondage to practical needs. Without ulterior purpose he contemplates things, the heavens, the world, and asks, what is all this? Where does it come from? From the answers to his questions he expects no profit but an intrinsic satisfaction.

Second: Once I have satisfied my wonderment and admiration by knowledge of what is, *doubt* arises. I have heaped up insights, but upon critical examination nothing is certain. Sensory perceptions are conditioned by our sense organs and hence deceptive; in any event they do not coincide with what exists in itself outside me, independently of my perception. Our categories are those of our human understanding. They become entangled in hopeless contradictions. Everywhere proposition stands against proposition. In my philosophical progress I seize upon doubt and attempt to apply it radically to everything, either taking pleasure in the sceptical negation which recognizes nothing but by itself cannot take a single step forward, or inquiring: Where then is there a certainty that rises above all doubt and withstands all critique?

Descartes' famous proposition, "I think, therefore I am," was for him a solid certainty, though he doubted everything else. For even a total fallacy in my thinking, a fallacy which may be beyond my understanding, cannot blind me to the realization that in order to be deluded in my thinking I must *be*.

Methodical doubt gives rise to a critical examination of all knowledge, and without radical doubt there can be no true philosophical thought. But the crucial question is: How and where has a foundation for certainty been gained through doubt itself?

And third: While I concentrate my energies upon the knowledge of things in the world, while I am engaged in doubt as a road to certainty, I am immersed in things; I do not think of myself, of my aims, my happiness, my salvation. In forgetfulness of my self I am content with the attainment of this knowledge.

This changes when I become aware of myself in my situation.

The Stoic Epictetus said, "Philosophy arises when we become *aware of our own weakness and helplessness*." How shall I help myself in my weakness? His answer was: By looking upon everything that is not within my power as necessary and indifferent to me, but by raising what does depend on me, namely the mode and content of my ideas, to clarity and freedom by thought.

And now let us take a look at our human state. We are always in situations. Situations change, opportunities arise. If they are missed they never return. I myself can work to change the situation. But there are situations which remain essentially the same even if their momentary aspect changes and their shattering force is obscured: I must die, I must suffer, I must struggle, I am subject to chance, I involve myself inexorably in guilt. We call these fundamental situations of our existence ultimate situations. That is to say, they are situations which we cannot evade or change. Along with wonder and doubt, awareness of these ultimate situations is the most profound source of philosophy. In our day-to-day lives we often evade them, by closing our eyes and living as if they did not exist. We forget that we must die, forget our guilt, and forget that we are at the mercy of chance. We face only concrete situations and master them to our profit, we react to them by planning and acting in the world, under the impulsion of our practical interests. But to ultimate situations we react either by obfuscation or, if we really apprehend them, by despair and rebirth: we become ourselves by a change in our consciousness of being.

Or we may define our human situation by saying that *no reliance can be placed in worldly existence.*

Ingenuously we mistake the world for being as such. In happy situations we rejoice at our strength, we are thoughtlessly confident, we know nothing but our actuality. In pain and weakness we despair. But if we come out of this situation alive we let ourselves slip back into forgetfulness of self and a life of happiness.

Such experience however has sharpened man's wits. The menace beneath which he lives drives him to seek security. He expects his mastery of nature and his community with other men to guarantee his existence.

Man gains power over nature in order to make it serve him; through science and technology he seeks to make it reliable.

But in man's domination of nature there remains an element of the incalculable which represents a constant threat, and the end is always failure: hard labour, old age, sickness and death cannot be done away with. Our dominated nature is reliable only in isolated cases; in the whole we can place no reliance.

Men band together in a community in order to limit and ultimately abolish the endless struggle of all against all; they seek to achieve security through mutual aid.

But here again there is a limit. Only if there were states in which every citizen stood to every other in a relation of absolute solidarity could justice and freedom be secure. For only then, if a citizen suffered injustice, would all others oppose it as one man. Such a state has never been seen. Those who have stood by one another in extremity and weakness have never been more than limited groups, and sometimes no more than a few individuals. No state, no church, no society offers absolute security. Such security has been a pleasing delusion of quiet times, in which the ultimate situations were veiled.

But there is a counterweight to the general unreliability of the world: there are in the world things worthy of faith, things that arouse confidence; there is a foundation which sustains us: home and country, parents and ancestors, brothers and sisters and friends, husbands and wives. There is a foundation of historical tradition, in native language, in faith, in the work of thinkers, poets, and artists. However, this tradition also gives no security, it is not absolutely reliable. For we encounter it always as the work of man; God is nowhere in the world. Tradition always implies a question. Keeping sight of the tradition, man must always derive what for him is certainty, being, the reliable, from his own primal source. But the precariousness of all worldly existence is a warning to us, it forbids us to content ourselves with the world; it points to something else.

The ultimate situations—death, chance, guilt, and the uncertainty of the world—confront me with the reality of failure. What do I do in the face of this absolute failure, which if I am honest I cannot fail to recognize?

The advice of the Stoic, to withdraw to our own freedom in the independence of the mind, is not adequate. The Stoic's perception of man's weakness was not radical enough. He failed to see that the mind in itself is empty, dependent on what is put into it, and he failed to consider the possibility of madness. The Stoic leaves us without consolation; the independent mind is barren, lacking all content. He leaves us without hope, because his doctrine affords us no opportunity of inner transformation, no fulfilment through self-conquest in love, no hopeful expectation of the possible.

And yet the Stoics' striving is toward true philosophy. Their thought, because its source is in ultimate situations, expresses the basic drive to find a revelation of true being in human failure.

Crucial for man is his attitude toward failure: whether it remains hidden from him and overwhelms him only objectively at the end or whether he perceives it unobscured as the constant limit of his existence; whether he snatches at fantastic solutions and consolations or faces it honestly, in silence before the unfathomable. The way in which man approaches his failure determines what he will become.

In ultimate situations man either perceives nothingness or senses true being in spite of and above all ephemeral worldly existence. Even despair, by the very fact that it is possible in the world, points beyond the world.

Or, differently formulated, man seeks redemption. Redemption is offered by the great, universal religions of redemption. They are characterized by an objective guarantee of the truth and reality of redemption. Their road leads to an act of individual conversion. This philosophy cannot provide. And yet all philosophy is a transcending of the world, analogous to redemption.

To sum up: The source of philosophy is to be sought in wonder, in doubt, in a sense of forsakenness. In any case it begins with an inner upheaval, which determines its goal.

Plato and Aristotle were moved by wonder to seek the nature of being.

Amid infinite uncertainty Descartes sought compelling certainty.

Amid the sufferings of life the Stoics sought the repose of the mind.

Each of these experiences has its own truth, clothed always in historical conceptions and language. In making these philosophies our own we penetrate the historical husk to the primal sources that are alive within us.

The inner drive is toward firm foundations, depth of being, eternity.

But for us perhaps none of these is the most fundamental, absolute source. The discovery that being can be revealed to wonder is a source of inspiration, but beguiles us into withdrawing from the world and succumbing to a pure, magical metaphysic. Compelling certainty is limited to the scientific knowledge by which we orient ourselves in the world. Stoic imperturbability serves us only as a makeshift in distress, as a refuge from total ruin, but in itself remains without content and life.

These three motives—wonder leading to knowledge, doubt leading to certainty, forsakenness leading to the self—cannot by themselves account for our present philosophical thought.

In this crucial turning point in history, in this age of unprecedented ruin and of potentialities that can only be darkly surmised, the three motives we have thus far considered remain in force, but they are not adequate. They can operate only if there is *communication* among men.

In all past history there was a self-evident bond between man and man, in stable communities, in institutions, and in universal ideas. Even the isolated individual was in a sense sustained in his isolation. The most visible sign of today's disintegration is that more and more men do not understand one another, that they meet and scatter, that they are indifferent to one another, that there is no longer any reliable community or loyalty.

Today a universal situation that has always existed in fact assumes crucial importance: That I can, and cannot, become one with the Other in truth; that my faith, precisely when I am certain, clashes with other men's faith; that there is always somewhere a limit beyond which there appears to be nothing but battle without hope of unity, ending inevitably in subjugation or annihilation; that softness and complaisance cause men without faith either to band blindly together or stubbornly to attack one another.

All this is not incidental or unimportant. It might be, if there were a truth that might satisfy me in my isolation. I should not suffer so deeply from lack of communication or find such unique pleasure in authentic communication if I for myself, in absolute solitude, could be certain of the truth. But I am only in conjunction with the Other, alone I am nothing.

Communication from understanding to understanding, from mind to mind, and also from existence to existence, is only a medium for impersonal meanings and values. Defence and attack then become means not by which men gain power but by which they approach one another. The contest is a loving contest in which each man surrenders his weapons to the other. The certainty of authentic being resides only in unreserved communication between men who live together and vie with one another in a free community, who regard their association with one another as but a preliminary stage, who take nothing for granted and question everything. Only in communication is all other truth fulfilled, only in communication am I myself not merely living but fulfilling life. God manifests Himself only indirectly, and only through man's love of man; compelling certainty is particular and relative, subordinated to the Whole. The Stoical attitude is in fact empty and rigid.

The basic philosophical attitude of which I am speaking is rooted in distress at the absence of communication, in the drive to authentic communication, and in the possibility of the loving contest which profoundly unites self and self.

And this philosophical endeavour is at the same time rooted in the three philosophical experiences we have mentioned, which must all be considered in the light of their meaning, whether favourable or hostile, for communication from man to man.

And so we may say that wonder, doubt, the experience of ultimate situations, are indeed sources of philosophy, but the ultimate source is the will to authentic communication, which embraces all the rest. This becomes apparent at the very outset, for does not all philosophy strive for communication, express itself, demand a hearing? And is not its very essence communicability, which is in turn inseparable from truth?

Communication then is the aim of philosophy, and in communication all its other aims are ultimately rooted: awareness of being, illumination through love, attainment of peace.

II

THE
CONSCIOUS
SELF

A. The Ego and the Id

Sigmund Freud

In this introductory chapter there is nothing new to be said and it will not be possible to avoid repeating what has often been said before.

The division of the psychical into what is conscious and what is unconscious is the fundamental premise of psycho-analysis, and it alone makes it possible for psycho-analysis to understand the pathological processes in mental life, which are as common as they are important, and to find a place for them in the framework of science. To put it once more, in a different way: psycho-analysis cannot situate the essence of the psychical in consciousness, but is obligated to regard consciousness as a quality of the psychical, which may be present in addition to other qualities or may be absent.

If I could suppose that everyone interested in psychology would read this book, I should also be prepared to find that at this point some of my readers would already stop short and would go no further; for here we have the first shibboleth of psycho-analysis. To most people who have been educated in philosophy the idea of anything psychical which is not also conscious is so inconceivable that it seems to them absurd and refutable simply by logic. I believe this is only because they have never studied the relevant phenomena of hypnosis and dreams, which—quite apart from pathological manifestations—necessitate this view. Their psychology of consciousness is incapable of solving the problems of dreams and hypnosis.

Being conscious is in the first place a purely descriptive term, resting on perception of the most immediate and certain character. Experience goes on to show that a psychical element (for instance, an idea) is not as a rule conscious for a protracted length of time. On the contrary, a state of consciousness is characteristically very transitory; an idea that is conscious now is no longer so a moment later, although it can become so again under certain conditions that are easily brought about. In the interval the idea was—we do not know what. We can say that it was latent, and by this we mean that it was capable of becoming conscious at any time. Or, if we say that it was unconscious, we shall also be giving a correct description of it. Here "unconscious" coincides with "latent and capable of becoming conscious." The philosophers would no doubt object: "No, the term 'unconscious' is not applicable here; so long as the idea was in a state of latency it was not anything psychical at all." To contradict them at this point would lead to nothing more profitable than a verbal dispute.

But we have arrived at the term or concept of the unconscious along another path, by considering certain experiences in which mental dynamics play a part. We have found—that is, we have been obliged to assume—that very powerful mental processes or ideas exist (and here a quantitative or economic factor comes into question for the first time) which can produce all the effects in mental life that ordinary ideas do (including effects that can in their turn become conscious as ideas), though they themselves do not become conscious. It is unnecessary to repeat in detail here what has been explained so often before. It is enough to say that at this point psycho-analytic theory steps in and asserts that the reason why such ideas cannot become conscious is that a certain force opposes them, that otherwise they could become conscious, and that it would then be apparent how little they differ from other elements which are admittedly psychical. The fact that in the technique of psycho-analysis a means has been found by which the opposing force can be removed and the ideas in question made conscious rendered this theory irrefutable. The state in which the ideas existed before being made conscious is called by us repression, and we assert that the force which instituted the repression and maintains it is perceived as resistance during the work of analysis.

Thus we obtain our concept of the unconscious from the theory of repression. The repressed is the prototype of the unconscious for us. We see, however, that we have two kinds of unconscious—the one which is latent but capable of becoming conscious, and the one which is repressed and which is not, in itself and without more ado, capable of becoming conscious. This piece of insight into psychical dynamics cannot fail to affect terminology and description. The latent, which is unconscious only descriptively, not in the dynamic sense, we call preconscious; we restrict the term unconscious to the dynamically unconscious repressed; so that now we have three terms, conscious (Cs.), preconscious (Pcs.), and unconscious (Ucs.), whose sense is no longer purely descriptive. The Pcs. is presumably a great deal closer to the Cs. than is the Ucs., and since we have called the Ucs. psychical we shall with even less hesitation call the latent Pcs. psychical. But why do we not rather, instead of this, remain in agreement with the philosophers and, in a consistent way, distinguish the Pcs. as well as the Ucs. from the conscious psychical? The philosophers would then propose that the Pcs. and Ucs. should be described as two species or stages of the "psychoid," and harmony would be established. But endless difficulties in exposition would follow; and the one important fact, that these two kinds of "psychoid" coincide in almost every other respect with what is admittedly psychical, would be forced into the background in the interests of a prejudice dating from a period in which these psychoids, or the most important part of them, were still unknown.

We can now play about comfortably with our three terms, Cs., Pcs., and Ucs., so long as we do not forget that in the descriptive sense there are two kinds of unconscious, but in the dynamic sense only one. For purposes of exposition this distinction can in some cases be ignored, but in others it is of course indispensable. At the same time, we have become more or less accustomed to this ambiguity of the unconscious and have managed pretty well with it. As far as I can see, it is impossible to avoid this ambiguity; the distinction between conscious and unconscious is in the last resort a question of perception, which must be answered "yes" or "no," and the act of perception itself tells us nothing of the reason why a thing is or is not perceived. No one has a right to complain because the actual phenomenon expresses the dynamic factor ambiguously.

In the further course of psycho-analytic work, however, even these distinctions have proved to be inadequate and, for practical purposes, insufficient. This has become clear in more ways than one; but the decisive instance is as follows. We have formed the idea that in each individual there is a coherent organization of mental processes; and we call this his ego. It is to this ego that consciousness is attached; the ego controls the approaches to motility—that is, to the discharge of excitations into the external world; it is the mental agency which supervises all its own constituent processes, and which goes to sleep at night, though even then it exercises the censorship on dreams. From this ego proceed the repressions, too, by means of which it is sought to exclude certain trends in the mind not merely from consciousness but also from other forms of effectiveness and activity. In analysis these trends which have been shut out stand in opposition to the ego, and the analysis is faced with the task of removing the resistances which the ego displays against concerning itself with the repressed. Now we find during analysis that, when we put certain tasks before the patient, he gets into difficulties; his associations fail when they should be coming near the repressed. We then tell him that he is dominated by a resistance; but he is quite unaware of the fact, and, even if he guesses from his unpleasurable feelings that a resistance is now at work in him, he does not know what it is or how to describe it. Since, however, there can be no question but that this resistance emanates from his ego and belongs to it, we find ourselves in an unforeseen situation. We have come upon something in the ego itself which is also unconscious which behaves exactly like the repressed—that is, which produces powerful effects without before it can be made conscious. From the point of view of analytic practice, the consequence of this discovery is that we land in endless obscurities and difficulties if we keep to our habitual forms of expression and try, for instance, to derive neuroses from a conflict between the conscious and the unconscious. We shall have to substitute for this antithesis another, taken from our insight into the structural conditions of the mind—the antithesis between the coherent ego and the repressed which is split off from it.

For our conception of the unconscious, however, the consequences of our discovery are even more important. Dynamic considerations caused us to make our first correction; our insight into the structure of the mind leads to the second. We recognize that the Ucs. does not coincide with the repressed; it is still true that all that is repressed is Ucs., but not all that is Ucs. is repressed. A part of the ego, too—and Heaven knows how important a part—may be Ucs., undoubtedly is Ucs. And this Ucs. belonging to the ego is not latent like the Pcs.; for if it were, it could not be activated without becoming Cs., and the process of making it conscious would not encounter such great difficulties. When we find ourselves thus confronted by the necessity of postulating a third Ucs., which is not repressed, we must admit that the characteristic of being unconscious begins to lose significance for us. It becomes a quality which can have many meanings, a quality which we are unable to make, as we should have hoped to do, the basis of far-reaching and inevitable conclusions. Nevertheless we must beware of ignoring this characteristic, for the property of being conscious or not is in the last resort our one beacon-light in the darkness of depth-psychology.

B. Meditations

Rene Descartes

And to these reasons for doubting I have recently added two other very general ones. The first is that I have never thought I perceived anything when awake that I might not sometimes also think I perceived when I am asleep; and since I do not believe that the things I seem to perceive when asleep proceed from objects outside of myself, I did not see any better reason why I ought to believe this about what I seem to perceive when awake. The other reason was that, not yet knowing, or rather pretending not to know the author of my being, I saw nothing to make it impossible that I was so constructed by nature that I should be mistaken even in the things which seemed to me most true.

And as for the reasons which had previously persuaded me that sensible objects truly existed, I did not find it very difficult to answer them. For as nature seemed to lead me to many conclusions from which reason dissuaded me, I did not believe that I ought to have much faith in the teachings of this nature. And although my sense perceptions do not depend upon my volition, I did not think that I should therefore conclude that they proceeded from things different from myself, since there might perhaps be some faculty in myself even though it has been thus far unknown to me, which could [be their cause and] produce them.

But now that I am beginning to know myself better and to discover more clearly the author of my origin, I do not think in truth that I ought rashly to admit everything which the senses seem to teach us, but on the other hand I do not think that I should doubt them all in general.

First, since I know that all the things I conceive clearly and distinctly can be produced by God exactly as I conceive them, it is sufficient that I can clearly and distinctly conceive one thing apart from another to be certain that the one is distinct [or different] from the other. For they can be made to exist separately, at least by [the omnipotence of] God, and we are obliged to consider them different no matter what power produces this separation. From the very fact that I know with certainty that I exist, and that I find that [absolutely] nothing else belongs [necessarily] to my nature or essence except that I am a thinking being, I readily conclude that my essence consists solely in being a body which thinks [or a substance whose whole essence or nature is only to think]. And although perhaps, or rather certainly, as I will soon show, I have a body with which I am very closely united, nevertheless, since on the one hand I have a clear and distinct idea of myself in so far as I am only a thinking and not an extended being, and since on the other hand I have a distinct idea of body in so far as it is only an extended being which does not think, it is certain that this "I" [—that is to say, my soul, by virtue of which I am what I am—] is entirely [and truly] distinct from my body and that it can [be or] exist without it.

Furthermore, I find in myself various faculties of thinking which each have their own particular characteristics [and are distinct from myself]. For example, I find in myself the faculties of imagination and of perception, without which I might no doubt conceive of myself, clearly and distinctly, as a whole being; but I could not, conversely, conceive of those faculties without me, that is to say, without an intelligent substance [to which they are attached or in which they inhere]. For [in our notion of them or, to use the scholastic vocabulary,] in their formal concept, they embrace some type of intellection. From all this I reach the conception that these faculties are distinct from me as [shapes, movements, and other] modes [or accidents of objects] are distinct from [the very] objects [that sustain them].

I also recognize [in myself] some other faculties, such as the power of changing location, of assuming various postures, and other similar ones; which cannot be conceived without some substance in which they inhere, any more than the preceding ones, and which therefore cannot exist without such a substance. But it is [quite] evident that these faculties, if [it is true that] they exist, must inhere in some corporeal or extended substance, and not in an intelligent substance, since their clear and distinct concept does actually involve some sort of extension, but no sort of intelligence whatsoever. Furthermore, I cannot doubt that there is in me a certain passive faculty of perceiving, that is, of receiving and recognizing the ideas of sensible objects; but [it would be valueless to me, and] I could in no way use it if there were not also in me, or in something else, another active faculty capable of forming and producing these ideas. But this active faculty cannot be in me [, in so far as I am a thinking being], since it does not at all presuppose [my] intelligence and also since those ideas often occur to me without my contributing to them in any way, and even frequently against my will. Thus it must necessarily exist in some substance different from myself, in which all the reality that exists objectively in the ideas produced by this faculty is formally or eminently contained, as I have said before. This substance is either a body—that is, a corporeal nature—in which is formally [and actually] contained all that which is contained objectively [and by representation] in these ideas; or else it is God himself, or some other creation more noble than the body, in which all this is eminently contained.

But since God is not a deceiver, it is very manifest that he does not send me these ideas directly by his own agency, nor by the mediation of some creation in which their objective reality does not exist formally but only eminently. For since he has not given me any faculty for recognizing what that creation might be, but on the contrary a very great inclination to believe that these ideas come from corporeal objects, I do not see how we could clear God of the charge of deceit if these ideas did in fact come from some other source [or were produced by other causes] than corporeal objects. Therefore we must conclude that corporeal objects exist. Nevertheless, they are not perhaps entirely what our senses perceive them to be, for there are many ways in which this sense perception is very obscure and confused; but [we must] at least [admit that] everything which I conceive clearly and distinctly [as occurring] in them—that is to say, everything, generally speaking, which is discussed in pure mathematics [or geometry]—does in truth occur in them.

As for the rest, there are other beliefs, which are very doubtful and uncertain, which are either merely particular—as, for example, that the sun is of such a size and such a shape—or else are conceived less clearly [and less distinctly]—such as light, sound, pain, and other similar things. Nevertheless, from the mere fact that God is not a deceiver, and that in consequence he has not permitted any falsity in my opinions without having given me some faculty capable of correcting it, [I think I can conclude with assurance that] I have some hope of learning the truth even about these matters [and the means of knowing them with certainty].

First, there is no doubt but that all that nature teaches me contains some truth. For by nature, considered in general, I now understand nothing else but God himself, or else the [order and] system that God has established for created things; and by my nature in particular I understand nothing else but the arrangement [or assemblage] of all that God has given me.

Now there is nothing that this nature teaches me more expressly [or more obviously] than that I have a body which is in poor condition when I feel pain, which needs food or drink when I have the feelings of hunger or thirst, and so on. And therefore I ought to have no doubt that in this there is some truth.

Nature also teaches me by these feelings of pain, hunger, thirst, and so on that I am not only residing in my body, as a pilot in his ship, but furthermore, that I am intimately connected with it, and that [the mixture is] so blended, as it were, that [something like] a single whole is produced. For if that were not the case, when my body is wounded I would not therefore feel pain, I, who am only a thinking being; but I would perceive that wound by the understanding alone, as a pilot perceives by sight if something in his vessel is broken. And when my body needs food or drink, I would simply know the fact itself, instead of [receiving notice of it by] having confused feelings of hunger and thirst. For actually all these feelings of hunger, thirst, pain, and so on are nothing else but certain confused modes of thinking, which have their origin in [and depend upon] the union and apparent fusion of the mind with the body.

Furthermore, nature teaches me that many other bodies exist in the vicinity of my own, of which I must seek some and avoid others. And certainly, from the fact that I perceive different kinds of colors, odors, tastes, sounds, heat, hardness, and so on, I very readily conclude that in the objects from which these various sense perceptions proceed there are some corresponding variations, although perhaps these variations are not really similar to the perceptions. And from the fact that some of these [various sense] perceptions are agreeable to me and others are disagreeable, there is absolutely no doubt that my body, or rather my whole self, in so far as I am composed of body and mind, can in various ways be benefited or harmed by the other objects which surround it.

But there are many other opinions that nature has apparently taught me which, however, I have not truly learned from her, but which were introduced into my mind by my habit of judging things inattentively. Thus it can easily happen that these opinions contain some falsity—as, for example, my opinion that all spaces in which there is nothing which [affects and] makes an impression on my senses are empty; that in an object which is hot there is some quality similar to my idea of heat; that in a white, [or black,] or green object there is the same whiteness, [or blackness,] or greenness that I perceive; that in a bitter or sweet object there is the same taste [or the same flavor], and so on for the other senses; and that stars, towers, and all other distant objects are the same shape and size that they appear [from afar] to our eyes, and so forth.

In order that there should be nothing in this matter that I do not conceive sufficiently distinctly, I should define more precisely what I properly mean when I say that nature teaches me something. For I am here using the word "nature" in a more restricted sense than when I use it to mean a combination [or assemblage] of everything God has given me, seeing that this [assemblage or] combination includes many things which pertain to the mind alone, to which I do not intend to refer here when speaking of nature—as [for example] my knowledge [of this truth] that what has [once] been done can never [after] not have been done, and all [of an infinity of] other [similar] truths known to me by the light of nature [without any aid of the body]. Such an assemblage also includes many other things which belong to body alone and are not here included under the name of "nature," such as its quality of being heavy and many other similar ones; for I am not concerned with these either, but only with those things which God has presented to me as a being composed of mind and body. This nature effectively teaches me to avoid things which produce in me the feeling of pleasure and so on. But I do not see that beyond this it teaches me that I should ever conclude anything from these various sense perceptions concerning things outside of ourselves, unless the mind has [carefully and] maturely examined them. For it seems to me that it is the business of the mind alone, and not of the being composed of mind and body, to decide the truth of such matters.

Thus, although a star makes no more impression on my eye than the flame of a candle, and there is no real or positive inclination [or natural faculty] in me that leads me to believe that it is larger than this flame, nevertheless I have so judged it from infancy for no adequate reason. And although in approaching the flame I feel heat, and even though in approaching it a little too closely I feel pain, there is still no reason that can convince me that there is some quality in the flame similar to this heat, any more than to this pain. I only have reason to believe there is some quality in it, whatever it may be, which arouses in me these feelings of heat or pain.

Similarly, although there are parts of space in which I find nothing that [excites and] affects my senses, I ought not therefore to conclude that they contain no objects. Thus I see that both here and in many other similar cases I am accustomed to [misunderstand and] misconstrue the order of nature, because although these [sensations or] sense perceptions were given to me only to indicate to my mind which objects are useful or harmful to the composite body of which it is a part, and are for that purpose sufficiently clear and distinct, I nevertheless use them as though they were very certain rules by which I could obtain direct information about the essence [and the nature] of external objects, about which they can of course give me no information except very obscurely and confusedly.

In the previous discussion I have already explained sufficiently how it happens, despite the supreme goodness of God, that error occurs in my judgments. One further difficulty, though, presents itself here. This concerns objects which I am taught by nature to seek or avoid and also the internal sensations which she has given me. For it seems to me that I have noticed error here [and thus that I am sometimes directly deceived by my nature]—as, for example, when the pleasant taste of some food in which poison has been mixed can induce me to take the poison, and so misleads me. It is nevertheless true that in this case nature [can be excused, for it] only leads me to desire the food in which a pleasant taste is found, and not to desire the poison which is unknown to it. Thus I cannot conclude anything from this except that my nature is not entirely and universally cognizant of all things. And at this there is no reason to be surprised, since man, being of a finite nature, is also restricted to a knowledge of a limited perfection.

But we also make mistakes sufficiently frequently even about matters of which we are directly informed by nature, as happens to sick people when they desire to drink or eat things which [can] later harm them. It might be argued here that the reason that they err is that their nature is corrupted. But this does not remove the difficulty, for a sick man is in truth no less the creation of God than is a man in full health, and therefore it is just as inconsistent with the goodness of God for him as for the other to have a [misleading and] faulty nature. A clock, composed of wheels and counterweights, is no less exactly obeying all the laws of nature when it is badly made and does not mark the time correctly than when it completely fulfills the intention of its maker; so also, the human body may be considered as a machine, so built and composed of bones, nerves, muscles, veins, blood, and skin that even if there were no mind in it, it would not cease to move in all the ways that it does at present when it is not moved under the direction of the will, nor consequently with the aid of the mind [, but only by the condition of its organs]. I readily recognize that it is quite natural, for example, for this body to suffer dryness in the throat as a result of a dropsical condition, and thus to produce a feeling of thirst in the mind and a consequent disposition on the part of the mind to stimulate the nerves and other parts in the manner requisite for drinking, and so to increase the body's illness [and injure itself]. It is just as natural, I say, as it is for it to be beneficially influenced to drink by a similar dryness of the throat, when it is not ill at all.

And although in considering the purpose for which a clock has been intended by its designer, I can say that it is false to its nature when it does not correctly indicate the time, and although in considering the mechanism of the human body in the same way as having been formed [by God] to provide all the customary activities, I have reason to think that it is not functioning according to its nature when its throat is dry and drinking injures its chances of self-preservation, I nevertheless recognize that this last usage of the word "nature" is very different from the other. For the latter is nothing else but an arbitrary appellation which depends entirely on my own idea in comparing a sick man and a poorly made clock, and contrasting them with my idea of a healthy man and a well-made clock; this appellation refers to nothing which is actually found in the objects of which we are talking. On the contrary, by the other usage of the word "nature," I mean something which is actually found in objects and which therefore is not without some truth.

But certainly, although as far as a dropsical body is concerned, it is only an arbitrary appellation to say that its nature is corrupted when, without needing to drink, it still has a dry and arid throat; nevertheless, when we consider the composite body [as a whole]—that is to say, the mind [or soul] united with the body—-it is not a pure appellation, but [truly] an actual error on the part of nature that it is thirsty when it is very harmful to it to drink. Therefore we must examine how it is that the goodness of God does not prevent man's nature, so considered, from being faulty [and deceptive].

[To begin this examination,] I first take notice here that there is a great difference between the mind and the body, in that the body, from its nature, is always divisible and the mind is completely indivisible. For in reality, when I consider the mind—that is, when I consider myself in so far as I am only a thinking being—I cannot distinguish any parts, but I recognize [and conceive very clearly] that I am a thing which is absolutely unitary and entire. And although the whole mind seems to be united with the whole body, nevertheless when a foot or an arm or some other part of the body is amputated, I recognize quite well that nothing has been lost to my mind on that account. Nor can the faculties of willing, perceiving, understanding, and so forth be [any more properly] called parts of the mind, for it is one and the same mind which [as a complete unit] wills, perceives, and understands [, and so forth]. But just the contrary is the case with corporeal or extended objects, for I cannot imagine any [, however small they might be,] which my mind does not very easily divide into [several] parts, and I consequently recognize these objects to be divisible. This alone would suffice to show me that the mind [or soul of man] is altogether different from the body, if I did not already know it sufficiently well for other reasons.

I also take notice that the mind does not receive impressions from all parts of the body directly, but only from the brain, or perhaps even from one of its smallest parts—the one, namely, where the senses in common have their seat. This makes the mind feel the same thing whenever it is in the same condition, even though the other parts of the body can be differently arranged, as is proved by an infinity of experiments which it is not necessary to describe here.

I furthermore notice that the nature of the body is such that no one of its parts can be moved by another part some little distance away without its being possible for it to be moved in the same way by any one of the intermediate parts, even when the more distant part does not act. For example, in the cord A B C D [which is thoroughly stretched], if we pull [and move] the last part D, the first part A will not be moved in any different manner from that in which it could also be moved if we pulled one of the middle parts B or C, while the last part D remained motionless. And in the same way, when I feel pain in my foot, physics teaches me that this sensation is communicated by means of nerves distributed through the foot. When these nerves are pulled in the foot, being stretched like cords from there to the brain, they likewise pull at the same time the internal part of the brain [from which they come and] where they terminate, and there produce a certain movement which nature has arranged to make my mind feel pain as though that pain were in my foot. But because these nerves must pass through the leg, the thigh, the loins, the back, and the neck, in order to extend from the foot to the brain, it can happen that even when the nerve endings in the foot are not stimulated, but only some of the intermediate parts [located in the loins or the neck], precisely the same movements are nevertheless produced in the brain that could be produced there by a wound received in the foot, as a result of which it necessarily follows that the mind feels the same pain [in the foot as though the foot had been wounded]. And we must make the same judgment about all our other sense perceptions.

Finally, I notice that since each one of the movements that occurs in the part of the brain from which the mind receives impressions directly can only produce in the mind a single sensation, we cannot [desire or] imagine any better arrangement than that this movement should cause the mind to feel that sensation, of all the sensations the movement is capable of causing, which is most effectively and frequently useful for the preservation of the human body when it is in full health. But experience shows us that all the sensations which nature has given us are such as I have just stated, and therefore there is nothing in their nature which does not show the power and the goodness of [the] God [who has produced them].

Thus, for example, when the nerves of the foot are stimulated violently and more than is usual, their movement, passing though the marrow of the backbone up to the interior of the brain, produces there an impression upon the mind which makes the mind feel something—namely, pain as though in the foot—by which the mind is [warned and] stimulated to do whatever it can to remove the cause, taking it to be very [dangerous and] harmful to the foot.

It is true that God could establish the nature of man in such a way that this same brain event would make the mind feel something quite different; for example, it might cause the movement to be felt as though it were in the brain, or in the foot, or else in some other intermediate location [between the foot and the brain], or finally it might produce any other feeling [that can exist]; but none of those would have contributed so well to the preservation of the body [as that which it does produce].

In the same way, when we need to drink, there results a certain dryness in the throat which affects its nerves and, by means of them, the interior of the brain. This brain event makes the mind feel the sensation of thirst, because under those conditions there is nothing more useful to us than to know that we need to drink for the conservation of our health. And similar reasoning applies to other sensations.

From this it is entirely manifest that, despite the supreme goodness of God, the nature of man, in so far as he is composed of mind and body, cannot escape being sometimes [faulty and] deceptive. For if there is some cause which produces, not in the foot, but in some other part of the nerve which is stretched from the foot to the brain, or even in the brain itself, the same effect which ordinarily occurs when the foot is injured, we will feel pain as though it were in the foot, and we will naturally be deceived by the sensation. The reason for this is that the same brain event can cause only a single sensation in the mind; and this sensation being much more frequently produced by a cause which wounds the foot than by another acting in a different location, it is much more reasonable that it should always convey to the mind a pain in the foot rather than one in any other part [of the body]. And if it happens that sometimes the dryness of the throat does not come in the usual manner from the fact that drinking is necessary for the health of the body, but from some quite contrary cause, as in the case of those afflicted with dropsy, nevertheless it is much better that we should be deceived in that instance than if, on the contrary, we were always deceived when the body was in health; and similarly for the other sensations.

And certainly this consideration is very useful to me, not only so that I can recognize all the errors to which my nature is subject, but also so that I may avoid them or correct them more easily. For knowing that each of my senses conveys truth to me more often than falsehood concerning whatever is useful or harmful to the body, and being almost always able to use several of them to examine the same object, and being in addition able to use my memory to bind and join together present information with what is past, and being able to use my understanding, which has already discovered all the causes of my errors, I should no longer fear to encounter falsity in the objects which are most commonly represented to me by my senses.

And I should reject all the doubts of these last few days as exaggerated and ridiculous, particularly that very general uncertainty about sleep, which I could not distinguish from waking life. For now I find in them a very notable difference, in that our memory can never bind and join our dreams together [one with another and all] with the course of our lives, as it habitually joins together what happens to us when we are awake. And so, in effect, if someone suddenly appeared to me when I was awake and afterward disappeared in the same way, as [do images that I see] in my sleep, so that I could not determine where he came from or where he went, it would not be without reason that I would consider it a ghost or a phantom produced in my brain [and similar to those produced there when I sleep], rather than truly a man.

But when I perceive objects in such a way that I distinctly recognize both the place from which they come and the place where they are, as well as the time when they appear to me; and when, without any hiatus, I can relate my perception of them with all the rest of my life, I am entirely certain that I perceive them wakefully and not in sleep. And I should not in any way doubt the truth of these things if, having made use of all my senses, my memory, and my understanding, to examine them, nothing is reported to me by any of them which is inconsistent with what is reported by the others. For, from the fact that God is not a deceiver, it necessarily follows that in this matter I am not deceived.

But because the exigencies of action frequently [oblige us to make decisions and] do not [always] allow us the leisure to examine these things with sufficient care, we must admit that human life is very often subject to error in particular matters; and we must in the end recognize the infirmity [and weakness] of our nature.

C. Concept of Mind

Gilbert Ryle

THE OFFICIAL DOCTRINE

There is a doctrine about the nature and place of minds which is so prevalent among theorists and even among laymen that it deserves to be described as the official theory. Most philosophers, psychologists and religious teachers subscribe, with minor reservations, to its main articles and, although they admit certain theoretical difficulties in it, they tend to assume that these can be overcome without serious modifications being made to the architecture of the theory. It will be argued here that the central principles of the doctrine are unsound and conflict with the whole body of what we know about minds when we are not speculating about them.

The official doctrine, which hails chiefly from Descartes, is something like this. With the doubtful exceptions of idiots and infants in arms every human being has both a body and a mind. Some would prefer to say that every human being is both a body and a mind. His body and his mind are ordinarily harnessed together, but after the death of the body his mind may continue to exist and function.

Human bodies are in space and are subject to the mechanical laws which govern all other bodies in space. Bodily processes and states can be inspected by external observers. So a man's bodily life is as much a public affair as are the lives of animals and reptiles and even as the careers of trees, crystals and planets.

But minds are not in space, nor are their operations subject to mechanical laws. The workings of one mind are not witnessable by other observers; its career is private. Only I can take direct cognizance of the states and processes of my own mind. A person therefore lives through two collateral histories, one consisting of what happens in and to his body, the other consisting of what happens in and to his mind. The first is public, the second private. The events in the first history are events in the physical world, those in the second are events in the mental world.

It has been disputed whether a person does or can directly monitor all or only some of the episodes of his own private history; but,

according to the official doctrine, of at least some of these episodes he
has direct and unchallengeable cognisance. In consciousness, self-consciousness and introspection he is directly and authentically apprised
of the present states and operations of his mind. He may have great or
small uncertainties about concurrent and adjacent episodes in the
physical world, but he can have none about at least part of what is
momentarily occupying his mind.

It is customary to express this bifurcation of his two lives and of
his two worlds by saying that the things and events which belong to
the physical world, including his own body, are external, while the
workings of his own mind are internal. This antithesis of outer and
inner is of course meant to be construed as a metaphor, since minds,
not being in space, could not be described as being spatially inside anything else, or as having things going on spatially inside themselves. But
relapses from this good intention are common and theorists are found
speculating how stimuli, the physical sources of which are yards or
miles outside a person's skin, can generate mental responses inside his
skull, or how decisions framed inside his cranium can set going movements of his extremities.

Even when 'inner' and 'outer' are construed as metaphors, the
problem how a person's mind and body influence one another is noto-
riously charged with theoretical difficulties. What the mind wills, the
legs, arms and the tongue execute; what affects the ear and the eye has
something to do with what the mind perceives; grimaces and smiles
betray the mind's moods and bodily castigations lead, it is hoped, to
moral improvement. But the actual transactions between the episodes
of the private history and those of the public history remain mysterious, since by definition they can belong to neither series. They could
not be reported among the happenings described in a person's auto-
biography of his inner life, but nor could they be reported among those
described in someone else's biography of that person's overt career.
They can be inspected neither by introspection nor by laboratory
experiment. They are theoretical shuttlecocks which are forever being
bandied from the physiologist back to the psychologist and from the
psychologist back to the physiologist.

Underlying this partly metaphorical representation of the bifurcation of a person's two lives there is a seemingly more profound and
philosophical assumption. It is assumed that there are two different
kinds of existence or status. What exists or happens may have the status of physical existence, or it may have the status of mental existence.
Somewhat as the faces of coins are either heads or tails, or somewhat
as living creatures are either male or female, so, it is supposed, some

existing is physical existing, other existing is mental existing. It is a necessary feature of what has physical existence that it is in space and time; it is a necessary feature of what has mental existence that it is in time but not in space. What has physical existence is composed of matter, or else is a function of matter; what has mental existence consists of consciousness, or else is a function of consciousness.

There is thus a polar opposition between mind and matter, an opposition which is often brought out as follows. Material objects are situated in a common field, known as 'space', and what happens to one body in one part of space is mechanically connected with what happens to other bodies in other parts of space. But mental happenings occur in insulated fields, known as 'minds', and there is, apart maybe from telepathy, no direct causal connection between what happens in one mind and what happens in another. Only through the medium of the public physical world can the mind of one person make a difference to the mind of another. The mind is its own place and in his inner life each of us lives the life of a ghostly Robinson Crusoe. People can see, hear and jolt one another's bodies, but they are irremediably blind and deaf to the workings of one another's minds and inoperative upon them.

What sort of knowledge can be secured of the workings of a mind? On the one side, according to the official theory, a person has direct knowledge of the best imaginable kind of the workings of his own mind. Mental states and processes are (or are normally) conscious states and processes, and the consciousness which irradiates them can engender no illusions and leaves the door open for no doubts. A person's present thinkings, feelings and willings, his perceivings, rememberings and imaginings are intrinsically 'phosphorescent'; their existence and their nature are inevitably betrayed to their owner. The inner life is a stream of consciousness of such a sort that it would be absurd to suggest that the mind whose life is that stream might be unaware of what is passing down it.

True, the evidence adduced recently by Freud seems to show that there exist channels tributary to this stream, which run hidden from their owner. People are actuated by impulses the existence of which they vigorously disavow; some of their thoughts differ from the thoughts which they acknowledge; and some of the actions which they think they will to perform they do not really will. They are thoroughly gulled by some of their own hypocrisies and they successfully ignore facts about their mental lives which on the official theory ought to be patent to them. Holders of the official theory tend, however, to maintain that anyhow in normal circumstances a person must be directly and authentically seized of the present state and workings of his own mind.

Besides being currently supplied with these alleged immediate data of consciousness, a person is also generally supposed to be able to exercise from time to time a special kind of perception, namely inner perception, or introspection. He can take a (non-optical) 'look' at what is passing in his mind. Not only can he view and scrutinize a flower through his sense of sight and listen to and discriminate the notes of a bell through his sense of hearing; he can also reflectively or introspectively watch, without any bodily organ of sense, the current episodes of his inner life. This self-observation is also commonly supposed to be immune from illusion, confusion or doubt. A mind's reports of its own affairs have a certainty superior to the best that is possessed by its reports of matters in the physical world. Sense-perceptions can, but consciousness and introspection cannot, be mistaken or confused.

On the other side, one person has no direct access of any sort to the events of the inner life of another. He cannot do better than make problematic inferences from the observed behaviour of the other person's body to the states of mind which, by analogy from his own conduct, he supposes to be signalised by that behaviour. Direct access to the workings of a mind is the privilege of that mind itself; in default of such privileged access, the workings of one mind are inevitably occult to everyone else. For the supposed arguments from bodily movements similar to their own to mental workings similar to their own would lack any possibility of observational corroboration. Not unnaturally, therefore, an adherent of the official theory finds it difficult to resist this consequence of his premises, that he has no good reason to believe that there do exist minds other than his own. Even if he prefers to believe that to other human bodies there are harnessed minds not unlike his own, he cannot claim to be able to discover their individual characteristics, or the particular things that they undergo and do. Absolute solitude is on this showing the ineluctable destiny of the soul. Only our bodies can meet.

As a necessary corollary of this general scheme there is implicitly prescribed a special way of construing our ordinary concepts of mental powers and operations. The verbs, nouns and adjectives, with which in ordinary life we describe the wits, characters and higher-grade performances of the people with whom we have do, are required to be construed as signifying special episodes in their secret histories, or else as signifying tendencies for such episodes to occur. When someone is described as knowing, believing or guessing something, as hoping, dreading, intending or shirking something, as designing this or being amused at that, these verbs are supposed to denote the occurrence of specific modifications in his (to us) occult stream of consciouness. Only his own privileged access to this stream in direct awareness and introspection could provide authentic testimony that these mental-conduct verbs were correctly or incorrectly applied. The onlooker, be he teacher, critic, biographer or friend, can never assure himself that his comments have any vestige of truth. Yet it was just because we do in fact all know how to make such comments, make them with general correctness and correct them when they turn out to be confused or mistaken, that philosophers found it necessary to construct their theories of the nature and place of minds. Finding mental-conduct concepts being regularly and effectively used, they properly sought to fix their logical geography. But the logical geography officially recommended would entail that there could be no regular or effective use of these mental-conduct concepts in our descriptions of, and prescriptions for, other people's minds.

THE ABSURDITY OF THE OFFICIAL DOCTRINE

Such in outline is the official theory. I shall often speak of it, with deliberate abusiveness, as 'the dogma of the Ghost in the Machine'. I hope to prove that it is entirely false, and false not in detail but in principle. It is not merely an assemblage of particular mistakes. It is one big mistake and a mistake of a special kind. It is, namely, a category-mistake. It represents the facts of mental life as if they belonged to one logical type or category (or range of types or categories), when they actually belong to another. The dogma is therefore a philosopher's myth. In attempting to explode the myth I shall probably be taken to be denying well-known facts about the mental life of human beings, and my plea that I aim at doing nothing more than rectify the logic of mental-conduct concepts will probably be disallowed as mere subterfuge.

I must first indicate what is meant by the phrase 'Category-mistake'. This I do in a series of illustrations.

A foreigner visiting Oxford or Cambridge for the first time is shown a number of colleges, libraries, playing fields, museums, scientific departments and administrative offices. He then asks 'But where is the University? I have seen where the members of the Colleges live, where the Registrar works, where the scientists experiment and the rest. But I have not yet seen the University in which reside and work the members of your University.' It has then to be explained to him that the University is not another collateral institution, some ulterior counterpart to the colleges, laboratories and offices which he has seen. The University is just the way in which all that he has already seen is organized. When they are seen and when their co-ordination is understood, the University has been seen. His mistake lay in his innocent assumption that it was correct to speak of Christ Church, the Bodleian Library, the Ashmolean Museum *and* the University, to speak, that is, as if 'the University' stood for an extra member of the class of which these other units are members. He was mistakenly allocating the University to the same category as that to which the other institutions belong.

The same mistake would be made by a child witnessing the march-past of a division, who, having had pointed out to him such and such battalions, batteries, squadrons, etc., asked when the division was going to appear. He would be supposing that a division was a counterpart to the units already seen, partly similar to them and partly unlike them. He would be shown his mistake by being told that in watching the battalions, batteries and squadrons marching past he had been watching the division marching past. The march-past was not a parade of battalions, batteries, squadrons *and* a division; it was a parade of the battalions, batteries and squadrons *of* a division.

One more illustration. A foreigner watching his first game of cricket learns what are the functions of the bowlers, the batsmen, the fielders, the umpires and the scorers. He then says 'But there is no one left on the field to contribute the famous element of team-spirit. I see who does the bowling, the batting and the wicket-keeping; but I do not see whose role it is to exercise *esprit de corps*.' Once more, it would have to be explained that he was looking for the wrong type of thing. Team-spirit is not another cricketing-operation supplementary to all of the other special tasks. It is, roughly, the keenness with which each of the special tasks is performed, and performing a task keenly is not performing two tasks. Certainly exhibiting team-spirit is not the same thing as bowling or catching, but nor is it a third thing such that we can say that the bowler first bowls *and* then exhibits team-spirit or that a fielder is at a given moment *either* catching *or* displaying *esprit de corps*.

These illustrations of category-mistakes have a common feature which must be noticed. The mistakes were made by people who did not know how to wield the concepts *University, division* and *team-spirit*. Their puzzles arose from inability to use certain items in the English vocabulary.

The theoretically interesting category-mistakes are those made by people who are perfectly competent to apply concepts, at least in the situations with which they are familiar, but are still liable in their abstract thinking to allocate those concepts to logical types to which they do not belong. An instance of a mistake of this sort would be the following story. A student of politics has learned the main differences between the British, the French and the American Constitutions, and has learned also the differences and connections between the Cabinet, Parliament, the various Ministries, the Judicature and the Church of England. But he still becomes embarrassed when asked questions about the connections between the Church of England, the Home Office and the British Constitution. For while the Church and the Home Office are institutions, the British Constitution is not another institution in the same sense of that noun. So inter-institutional relations which can be asserted or denied to hold between the Church and the Home Office cannot be asserted or denied to hold between either of them and the British Constitution. 'The British Constitution' is not a term of the same logical type as 'the Home Office' and 'the Church of England'. In a partially similar way, John Doe may be a relative, a friend, an enemy or a stranger to Richard Roe; but he cannot be any of these things to the Average Taxpayer. He knows how to talk sense in certain sorts of discussions about the Average Taxpayer, but he is baffled to say why he could not come across him in the street as he can come across Richard Roe.

It is pertinent to our main subject to notice that, so long as the student of politics continues to think of the British Constitution as a counterpart to the other institutions, he will tend to describe it as a mysteriously occult institution; and so long as John Doe continues to think of the Average Taxpayer as a fellow-citizen, he will tend to think of him as an elusive insubstantial man, a ghost who is everywhere yet nowhere.

My destructive purpose is to show that a family of radical category-mistakes is the source of the double-life theory. The representation of a person as a ghost mysteriously ensconced in a machine derives from this argument. Because, as is true, a person's thinking, feeling and purposive doing cannot be described solely in the idioms of physics, chemistry and physiology, therefore they must be described in counterpart idioms. As the human body is a complex organised unit, so the human mind must be another complex organised unit, though one made of a different sort of stuff and with a different sort of structure. Or, again, as the human body, like any other parcel of matter, is a field of causes and effects, so the mind must be another field of causes and effects, though not (Heaven be praised) mechanical causes and effects.

D. Time and Free Will

Henri Bergson

Now, if space is to be defined as the homogeneous, it seems that inversely every homogeneous and unbounded medium will be space. For, homogeneity here consisting in the absence of every quality, it is hard to see how two forms of the homogeneous could be distinguished from one another. Nevertheless it is generally agreed to regard time as an unbounded medium, different from space but homogeneous like the latter: the homogeneous is thus supposed to take two forms, according as its contents co-exist or follow one another. It is true that, when we make time a homogeneous medium in which conscious states unfold themselves, we take it to be given all at once, which amounts to saying that we abstract it from duration. This simple consideration ought to warn us that we are thus unwittingly falling back upon space, and really giving up time. Moreover, we can understand that material objects, being exterior to one another and to ourselves, derive both exteriorities from the homogeneity of a medium which inserts intervals between them and sets off their outlines: but states of consciousness, even when successive, permeate one another, and in the simplest of them the whole soul can be reflected. We may therefore surmise that time, conceived under the form of a homogeneous medium, is some spurious concept, due to the trespassing of the idea of space upon the field of pure consciousness. At any rate we cannot finally admit two forms of the homogeneous, time and space, without first seeking whether one of them cannot be reduced to the other. Now, externality is the distinguishing mark of things which occupy space, while states of consciousness are not essentially external to one another, and become so only by being spread out in time, regarded as a homogeneous medium. If, then, one of these two supposed forms of the homogeneous, namely time and space, is derived from the other, we can surmise *a priori* that the idea of space is the fundamental datum. But, misled by the apparent simplicity of the idea of time, the philosophers who have tried to reduce one of these ideas to the other have thought that they could make extensity out of duration. While showing how they have been misled, we shall see that time, conceived under the form of an unbounded and homogeneous medium, is nothing but the ghost of space haunting the reflective consciousness.

The English school tries, in fact, to reduce relations of extensity to more or less complex relations of succession in time. When, with our eyes shut, we run our hands along a surface, the rubbing of our fingers against the surface, and especially the varied play of our joints, provide a series of sensations, which differ only by their *qualities* and which exhibit a certain order in time. Moreover, experience teaches us that this series can be reversed, that we can, by an effort of a different kind (or, as we shall call it later, *in an opposite direction*), obtain the same sensations over again in an inverse order: relations of position in space might then be defined as reversible relations of succession in time. But such a definition involves a vicious circle, or at least a very superficial idea of time. There are, indeed, as we shall show a little later, two possible conceptions of time, the one free from all alloy, the other surreptitiously bringing in the idea of space. Pure duration is the form which the succession of our conscious states assumes when our ego lets itself *live,* when it refrains from separating its present state from its former states. For this purpose it need not be entirely absorbed in the passing sensation or idea; for then, on the contrary, it would no longer *endure.* Nor need it forget its former states: it is enough that, in recalling these states, it does not set them alongside its actual state as one point alongside another, but forms both the past and the present states into an organic whole, as happens when we recall the notes of a tune, melting, so to speak, into one another. Might it not be said that, even if these notes succeed one another, yet we perceive them in one another, and that their totality may be compared to a living being whose parts, although distinct, permeate one another just because they are so closely connected? The proof is that, if we interrupt the rhythm by dwelling longer than is right on one note of the tune, it is not its exaggerated length, as length, which will warn us of our mistake, but the qualitative change thereby caused in the whole of the musical phrase. We can thus conceive of succession without distinction, and think of it as a mutual penetration, an interconnexion and organization of elements, each one of which represents the whole, and cannot be distinguished or isolated from it except by abstract thought. Such is the account of duration which would be given by a being who was ever the same and ever changing, and who had no idea of space. But, familiar with the latter idea and indeed beset by it, we introduce it unwittingly into our feeling of pure succession; we set our states of consciousness side by side in such a way as to perceive them simultaneously, no longer in one another, but alongside one another; in a word, we project time into space, we express duration in terms of extensity, and succession thus takes the form of a continuous line or a chain, the parts of which touch without penetrating one another. Note that the mental image thus shaped implies the perception, no longer successive, but simultaneous, of a *before* and *after,* and that it would be a contradiction to suppose a succession which was only a succession, and which nevertheless was contained in one and the same instant. Now, when we speak of an *order* of succession in duration, and of the reversibility of this order, is the succession we are dealing with pure succession, such as we have just defined it, without any admixture of extensity, or is it succession developing in space, in such a way that we can take in at once a number of elements which are both distinct and set side by side? There is no doubt about the answer: we could not introduce *order* among terms without first distinguishing them and then comparing the places which they occupy; hence we must perceive them as multiple, simultaneous and distinct; in a word, we set them side by side, and if we introduce an order in what is successive, the reason is that succession is converted into simultaneity and is projected into space. In short, when the movement of my finger along a surface or a line provides me with a series of sensations of different qualities, one of two things happens: either I picture these sensations to myself as in duration only, and in that case they succeed one another in such a way that I cannot at a given moment perceive a number of them as simultaneous and yet distinct; or else I make out an order of succession, but in that case I display the faculty not only of perceiving a succession of elements, but also of setting them out in line after having distinguished them: in a word, I already possess the idea of space. Hence the idea of a reversible series in duration, or even simply of a certain *order* of succession in time, itself implies the representation of space, and cannot be used to define it.

To give this argument a stricter form, let us imagine a straight line of unlimited length, and on this line a material point A, which moves. If this point were conscious of itself, it would feel itself change, since it moves: it would perceive a succession; but would this succession assume for it the form of a line? No doubt it would, if it could rise, so to speak, above the line which it traverses, and perceive simultaneously several points of it in juxtaposition: but by doing so it would form the idea of space, and it is in space and not in pure duration that it would see displayed the changes which it undergoes. We here put our finger on the mistake of those who regard pure duration as something similar to space, but of simpler nature. They are fond of setting psychic states side by side, of forming a chain or a line of them, and do not imagine that they are introducing into this operation the idea of space properly so called, the idea of space in its totality, because space is a medium of three dimensions. But how can they fail to notice that, in order to perceive a line as a line, it is necessary to take up a position outside it, to take account of the void which surrounds it, and consequently to think a space of three dimensions? If our conscious point A does not yet possess the idea of space—and this is the hypothesis which we have agreed to adopt—the succession of states through which it passes cannot assume for it the form of a line; but its sensations will add themselves dynamically to one another and will organize themselves, like the successive notes of a tune by which we allow ourselves to be lulled and soothed. In a word, pure duration might well be nothing but a succession of qualitative changes, which melt into and permeate one another, without precise outlines, without any tendency to externalize themselves in relation to one another, without any affiliation with number: it would be pure heterogeneity. But for the present we shall not insist upon this point; it is enough for us to have shown that, from the moment when you attribute the least homogeneity to duration, you surreptitiously introduce space.

It is true that we count successive moments of duration, and that, because of its relations with number, time at first seems to us to be a measurable magnitude, just like space. But there is here an important distinction to be made. I say, e.g., that a minute has just elapsed, and I mean by this that a pendulum, beating the seconds, has completed sixty oscillations. If I picture these sixty oscillations to myself all at once by a single mental perception, I exclude by hypothesis the idea of a succession. I do not think of sixty strokes which succeed one another, but of sixty points on a fixed line, each one of which symbolizes, so to speak, an oscillation of the pendulum. If, on the other hand, I wish to picture these sixty oscillations in succession, but without altering the way they are produced in space, I shall be compelled to think of each oscillation to the exclusion of the recollection of the preceding one, for space has preserved no trace of it; but by doing so I shall condemn myself to remain for ever in the present; I shall give up the attempt to think a succession or a duration. Now if, finally, I retain the recollection of the preceding oscillation together with the image of the present oscillation, one of two things will happen. Either I shall set the two images side by side, and we then fall back on our first hypothesis, or I shall perceive one in the other, each permeating the other and organizing themselves like the notes of a tune, so as to form what we shall call a continuous or qualitative multiplicity with no resemblance to number. I shall thus get the image of pure duration; but I shall have entirely got rid of the idea of a homogeneous medium or a measurable quantity. By carefully examining our consciousness we shall recognize that it proceeds in this way whenever it refrains from representing duration symbolically. When the regular oscillations of the pendulum make us sleepy, is it the last sound heard, the last movement perceived, which produces this effect? No, undoubtedly not, for why then should not the first have done the same? Is it the recollection of the preceding sounds or movements, set in juxtaposition to the last one? But this same recollection, if it is later on set in juxtaposition to a single sound or movement, will remain without effect. Hence we must admit that the sounds combined with one another and acted, not by their quantity as quantity, but by the quality which their quantity exhibited, i.e. by the rhythmic organization of the whole. Could the effect of a slight but continuous stimulation be understood in any other way? If the sensation remained always the same, it would continue to be indefinitely slight and indefinitely bearable. But the fact is that each increase of stimulation is taken up into the preceding stimulations, and that the whole produces on us the effect of a musical phrase which is constantly on the point of ending and constantly altered in its totality by the addition of some new note. If we assert that it is always the *same* sensation, the reason is that we are thinking, not of the sensation itself, but of its objective cause situated in space. We then set it out in space in its turn, and in place of an organism which develops, in place of changes which permeate one another, we perceive one and the same sensation stretching itself out lengthwise, so to speak, and setting itself in juxtaposition to itself without limit. Pure duration, that which consciousness perceives, must thus be reckoned among the so-called intensive magnitudes, if intensities can be called magnitudes: strictly speaking, however, it is not a quantity, and as soon as we try to measure it, we unwittingly replace it by space.

But we find it extraordinarily difficult to think of duration in its original purity; this is due, no doubt, to the fact that we do not *endure* alone; external objects, it seems, *endure* as we do, and time, regarded from this point of view, has every appearance of a homogeneous medium. Not only do the moments of this duration seem to be external to one another, like bodies in space, but the movement perceived by our senses is the, so to speak, palpable sign of a homogeneous and measurable duration. Nay more, time enters into the formulae of mechanics, into the calculations of the astronomer, and even of the physicist, under the form of a quantity. We measure the velocity of a movement, implying that time itself is a magnitude. Indeed, the analysis which we have just attempted requires to be completed, for if duration properly so-called cannot be measured, what is it that is measured by the oscillations of the pendulum? Granted that inner duration, perceived by consciousness, is nothing else but the melting of states of consciouness into one another, and the gradual growth of the ego, it will be said, notwithstanding, that the time which the astronomer introduces into his formulae, the time which our clocks divide into equal portions, this time, at least, is something different: it must be a measurable and therefore homogeneous magnitude.—It is nothing of the sort, however, and a close examination will dispel this last illusion.

When I follow with my eyes on the dial of a clock the movement of the hand which corresponds to the oscillations of the pendulum, I do not measure duration, as seems to be thought; I merely count simultaneities, which is very different. Outside of me, in space, there is never more than a single position of the hand and the pendulum, for nothing is left of the past positions. Within myself a process of organization or interpenetration of conscious states is going on, which constitutes true duration. It is because I *endure* in this way that I picture to myself what I call the past oscillations of the pendulum at the same time as I perceive the present oscillation. Now, let us withdraw for a moment the ego which thinks these so-called successive oscillations: there will never be more than a single oscillation, and indeed only a single position, of the pendulum, and hence no duration. Withdraw, on the other hand, the pendulum and its oscillations; there will no longer be anything but the heterogeneous duration of the ego, without moments external to one another, without relation to number. Thus, within our ego, there is succession without mutual externality; outside the ego, in pure space, mutual externality without succession: mutual externality, since the present oscillation is radically distinct from the previous oscillation, which no longer exists; but no succession, since succession exists solely for a conscious spectator who keeps the past in mind and sets the two oscillations or their symbols side by side in an auxiliary space. Now, between this succession without externality and this externality without succession, a kind of exchange takes place, very similar to what physicists call the phenomenon of endosmosis. As the successive phases of our conscious life, although interpenetrating, correspond individually to an oscillation of the pendulum which occurs at the same time, and as, moreover, these oscillations are sharply distinguished from one another, we get into the habit of setting up the same distinction between the successive moments of our conscious life: the oscillations of the pendulum break it up, so to speak, into parts external to one another: hence the mistaken idea of a homogeneous inner duration, similar to space, the moments of which are identical and follow, without penetrating, one another. But, on the other hand, the oscillations of the pendulum, which are distinct only because one has disappeared when the other appears on the scene, profit, as it were, from the influence which they have thus exercised over our conscious life. Owing to the fact that our consciousness has organized them as a whole in memory, they are first preserved and afterwards disposed in a series: in a word, we create for them a fourth dimension of space, which we call homogeneous time, and which enables the movement of the pendulum, although taking place at one spot, to be continually set in juxtaposition to itself. Now, if we try to determine the exact part played by the real and the imaginary in this very complex process, this is what we find. There is a real space, without duration, in which phenomena appear and disappear simultaneously with our states of consciousness. There is a real duration, the heterogeneous moments of which permeate one another; each moment, however, can be brought into relation with a state of the external world which is contemporaneous with it, and can be separated from the other moments in consequence of this very process. The comparison of these two realities gives rise to a symbolical representation of duration, derived from space. Duration thus assumes the illusory form of a homogeneous medium, and the connecting link between these two terms, space and duration, is simultaneity, which might be defined as the intersection of time and space.

But another conclusion results from this analysis, namely, that the multiplicity of conscious states, regarded in its original purity, is not at all like the discrete multiplicity which goes to form a number. In such a case there is, as we said, a qualitative multiplicity. In short, we must admit two kinds of multiplicity, two possible senses of the word "distinguish," two conceptions, the one qualitative and the other quantitative, of the difference between *same* and *other.* Sometimes this multiplicity, this distinctness, this heterogeneity contains number only potentially, as Aristotle would have said. Consciousness, then, makes a qualitative discrimination without any further thought of counting the qualities or even of distinguishing them as *several.* In such a case we have multiplicity without quantity. Sometimes, on the other hand, it is a question of a multiplicity of terms which are counted or which are conceived as capable of being counted; but we think then of the possibility of externalizing them in relation to one another, we set them out in space. Unfortunately, we are so accustomed to illustrate one of these two meanings of the same word by the other, and even to perceive the one in the other, that we find it extraordinarily difficult to distinguish between them or at least to express this distinction in words. Thus I said that several conscious states are organized into a whole, permeate one another, gradually gain a richer content, and might thus give any one ignorant of space the feeling of pure duration; but the very use of the word "several" shows that I had already isolated these states, externalized them in relation to one another, and, in a word, set them side by side; thus, by the very language which I was compelled to use, I betrayed the deeply ingrained habit of setting out time in space. From this spatial setting out, already accomplished, we are compelled to borrow the terms which we use to describe the state of a mind which has not yet accomplished it: these terms are thus misleading from the very beginning, and the idea of a multiplicity without relation to number or space, although clear for pure reflective thought, cannot be translated into the language of common sense. And yet we cannot even form the idea of discrete multiplicity without considering at the same time a qualitative multiplicity. When we explicitly count units by stringing them along a spatial line, is it not the case that, alongside this addition of identical terms standing out from a homogeneous background, an organization of these units is going on in the depths of the soul, a wholly dynamic process, not unlike the purely qualitative way in which an anvil, if it could feel, would realize a series of blows from a hammer? In this sense we might almost say that the numbers in daily use have each their emotional equivalent. Tradesmen are well aware of it, and instead of indicating the price of an object by a round number of shillings, they will mark the next smaller number, leaving themselves to insert afterwards a sufficient number of pence and farthings. In a word, the process by which we count units and make them into a discrete multiplicity has two sides; on the one hand we assume that they are identical, which is conceivable only on condition that these units are ranged alongside each other in a homogeneous medium; but on the other hand the third unit, for example, when added to the other two, alters the nature, the appearance and, as it were, the rhythm of the whole; without this interpenetration and this, so to speak, qualitative progress, no addition would be possible. Hence it is through the quality of quantity that we form the idea of quantity without quality.

It is therefore obvious that, if it did not betake itself to a symbolical substitute, our consciousness would never regard time as a homogeneous medium, in which the terms of a succession remain outside one another. But we naturally reach this symbolical representation by the mere fact that; in a series of identical terms, each term assumes a double aspect for our consciousness: one aspect which is the same for all of them, since we are thinking then of the sameness of the external object, and another aspect which is characteristic of each of them, because the supervening of each term brings about a new organization of the whole. Hence the possibility of setting out in space, under the form of numerical multiplicity, what we have called a qualitative multiplicity, and of regarding the one as the equivalent of the other. Now, this twofold process is nowhere accomplished so easily as in the perception of the external phenomenon which takes for us the form of motion. Here we certainly have a series of identical terms, since it is always the same moving body; but, on the other hand, the synthesis carried out by our consciousness between the actual position and what our memory calls the former positions, causes these images to permeate, complete, and, so to speak, continue one another. Hence, it is principally by the help of motion that duration assumes the form of a homogenous medium, and that time is projected into space. But, even if we leave out motion, any repetition of a well-marked external phenomenon would suggest to consciousness the same mode of representation. Thus, when we hear a series of blows of a hammer, the sounds form an indivisible melody in so far as they are pure sensations, and, here again, give rise to a dynamic progress; but, knowing that the same objective cause is at work, we cut up this progress into phases which we then regard as identical; and this multiplicity of elements no longer being conceivable except by being set out in space, since they have now become identical, we are necessarily led to the idea of a homogeneous time, the symbolical image of real duration. In a word, our ego comes in contact with the external world at its surface; our successive sensations, although dissolving into one another, retain something of the mutual externality which belongs to their objective causes; and thus our superficial psychic life comes to be pictured without any great effort as set out in a homogeneous medium. But the symbolical character of such a picture becomes more striking as we advance further into the depths of consciousness: the deep-seated self which ponders and decides, which heats and blazes up, is a self whose states and changes permeate one another and undergo a deep alteration as soon as we separate them from one another in order to set them out in space. But as this deeper self forms one and the same person with the superficial ego, the two seem to *endure* in the same way. And as the repeated picture of one identical objective phenomenon, ever recurring, cuts up our superficial psychic life into parts external to one another, the moments which are thus determined determine in their turn distinct segments in the dynamic and undivided progress of our more personal conscious states. Thus the mutual externality which material objects gain from their juxtaposition in homogeneous space reverberates and spreads into the depths of consciousness: little by little our sensations are distinguished from one another like the external causes which gave rise to them, and our feelings or ideas come to be separated like the sensations with which they are contemporaneous.

That our ordinary conception of duration depends on a gradual incursion of space into the domain of pure consciousness is proved by the fact that, in order to deprive the ego of the faculty of perceiving a homogeneous time, it is enough to take away from it this outer circle of psychic states which it uses as a balance-wheel. These conditions are realized when we dream; for sleep, by relaxing the play of the organic functions, alters the communicating surface between the ego and external objects. Here we no longer measure duration, but we feel it; from quantity it returns to the state of quality; we no longer estimate past time mathematically: the mathematical estimate gives place to a confused instinct, capable, like all instincts, of committing gross errors, but also of acting at times with extraordinary skill. Even in the waking state, daily experience ought to teach us to distinguish between duration as quality, that which consciousness reaches immediately and which is probably what animals perceive, and time so to speak materialized, time that has become quantity by being set out in space. Whilst I am writing these lines, the hour strikes on a neighbouring clock, but my inattentive ear does not perceive it until several strokes have made themselves heard. Hence I have not counted them; and yet I only have to turn my attention backwards to count up the four strokes which have already sounded and add them to those which I hear. If, then, I question myself carefully on what has just taken place, I perceive that the first four sounds had struck my ear and even affected my consciousness, but that the sensations produced by each one of them, instead of being set side by side, had melted into one another in such a way as to give the whole a peculiar quality, to make a kind of musical phrase out of it. In order, then, to estimate retrospectively the number of strokes sounded, I tried to reconstruct this phrase in thought: my imagination made one stroke, then two, then three, and as long as it did not reach the exact number four, my feeling, when consulted, answered that the total effect was qualitatively different. It had thus ascertained in its own way the succession of four strokes, but quite otherwise than by a process of addition, and without bringing in the image of a juxtaposition of distinct terms. In a word, the number of strokes was perceived as a quality and not as a quantity: it is thus that duration is presented to immediate consciousness, and it retains this form so long as it does not give place to a symbolical representation derived from extensity.

We should therefore distinguish two forms of multiplicity, two very different ways of regarding duration, two aspects of conscious life. Below homogeneous duration, which is the extensive symbol of true duration, a close psychological analysis distinguishes a duration whose heterogeneous moments permeate one another; below the numerical multiplicity of conscious states, a qualitative multiplicity; below the self with well-defined states, a self in which *succeeding each other* means *melting into one another* and forming an organic whole. But we are generally content with the first, i.e. with the shadow of the self projected into homogeneous space. Consciousness, goaded by an insatiable desire to separate, substitutes the symbol for the reality, or perceives the reality only through the symbol. As the self thus refracted, and thereby broken to pieces, is much better adapted to the requirements of social life in general and language in particular, consciousness prefers it, and gradually loses sight of the fundamental self.

In order to recover this fundamental self, as the unsophisticated consciousness would perceive it, a vigorous effort of analysis is necessary, which will isolate the fluid inner states from their image, first refracted, then solidified in homogeneous space. In other words, our perceptions, sensations, emotions and ideas occur under two aspects: the one clear and precise, but impersonal; the other confused, ever changing, and inexpressible, because language cannot get hold of it without arresting its mobility or fit it into its common-place forms without making it into public property. If we have been led to distinguish two forms of multiplicity, two forms of duration, we must expect each conscious state, taken by itself, to assume a different aspect according as we consider it within a discrete multiplicity or a confused multiplicity, in the time as quality, in which it is produced, or in the time as quantity, into which it is projected.

E. Existence and the Existent

Jacques Maritain

B y sense or experience, science or philosophy, each of us, as I said a moment ago, knows the environing world of subjects, supposita, and persons in their rôle as objects. The paradox of consciousness and personality is that each of us is situated precisely *at the centre* of this world. Each is at the centre of infinity. And this privileged subject, the thinking self, is to itself not object but subject; in the midst of all the subjects which it knows only as objects, it alone is subject as subject. We are thus confronted by subjectivity as subjectivity.

I know myself as subject by consciousness and reflexivity, but my substance is obscure to me. St. Thomas explains that in spontaneous reflection, which is a prerogative of the life of the intellect, each of us knows (by a kind of knowledge that is not scientific but experimental and incommunicable) that his soul exists, knows the singular existence of this subjectivity that perceives, suffers, loves, thinks. When a man is awake to the intuition of being he is awake at the same time to the intuition of subjectivity; he grasps, in a flash that will never be dimmed, the fact that *he is a self,* as Jean-Paul said. The force of such a perception may be so great as to sweep him along to that heroic asceticism of the void and of annihilation in which he will achieve ecstasy in the substantial existence of the *self* and the 'presence of immensity' of the divine Self at one and the same time—which in my view characterises the natural mysticism of India.

But the intuition of subjectivity is an existential intuition which surrenders no essence to us. We know *that which* we are by our phenomena, our operations, our flow of consciousness. The more we grow accustomed to the inner life, the better we decipher the astonishing and fluid multiplicity which is thus delivered to us; the more, also, we feel that it leaves us ignorant of the essence of our self. Subjectivity *as subjectivity* is inconceptualisable; is an unknowable abyss. It is unknowable by the mode of notion, concept, or representation, or by any mode of any science whatsoever—introspection, psychology, or philosophy. How could it be otherwise, seeing that every reality known through a concept, a notion, or a representation is known as object and not as subject? Subjectivity as such escapes by definition from that which we know about ourselves by means of notions.

Yet it is known in a way, or rather in certain ways, which I should like briefly to enumerate. At the very beginning and above all, subjectivity is known or rather felt in virtue of a formless and diffuse knowledge which, in relation to reflective consciousness, we may call unconscious or pre-conscious knowledge. This is knowledge of the 'concomitant' or spontaneous consciousness, which, without giving rise to a distinct act of thought, envelops in fact, *in actu exercito,* our inner world in so far as it is integrated into the vital activity of our spiritual faculties. Even for the most superficial persons, it is true that from the moment when they say *I,* the whole unfolding of their states of consciousness and their operations, their musings, memories, and acts, is subsumed by a virtual and ineffable knowledge, a vital and existential knowledge of the totality immanent in each of its parts, and immersed, without their troubling to become aware of it, in the diffuse glow, the unique freshness, the maternal connivance as it were, which emanates from subjectivity. Subjectivity is not known, it is felt as a propitious and enveloping night.

There is, secondly, a knowledge of subjectivity as such, imperfect and fragmentary of course, but in this instance formed and actually given to the mind, and which is thrown into relief by what St. Thomas calls knowledge by mode of inclination, sympathy, or connaturality, not by mode of knowledge. It appears before us under three specifically distinct forms: (1) practical knowledge, which judges both moral matters and the subject itself, by the inner inclinations of the subject. I mentioned this some pages back in connection with moral conscience and prudence; (2) poetic knowledge, in which subjectivity and the things of this world are known together in creative intuition-emotion and are revealed and expressed together, not in a word or concept but in a created work; (3) mystical knowledge, which is not directed towards the subject but towards things divine, and does not of itself issue in any expression, but in which God is known by union and by connaturality of love, and in which this very love that becomes the formal means of knowledge of the divine Self, simultaneously renders the human self transparent in its spiritual depths. Let the mystic reflect an instant upon himself, and a St. Theresa or a St. John of the Cross will show us to what extent the divine light gives him a lucid and inexhaustible knowledge of his own subjectivity.

But in none of these instances is the knowledge of subjectivity as subjectivity, however real it be, a knowledge by mode of knowledge, which is to say, by mode of conceptual objectisation.

In none of these instances is it philosophical knowledge. It would be a contradiction in terms to seek to make a philosophy of that sort of knowledge, since every philosophy—like it or not—proceeds by concepts. This is the first point to which the consideration of subjectivity as subjectivity draws our attention; and it is a point of capital importance. Subjectivity marks the frontier which separates the world of philosophy from the world of religion. This is what Kierkegaard felt so deeply in his polemic against Hegel. Philosophy runs against an insurmountable barrier in attempting to deal with subjectivity, because while philosophy of course knows subjects, it knows them only as objects. Philosophy is registered whole and entire in the relation of intelligence to object; whereas religion enters into the relation of subject to subject. For this reason, every philosophical religion, or every philosophy which, like Hegel's, claims to assume and integrate religion into itself, is in the last analysis a mystification.

When philosophy, taking its start in the being of things, attains to God as the cause of being, it has then, thanks to ana-noetic knowledge, rendered the divine Self an object of philosophical knowledge expressed in concepts. These concepts do not circumscribe the supreme reality presented by them. On the contrary, that divine reality infinitely overflows the banks of conceptual knowledge. But philosophy knows thereby, or ought to know, that the reality thus objectised 'through a glass, darkly,' is the reality of a transcendent Self inscrutable in its being and its goodness, in its liberty and its glory. And all the other intelligent *selves* who know it, from the instant that they do know it, owe to it, as their first duty, obedience and adoration. St. Paul blamed pagan wisdom for not recognising that glory of God of which it was in fact aware. But in fact, to recognise that glory is already to adore it. It is something to know that God is a transcendent and sovereign Self; but it is something else again to enter oneself and with all one's baggage—one's own existence and flesh and blood—into the vital relationship in which created subjectivity is brought face to face with this transcendent subjectivity and, trembling and loving, looks to it for salvation. This is the business of religion.

Religion is essentially that which no philosophy can be: a relation of person to person with all the risk, the mystery, the dread, the confidence, the delight, and the torment that lie in such a relationship. And this very relationship of subject to subject demands that into the knowledge of uncreated subjectivity which the created subjectivity possesses there shall be transferred something of that which the latter is as *subjectivity,* i.e., as that uncreated subjectivity is in the mystery of its personal life. Whence all religion comports an element of revelation. Therefore in the true faith it is the First Truth in Person which makes known to man the mystery of the divine subjectivity: *unigenitus filius, qui est in sinu patris, ipse enarravit.* This knowledge is still 'through a glass, darkly,' and therein the divine subjectivity is still objectised in order to be grasped by us. But this time it is in the glass of the super-analogy of faith, in concepts which God Himself has chosen as His means of speaking to us about Himself—until at the last every glass falls away and then we know truly as we are known. Then shall we truly know the divine subjectivity as subjectivity in the vision in which the divine essence itself actuates our intellect and transports us in ecstasy within itself. While awaiting this state, the connaturality of love gives us, in apophatic contemplation, a dim sort of substitute and obscure foretaste of such a union.

III

THE EXISTENTIAL SELF

A. Existentialism and Human Emotions

Jean-Paul Sartre

A theistic existentialism, which I represent, is more coherent. It states that if God does not exist, there is at least one being in whom existence precedes essence, a being who exists before he can be defined by any concept, and that this being is man, or, as Heidegger says, human reality. What is meant here by saying that existence precedes essence? It means that, first of all, man exists, turns up, appears on the scene, and, only afterwards, defines himself. If man, as the existentialist conceives him, is indefinable, it is because at first he is nothing. Only afterward will he be something, and he himself will have made what he will be. Thus, there is no human nature, since there is no God to conceive it. Not only is man what he conceives himself to be, but he is also only what he wills himself to be after this thrust toward existence.

Man is nothing else but what he makes of himself. Such is the first principle of existentialism. It is also what is called subjectivity, the name we are labeled with when charges are brought against us. But what do we mean by this, if not that man has a greater dignity than a stone or table? For we mean that man first exists, that is, that man first of all is the being who hurls himself toward a future and who is conscious of imagining himself as being in the future. Man is at the start a plan which is aware of itself, rather than a patch of moss, a piece of garbage, or a cauliflower; nothing exists prior to this plan; there is nothing in heaven; man will be what he will have planned to be. Not what he will want to be. Because by the word "will" we generally mean a conscious decision, which is subsequent to what we have already made of ourselves. I may want to belong to a political party, write a book, get married; but all that is only a mainifestation of an earlier, more spontaneous choice that is called "will." But if existence really does precede essence, man is responsible for what he is. Thus, existentialism's first move is to make every man aware of what he is and to make the full responsibility of his existence rest on him. And when we say that a man is responsible for himself, we do not only mean that he is responsible for his own individuality, but that he is responsible for all men.

The word subjectivism has two meanings, and our opponents play on the two. Subjectivism means, on the one hand, that an individual chooses and makes himself; and, on the other, that it is impossible for man to transcend human subjectivity. The second of these is the essential meaning of existentialism. When we say that man chooses his own self, we mean that every one of us does likewise; but we also mean by that that in making this choice he also chooses all men. In fact, in creating the man that we want to be, there is not a single one of our acts which does not at the same time create an image of man as we think he ought to be. To choose to be this or that is to affirm at the same time the value of what we choose, because we can never choose evil. We always choose the good, and nothing can be good for us without being good for all.

If, on the other hand, existence precedes essence, and if we grant that we exist and fashion our image at one and the same time, the image is valid for everybody and for our whole age. Thus, our responsibility is much greater than we might have supposed, because it involves all mankind. If I am a workingman and choose to join a Christian trade-union rather than be a communist, and if by being a member I want to show that the best thing for man is resignation, that the kingdom of man is not of this world, I am not only involving my own case—I want to be resigned for everyone. As a result, my action has involved all humanity. To take a more individual matter, if I want to marry, to have children; even if this marriage depends solely on my own circumstances or passion or wish, I am involving all humanity in monogamy and not merely myself. Therefore, I am responsible for myself and for everyone else. I am creating a certain image of man of my own choosing. In choosing myself, I choose man.

This helps us understand what the actual content is of such rather grandiloquent words as anguish, forlornness, despair. As you will see, it's all quite simple.

First, what is meant by anguish? The existentialists say at once that man is anguish. What that means is this: the man who involves himself and who realizes that he is not only the person he chooses to be, but also a lawmaker who is, at the same time, choosing all mankind as well as himself, can not help escape the feeling of his total and deep responsibility. Of course, there are many people who are not anxious; but we claim that they are hiding their anxiety, that they are fleeing from it. Certainly, many people believe that when they do something, they themselves are the only ones involved, and when someone says to them, "What if everyone acted that way?" they shrug their shoulders and answer, "Everyone doesn't act that way." But really, one should always ask himself, "What would happen if everybody looked at things that way?" There is no escaping this disturbing thought except by a kind of double-dealing. A man who lies and makes excuses for himself by saying "not everybody does that," is someone with an uneasy conscience, because the act of lying implies that a universal value is conferred upon the lie.

Anguish is evident even when it conceals itself. This is the anguish that Kierkegaard called the anguish of Abraham. You know the story: an angel has ordered Abraham to sacrifice his son; if it really were an angel who has come and said, "You are Abraham, you shall sacrifice your son," everything would be all right. But everyone might first wonder, "Is it really an angel, and am I really Abraham? What proof do I have?"

There was a madwoman who had hallucinations; someone used to speak to her on the telephone and give her orders. Her doctor asked her, "Who is it who talks to you?" She answered, "He says it's God." What proof did she really have that it was God? If an angel comes to me, what proof is there that it's an angel? And if I hear voices, what proof is there that they come from heaven and not from hell, or from the subconscious, or a pathological condition? What proves that they are addressed to me? What proof is there that I have been appointed to impose my choice and my conception of man on humanity? I'll never find any proof or sign to convince me of that. If a voice addresses me, it is always for me to decide that this is the angel's voice; if I consider that such an act is a good one, it is I who will choose to say that it is good rather than bad.

Now, I'm not being singled out as an Abraham, and yet at every moment I'm obliged to perform exemplary acts. For every man, everything happens as if all mankind had its eyes fixed on him and were guiding itself by what he does. And every man ought to say to himself, "Am I really the kind of man who has the right to act in such a way that humanity might guide itself by my actions?" And if he does not say that to himself, he is masking his anguish.

There is no question here of the kind of anguish which would lead to quietism, to inaction. It is a matter of a simple sort of anguish that anybody who has had responsibilities is familiar with. For example, when a military officer takes the responsibility for an attack and sends a certain number of men to death, he chooses to do so, and in the main he alone makes the choice. Doubtless, orders come from above, but they are too broad; he interprets them, and on this interpretation depend the lives of ten or fourteen or twenty men. In making a decision he can not help having a certain anguish. All leaders know this anguish. That doesn't keep them from acting; on the contrary, it is the very condition of their action. For it implies that they envisage a number of possibilities, and when they choose one, they realize that it has value only because it is chosen. We shall see that this kind of anguish, which is the kind that existentialism describes, is explained, in addition, by a direct responsibility to the other men whom it involves. It is not a curtain separating us from action, but is part of action itself.

When we speak of forlornness, a term Heidegger was fond of, we mean only that God does not exist and that we have to face all the consequences of this. The existentialist is strongly opposed to a certain kind of secular ethics which would like to abolish God with the least possible expense. About 1880, some French teachers tried to set up a secular ethics which went something like this: God is a useless and costly hypothesis; we are discarding it; but, meanwhile, in order for there to be an ethics, a society, a civilization, it is essential that certain values be taken seriously and that they be considered as having *a priori* existence. It must be obligatory, *a priori,* to be honest, not to lie, not to beat your wife, to have children, etc., etc. So we're going to try a little device which will make it possible to show that values exist all the same, inscribed in a heaven of ideas, though otherwise God does not exist. In other words—and this, I believe, is the tendency of everything called reformism in France—nothing will be changed if God does not exist. We shall find ourselves with the same norms of honesty, progress, and humanism, and we shall have made of God an outdated hypothesis which will peacefully die off by itself.

The existentialist, on the contrary, thinks it very distressing that God does not exist, because all possibility of finding values in a heaven of ideas disappears along with Him; there can no longer be an *a priori* Good, since there is no infinite and perfect consciousness to think it. Nowhere is it written that the Good exists, that we must be honest, that we must not lie; because the fact is we are on a plane where there are only men. Dostoievsky said, "If God didn't exist, everything would be possible." That is the very starting point of existentialism. Indeed, everything is permissible if God does not exist, and as a result man is forlorn, because neither within him nor without does he find anything to cling to. He can't start making excuses for himself.

If existence really does precede essence, there is no explaining things away by reference to a fixed and given human nature. In other words, there is no determinism, man is free, man is freedom. On the other hand, if God does not exist, we find no values or commands to turn to which legitimize our conduct. So, in the bright realm of values, we have no excuse behind us, nor justification before us. We are alone, with no excuses.

That is the idea I shall try to convey when I say that man is condemned to be free. Condemned, because he did not create himself, yet, in other respects is free; because, once thrown into the world, he is responsible for everything he does. The existentialist does not believe in the power of passion. He will never agree that a sweeping passion is a raving torrent which fatally leads a man to certain acts and is therefore an excuse. He thinks that man is responsible for his passion.

The existentialist does not think that man is going to help himself by finding in the world some omen by which to orient himself. Because he thinks that man will interpret the omen to suit himself. Therefore, he thinks that man, with no support and no aid, is condemned every moment to invent man. Ponge, in a very fine article, has said, "Man is the future of man." That's exactly it. But if it is taken to mean that this future is recorded in heaven, that God sees it, then it is false, because it would really no longer be a future. If it is taken to mean that, whatever a man may be, there is a future to be forged, a virgin future before him, then this remark is sound. But then we are forlorn.

B. The German Ideology

Karl Marx

M en can be distinguished from animals by consciousness, by religion or anything else you like. They themselves begin to distinguish themselves from animals as soon as they begin to *produce* their means of subsistence, a step which is conditioned by their physical organisation. By producing their means of subsistence men are indirectly producing their actual material life.

The way in which men produce their means of subsistence depends first of all on the nature of the actual means of subsistence they find in existence and have to reproduce. This mode of production must not be considered simply as being the reproduction of the physical existence of individuals. Rather it is a definite form of activity of these individuals, a definite form of expressing their life, a definite *mode of life* on their part. As individuals express their life, so they are. What they are, therefore, coincides with their production, both with *what* they produce and with *how* they produce. The nature of individuals thus depends on the material conditions determining their production.

This production only makes its appearance with the *increase of population*. In its turn this presupposes the *intercourse* [*Verkehr*] of individuals with one another. The form of this intercourse is again determined by production.

The relations of different nations among themselves depend upon the extent to which each has developed its productive forces, the division of labour and internal intercourse. This statement is generally recognised. But not only the relation of one nation to others, but also the whole internal structure of the nation itself depends on the stage of development reached by its production and its internal and external intercourse. How far the productive forces of a nation are developed is shown most manifestly by the degree to which the division of labour has been carried. Each new productive force, insofar as it is not merely a quantitative extension of productive forces already known (for instance the bringing into cultivation of fresh land), causes a further development of the division of labour.

The division of labour inside a nation leads at first to the separation of industrial and commercial from agricultural labour, and hence

to the separation of *town* and *country* and to the conflict of their interests. Its further development leads to the separation of commercial
from industrial labour. At the same time through the division of
labour inside these various branches there develop various divisions
among the individuals co-operating in definite kinds of labour. The
relative position of these individual groups is determined by the methods employed in agriculture, industry and commerce (patriarchalism,
slavery, estates, classes). These same conditions are to be seen (given
a more developed intercourse) in the relations of different nations to
one another.

The various stages of development in the division of labour are
just so many different forms of ownership, i.e., the existing stage in the
division of labour determines also the relations of individuals to one
another with reference to the material, instrument, and product of
labour.

The first form of ownership is tribal [*Stammeigentum*] ownership.
It corresponds to the undeveloped stage of production, at which a people lives by hunting and fishing, by the rearing of beasts or, in the highest stage, agriculture. In the latter case it presupposes a great mass of
uncultivated stretches of land. The division of labour is at this stage
still very elementary and is confined to a further extension of the natural division of labour existing in the family. The social structure is,
therefore, limited to an extension of the family; patriarchal family
chieftains, below them the members of the tribe, finally slaves. The
slavery latent in the family only develops gradually with the increase
of population, the growth of wants, and with the extension of external
relations, both of war and of barter.

The second form is the ancient communal and State ownership
which proceeds especially from the union of several tribes into a *city*
by agreement or by conquest, and which is still accompanied by slavery. Beside communal ownership we already find movable, and later
also immovable, private property developing, but as an abnormal
form subordinate to communal ownership. The citizens hold power
over their labouring slaves only in their community, and on this
account alone, therefore, they are bound to the form of communal
ownership. It is the communal private property which compels the
active citizens to remain in this spontaneously derived form of association over against their slaves. For this reason the whole structure of
society based on this communal ownership, and with it the power of
the people, decays in the same measure as, in particular, immovable
private property evolves. The division of labour is already more developed. We already find the antagonism of town and country; later the

antagonism between those states which represent town interests and those which represent country interests, and inside the towns themselves the antagonism between industry and maritime commerce. The class relation between citizens and slaves is not completely developed.

This whole interpretation of history appears to be contradicted by the fact of conquest. Up till now violence, war, pillage, murder and robbery, etc., have been accepted as the driving force of history. Here we must limit ourselves to the chief points and take, therefore, only the most striking example—the destruction of an old civilisation by a barbarous people and the resulting formation of an entirely new organisation of society. (Rome and the barbarians; feudalism and Gaul; the Byzantine Empire and the Turks.) With the conquering barbarian people war itself is still, as indicated above, a regular form of intercourse, which is the more eagerly exploited as the increase in population together with the traditional and, for it, the only possible, crude mode of production gives rise to the need for new means of production. In Italy, on the other hand, the concentration of landed property (caused not only by buying-up and indebtedness but also by inheritance, since loose living being rife and marriage rare, the old families gradually died out and their possessions fell into the hands of a few) and its conversion into grazing-land (caused not only by the usual economic forces still operative today but by the importation of plundered and tribute corn and the resultant lack of demand for Italian corn) brought about the almost total disappearance of the free population. The very slaves died out again and again, and had constantly to be replaced by new ones. Slavery remained the basis of the whole productive system. The plebeians, midway between freemen and slaves, never succeeded in becoming more than a proletarian rabble. Rome indeed never became more than a city; its connection with the provinces was almost exclusively political and could, therefore, easily be broken again by political events.

With the development of private property, we find here for the first time the same conditions which we shall find again, only on a more extensive scale, with modern private property. On the one hand, the concentration of private property, which began very early in Rome (as the Licinian agrarian law proves) and proceeded very rapidly from the time of the civil wars and especially under the Emperors; on the other hand, coupled with this, the transformation of the plebeian small peasantry into a proletariat, which, however, owing to its intermediate position between propertied citizens and slaves, never achieved an independent development.

The third form of ownership is feudal or estate property. If antiquity started out from the town and its little territory, the Middle Ages started out from the *country*. This different starting-point was determined by the sparseness of the population at that time, which was scattered over a large area and which received no large increase from the conquerors. In contrast to Greece and Rome, feudal development at the outset, therefore, extends over a much wider territory, prepared by the Roman conquests and the spread of agriculture at first associated with them. The last centuries of the declining Roman Empire and its conquest by the barbarians destroyed a number of productive forces; agriculture had declined, industry had decayed for want of a market, trade had died out or been violently suspended, the rural and urban population had decreased. From these conditions and the mode of organisation of the conquest determined by them, feudal property developed under the influence of the Germanic military constitution. Like tribal and communal ownership, it is based again on a community; but the directly producing class standing over against it is not, as in the case of the ancient community, the slaves, but the enserfed small peasantry. As soon as feudalism is fully developed, there also arises antagonism to the towns. The hierarchical structure of landownership, and the armed bodies of retainers associated with it, gave the nobility power over the serfs. This feudal organisation was, just as much as the ancient communal ownership, an association against a subjected producing class; but the form of association and the relation to the direct producers were different because of the different conditions of production.

This feudal system of landownership had its counterpart in the *towns* in the shape of corporative property, the feudal organisation of trades. Here property consisted chiefly in the labour of each individual person. The necessity for association against the organised robber nobility, the need for communal covered markets in an age when the industrialist was at the same time a merchant, the growing competition of the escaped serfs swarming into the rising towns, the feudal structure of the whole country: these combined to bring about the *guilds*. The gradually accumulated small capital of individual craftsmen and their stable numbers, as against the growing population, evolved the relation of journeyman and apprentice, which brought into being in the towns a hierarchy similar to that in the country.

Thus the chief form of property during the feudal epoch consisted on the one hand of landed property with serf labour chained to it, and on the other of the labour of the individual with small capital commanding the labour of journeymen. The organisation of both was determined by the restricted conditions of production—the small-scale and primitive cultivation of the land, and the craft type of industry. There was little division of labour in the heyday of feudalism. Each country bore in itself the antithesis of town and country; the division into estates was certainly strongly marked; but apart from the differentiation of princes, nobility, clergy and peasants in the country, and masters, journeymen, apprentices and soon also the rabble of casual labourers in the towns, no division of importance took place. In agriculture it was rendered difficult by the strip-system, beside which the cottage industry of the peasants themselves emerged. In industry there was no division of labour at all in the individual trades themselves, and very little between them. The separation of industry and commerce was found already in existence in older towns; in the newer it only developed later, when the towns entered into mutual relations.

The grouping of larger territories into feudal kingdoms was a necessity for the landed nobility as for the towns. The organisation of the ruling class, the nobility, had, therefore, everywhere a monarch at its head.

The fact is, therefore, that definite individuals who are productively active in a definite way enter into these definite social and political relations. Empirical observation must in each separate instance bring out empirically, and without any mystification and speculation, the connection of the social and political structure with production. The social structure and the State are continually evolving out of the life process of definite individuals, but of individuals, not as they may appear in their own or other people's imagination, but as they *really* are; i.e., as they operate, produce materially, and hence as they work under definite material limits, presuppositions and conditions independent of their will.

The production of ideas, of conceptions, of consciousness, is at first directly interwoven with the material activity and the material intercourse of men, the language of real life. Conceiving, thinking, the mental intercourse of men, appear at this stage as the direct efflux of their material behaviour. The same applies to mental production as expressed in the language of politics, laws, morality, religion, metaphysics, etc., of a people. Men are the producers of their conceptions, ideas, etc.—real, active men, as they are conditioned by a definite development of their productive forces and of the intercourse corresponding to these, up to its furthest forms. Consciousness can never be anything else than conscious existence, and the existence of men is their actual life-process. If in all ideology men and their circumstances appear upside-down as in a *camera obscura,* this phenomenon arises just as much from their historical life-process as the inversion of objects on the retina does from their physical life-process.

In direct contrast to German philosophy which descends from heaven to earth, here we ascend from earth to heaven. That is to say, we do not set out from what men say, imagine, conceive, nor from men as narrated, thought of, imagined, conceived, in order to arrive at men in the flesh. We set out from real, active men, and on the basis of their real life-process we demonstrate the development of the ideological reflexes and echoes of this life-process. The phantoms formed in the human brain are also, necessarily, sublimates of their material life-process, which is empirically verifiable and bound to material premises. Morality, religion, metaphysics, all the rest of ideology and their corresponding forms of consciousness, thus no longer retain the semblance of independence. They have no history, no development; but men, developing their material production and their material intercourse, alter, along with this their real existence, their thinking and the products of their thinking. Life is not determined by consciousness, but consciousness by life. In the first method of approach the starting-point is consciousness taken as the living individual; in the second method, which conforms to real life, it is the real living individuals themselves, and consciousness is considered solely as *their* consciousness.

This method of approach is not devoid of premises. It starts out from the real premises and does not abandon them for a moment. Its premises are men, not in any fantastic isolation and rigidity, but in their actual, empirically perceptible process of development under definite conditions. As soon as this active life-process is described, history ceases to be a collection of dead facts as it is with the empiricists (themselves still abstract), or an imagined activity of imagined subjects, as with the idealists.

Where speculation ends—in real life—there real, positive science begins: the representation of the practical activity, of the practical process of development of men. Empty talk about consciousness ceases, and real knowledge has to take its place. When reality is depicted, philosophy as an independent branch of knowledge loses its medium of existence. At the best its place can only be taken by a summing-up of the most general results, abstractions which arise from the observation of the historical development of men. Viewed apart from real history, these abstractions have in themselves no value whatsoever. They can only serve to facilitate the arrangement of historical material, to indicate the sequence of its separate strata. But they by no means afford a recipe or schema, as does philosophy, for neatly trimming the epochs of history. On the contrary, our difficulties begin only when we set about the observation and the arrangement—the real depiction—of our historical material, whether of a past epoch or of the present. The removal of these difficulties is governed by premises which it is quite impossible to state here, but which only the study of the actual life-process and the activity of the individuals of each epoch will make evident. We shall select here some of these abstractions, which we use in contradistinction to the ideologists, and shall illustrate them by historical examples.

HISTORY

Since we are dealing with the Germans, who are devoid of premises, we must begin by stating the first premise of all human existence and, therefore, of all history, the premise, namely, that men must be in a position to live in order to be able to "make history." But life involves before everything else eating and drinking, a habitation, clothing and many other things. The first historical act is thus the production of the means to satisfy these needs, the production of material life itself. And indeed this is an historical act, a fundamental condition of all history, which today, as thousands of years ago, must daily and hourly be fulfilled merely in order to sustain human life. Even when the sensuous world is reduced to a minimum, to a stick as with Saint Bruno, it presupposes the action of producing the stick. Therefore in any interpretation of history one has first of all to observe this fundamental fact in all its significance and all its implications and to accord it its due importance. It is well known that the Germans have never done this, and they have never, therefore, had an *earthly* basis for history and consequently never a historian. The French and the English, even if they have conceived the relation of this fact with so-called history only in an extremely one-sided fashion, particularly as long as they remained in the toils of political ideology, have nevertheless made the first attempts to give the writing of history a materialistic basis by being the first to write histories of civil society, of commerce and industry.

The second point is that the satisfaction of the first need (the action of satisfying, and the instrument of satisfaction which has been acquired) leads to new needs; and this production of new needs is the first historical act. Here we recognise immediately the spiritual ancestry of the great historical wisdom of the Germans who, when they run out of positive material and when they can serve up neither theological nor political nor literary rubbish, assert that this is not history at all, but the "prehistoric era." They do not, however, enlighten us as to how we proceed from this nonsensical "prehistory" to history proper; although, on the other hand, in their historical speculation they seize upon this "prehistory" with especial eagerness because they imagine themselves safe there from interference on the part of "crude facts," and, at the same time, because there they can give full rein to their speculative impulse and set up and knock down hypotheses by the thousand.

The third circumstance which, from the very outset, enters into historical development, is that men, who daily remake their own life, begin to make other men, to propagate their kind: the relation between man and woman, parents and children, the *family*. The family, which to begin with is the only social relationship, becomes later, when increased needs create new social relations and the increased population new needs, a subordinate one (except in Germany), and must then be treated and analysed according to the existing empirical data, not according to "the concept of the family," as is the custom in Germany. These three aspects of social activity are not of course to be taken as three different stages, but just as three aspects or, to make it clear to the Germans, three "moments," which have existed simultaneously since the dawn of history and the first men, and which still assert themselves in history today.

The production of life, both of one's own in labour and of fresh life in procreation, now appears as a double relationship: on the one hand as a natural, on the other as a social relationship. By social we understand the co-operation of several individuals, no matter under what conditions, in what manner and to what end. It follows from this that a certain mode of production, or industrial stage, is always combined with a certain mode of co-operation, or social stage, and this mode of co-operation is itself a "productive force." Further, that the multitude of productive forces accessible to men determines the nature of society, hence, that the "history of humanity" must always be studied and treated in relation to the history of industry and exchange. But it is also clear how in Germany it is impossible to write this sort of history, because the Germans lack not only the necessary power of comprehension and the material but also the "evidence of their senses," for across the Rhine you cannot have any experience of these things since history has stopped happening. Thus it is quite obvious from the start that there exists a materialistic connection of men with one another, which is determined by their needs and their mode of production, and which is as old as men themselves. This connection is ever taking on new forms, and thus presents a "history" independently of the existence of any political or religious nonsense which would especially hold men together.

Only now, after having considered four moments, four aspects of the primary historical relationships, do we find that man also possesses "consciousness," but, even so, not inherent, not "pure" consciousness. From the start the "spirit" is afflicted with the curse of being "burdened" with matter, which here makes its appearance in the form of agitated layers of air, sounds, in short, of language. Language is as old as consciousness, language *is* practical consciousness that exists also for other men, and for that reason alone it really exists for me personally as well; language, like consciousness, only arises from the need, the necessity, of intercourse with other men. Where there exists a relationship, it exists for me: the animal does not enter into *"relations"* with anything, it does not enter into any relation at all. For the animal, its relation to others does not exist as a relation. Consciousness is, therefore, from the very beginning a social product, and remains so as long as men exist at all. Consciousness is at first, of course, merely consciousness concerning the *immediate* sensuous environment and consciousness of the limited connection with other persons and things outside the individual who is growing self-conscious. At the same time it is consciousness of nature, which first appears to men as a completely alien, all-powerful and unassailable force, with which men's relations are purely animal and by which they are overawed like beasts; it is thus a purely animal consciousness of nature (natural religion).

We see here immediately: this natural religion or this particular relation of men to nature is determined by the form of society and vice versa. Here, as everywhere, the identity of nature and man appears in such a way that the restricted relation of men to nature determines their restricted relation to one another, and their restricted relation to one another determines men's restricted relation to nature, just because nature is as yet hardly modified historically; and, on the other hand, man's consciousness of the necessity of associating with the individuals around him is the beginning of the consciousness that he is living in society at all. This beginning is as animal as social life itself at this stage. It is mere herd-consciousness, and at this point man is only distinguished from sheep by the fact that with him consciousness takes the place of instinct or that his instinct is a conscious one. This sheep-like or tribal consciousness receives its further development and extension through increased productivity, the increase of needs, and, what is fundamental to both of these, the increase of population. With these there develops the division of labour, which was originally nothing but the division of labour in the sexual act, then that division of labour which develops spontaneously or "naturally" by virtue of natural predisposition (e.g., physical strength), needs, accidents, etc., etc. Division of labour only becomes truly such from the moment when a division of material and mental labour appears. From this moment onwards consciousness *can* really flatter itself that it is something other than consciousness of existing practice, that it *really* represents something without representing something real; from now on consciousness is in a position to emancipate itself from the world and to proceed to the formation of "pure" theory, theology, philosophy, ethics, etc. But even if this theory, theology, philosophy, ethics, etc., comes into contradiction with the existing relations, this can only occur because existing social relations have come into contradiction with existing forces of production; this, moreoever, can also occur in a particular national sphere of relations through the appearance of the contradiction, not within the national orbit, but between this national consciousness and the practice of other nations, i.e., between the national and the general consciousness of a nation (as we see it now in Germany).

Moreover, it is quite immaterial what consciousness starts to do on its own: out of all such muck we get only the one inference that these three moments, the forces of production, the state of society, and consciousness, can and must come into contradiction with one another, because the *division of labour* implies the possibility, nay the fact that intellectual and material activity—enjoyment and labour, production and consumption—devolve on different individuals, and that the only possibility of their not coming into contradiction lies in the negation in its turn of the division of labour. It is self-evident, moreover, that "spectres," "bonds," "the higher being," "concept," "scruple," are merely the idealistic, spiritual expression, the conception apparently of the isolated individual, the image of very empirical fetters and limitations, within which the mode of production of life and the form of intercourse coupled with it move.

With the division of labour, in which all these contradictions are implicit, and which in its turn is based on the natural division of labour in the family and the separation of society into individual families opposed to one another, is given simultaneously the *distribution,* and indeed the *unequal* distribution, both quantitative and qualitative, of labour and its products, hence property: the nucleus, the first form, of which lies in the family, where wife and children are the slaves of the husband. This latent slavery in the family, though still very crude, is the first property, but even at this early stage it corresponds perfectly to the definition of modern economists who call it the power of disposing of the labour-power of others. Division of labour and private property are, moreover, identical expressions: in the one the same thing is affirmed with reference to activity as is affirmed in the other with reference to the product of the activity.

Further, the division of labour implies the contradiction between the interest of the separate individual or the individual family and the communal interest of all individuals who have intercourse with one another. And indeed, this communal interest does not exist merely in the imagination, as the "general interest," but first of all in reality, as the mutual interdependence of the individuals among whom the labour is divided. And finally, the division of labour offers us the first example of how, as long as man remains in natural society, that is, as long as a cleavage exists between the particular and the common interest, as long, therefore, as activity is not voluntarily, but naturally, divided, man's own deed becomes an alien power opposed to him, which enslaves him instead of being controlled by him. For as soon as the distribution of labour comes into being, each man has a particular, exclusive sphere of activity, which is forced upon him and from which he cannot escape. He is a hunter, a fisherman, a shepherd, or a critical critic, and must remain so if he does not want to lose his means of livelihood; while in communist society, where nobody has one exclusive sphere of activity but each can become accomplished in any branch he wishes, society regulates the general production and thus makes it possible for me to do one thing today and another tomorrow, to hunt in the morning, fish in the afternoon, rear cattle in the evening, criticise after dinner, just as I have a mind, without ever becoming hunter, fisherman, shepherd or critic. This fixation of social activity, this consolidation of what we ourselves produce into an objective power above us, growing out of our control, thwarting our expectations, bringing to naught our calculations, is one of the chief factors in historical development up till now.

And out of this very contradication between the interest of the individual and that of the community the latter takes an independent form as the *State,* divorced from the real interests of individual and community, and at the same time as an illusory communal life, always based, however, on the real ties existing in every family and tribal conglomeration—such as flesh and blood, language, division of labour on a larger scale, and other interests—and especially, as we shall enlarge upon later, on the classes, already determined by the division of labour, which in every such mass of men separate out, and of which one dominates all the others. It follows from this that all struggles within the State, the struggle beween democracy, aristocracy, and monarchy, the struggle for the franchise, etc., etc., are merely the illusory forms in which the real struggles of the different classes are fought out among one another (of this the German theoreticians have not the faintest inkling, although they have received a sufficient introduction to the subject in the *Deutsch-Französische Jahrbücher* and *Die heilige Familie*). Further, it follows that every class which is stuggling for mastery, even when its domination, as is the case with the proletariat, postulates the abolition of the old form of society in its entirety and of domination itself, must first conquer for itself political power in order to represent its interest in turn as the general interest, which in the first moment it is forced to do. Just because individuals seek *only* their particular interest, which for them does not coincide with their communal interest (in fact the general is the illusory form of communal life), the latter will be imposed on them as an interest "alien" to them, and "independent" of them, as in its turn a particular, peculiar "general" interest; or they themselves must remain within this discord, as in democracy. On the other hand, too, the *practical* struggle of these particular interests, which constantly *really* run counter to the communal and illusory communal interests, makes *practical* intervention and control necessary through the illusory "general" interest in the form of the State. The social power, i.e., the multiplied productive force, which arises through the co-operation of different individuals as it is determined by the division of labour, appears to these individuals, since their co-operation is not voluntary but has come about naturally, not as their own united power,but as an alien force existing outside them, of the origin and goal of which they are ignorant, which they thus cannot control, which on the contrary passes through a peculiar series of phases and stages independent of the will and the action of man, nay even being the prime governor of these.

This *"estrangement"* (to use a term which will be comprehensible to the philosophers) can, of course, only be abolished given two *practical* premises. For it to become an "intolerable" power, i.e., a power against which men make a revolution, it must necessarily have rendered the great mass of humanity "propertyless," and produced, at the same time, the contradiction of an existing world of wealth and culture, both of which conditions presuppose a great increase in productive power, a high degree of its development. And, on the other hand, this development of productive forces (which itself implies the actual empirical existence of men in their *world-historical,* instead of local, being) is an absolutely necessary practical premise because without it *want* is merely made general, and with *destitution* the struggle for necessities and all the old filthy business would necessarily be reproduced; and furthermore, because only with this universal development of productive forces is a *universal* intercourse between men established, which produces in all nations simultaneously the phenomenon of the "propertyless" mass (universal competition), makes each nation dependent on the revolutions of the others, and finally has put *world-historical,* empirically universal individuals in place of local ones. Without this, (1) communism could only exist as a local event; (2) the *forces* of intercourse themselves could not have developed as *universal,* hence intolerable powers: they would have remained home-bred conditions surrounded by superstition; and (3) each extension of intercourse would abolish local communism. Empirically, communism is only possible as the act of the dominant peoples "all at once" and simultaneously, which presupposes the universal development of productive forces and the world intercourse bound up with communism. How otherwise could for instance property have had a history at all, have taken on different forms, and landed property, for example, according to the different premises given, have proceeded in France from parcellation to centralisation in the hands of a few, in England from centralisation in the hands of a few to parcellation, as is actually the case today? Or how does it happen that trade, which after all is nothing more than the exchange of products of various individuals and countries, rules the whole world through the relation of supply and demand—a relation which, as an English economist says, hovers over the earth like the fate of the ancients, and with invisible hand allots fortune and misfortune to men, sets up empires and overthrows empires, causes nations to rise and to disappear—while with the abolition of the basis of private property, with the communistic regulation of productions (and, implicit in this, the destruction of the alien relation between men and what they themselves produce), the power of the relation of supply and demand is dissolved into nothing, and men get exchange, production, the mode of their mutual relation, under their own control again?

Communism is for us not a *state of affairs* which is to be established, an *ideal* to which reality [will] have to adjust itself. We call communism the *real* movement which abolishes the present state of things. The conditions of this movement result from the premises now in existence. Moreover, the mass of *propertyless* workers—the utterly precarious position of labour-power on a mass scale cut off from capital or from even a limited satisfaction and, therefore, no longer merely temporarily deprived of work itself as a secure source of life—presupposes the *world market* through competition. The proletariat can thus only exist *world-historically,* just as communism, its activity, can only have a "world-historical" existence. World-historical existence of individuals, i.e., existence of individuals which is directly linked up with world history.

The form of intercourse determined by the existing productive forces at all previous historical stages, and in its turn determining these, is *civil society*. The latter, as is clear from what we have said above, has as its premises and basis the simple family and the multiple, the so-called tribe, and the more precise determinants of this society are enumerated in our remarks above. Already here we see how this civil society is the true source and theatre of all history, and how absurd is the conception of history held hitherto, which neglects the real relationships and confines itself to high-sounding dramas of princes and states.

Civil society embraces the whole material intercourse of individuals within a definite stage of the development of productive forces. It embraces the whole commercial and industrial life of a given stage and, insofar, transcends the State and the nation, though, on the other hand again, it must assert itself in its foreign relations as nationality, and inwardly must organise itself as State. The term "civil society" [buŕgerliche Gesellschaft] emerged in the eighteenth century, when property relationships had already extricated themselves from the ancient and medieval community society. Civil society as such only develops with the bourgeoisie; the social organisation evolving directly out of production and commerce, which in all ages forms the basis of the State and of the rest of the idealistic superstructure, has, however, always been designated by the same name.

C. Ressentiment

Max Scheler

F riedrich Nietzsche characterizes the idea of Christian love as the most delicate flower of ressentiment.

He believes that through this idea the ressentiment accumulated by an oppressed and at the same time vindictive nation, whose God was the "God of revenge" even when it was still politically and socially independent, is justified before this nation's consciousness.

If we fully appreciate the revolutionary character of the change which leads from the ancient to the Christian idea of love—Nietzsche himself has done this only vaguely and inexactly—the Nietzschean statement is much less paradoxical than would appear at first sight. Indeed, his discovery is one of the most profound which has ever been made on this question and is fully worthy of the most serious consideration. I stress this all the more because I consider his theory to be completely mistaken.

The Greek and Roman philosophers and poets have expressed the significance and value of love in ancient morality with admirable clarity. A brief summary, without reference to specific sources, will be sufficient here. First of all, logical form, law, justice—in short, the element of measure and equality in the distribution of goods and evils—are superior to love. Even though Plato, in the Symposium for example, establishes great differences in value between the various kinds of love, in Greek eyes the whole phenomenon of "love" belongs to the domain of the senses. It is a form of "desire," of "need," etc., which is foreign to the most perfect kind of being. This view is the natural corollary of the extremely questionable ancient division of human nature into "reason" and "sensuality," into a part that is formative and one that is formed. In the sphere of Christian morality, on the other hand, love is explicitly placed above the rational domain—love "that makes more blessed than all reason" (Augustine). This comes out quite clearly in the parable of the prodigal son. "Agape" and "caritas" are sharply and dualistically separated from "eros" and "amor," whereas the Greeks and Romans—though they do acknowledge distinctions in value— rather see a continuity between these types of love. Christian love is a spiritual intentionality which transcends the natural sphere, defeating and superseding the psychological mechanism of the natural instincts (such as hatred against one's enemies, revenge, and desire for retaliation). It can place a man in a completely new state of life. But that is not essential here. The most important difference between the ancient and Christian views of love lies in the direction of its movement. All ancient philosophers, poets, and moralists agree that love is a striving, an aspiration of the "lower" toward the "higher," the "unformed" toward the "formed," the μὴ ὄν toward the ὄν, "appearance" toward "essence," "ignorance" toward "knowledge," a "mean between fullness and privation," as Plato says in the Symposium. Thus in all human love relations, such as marriage or friendship, a distinction must be made between a "lover" and a "beloved," and the latter is always nobler and more perfect. He is the model for the lover's being, willing, and acting. This conception, which grew from the relations of life in antiquity, finds its clearest expression in the numerous forms of Greek metaphysics. Already Plato says: "We would not live if we were Gods." For the most perfect form of being cannot know "aspiration" or "need." Here love is only a road to something else, a "methodos." And according to Aristotle, in all things there is rooted an urge (ὀρέγεσθαι and ἐφίεσθαι) toward the deity, the Nous, the self-sufficient thinker who "moves" the world as "prime mover." He does not move it as a being whose will and activity is directed toward the outside, but "as the beloved moves the lover" (Aristotle), as it were attracting, enticing, and tempting it. In this idea, with its unique sublimity, beauty, and ancient coolness, the essence of the ancient conception of love is raised into the absolute and boundless. The universe is a great chain of dynamic spiritual entities, of forms of being ranging from the "prima materia" up to man—a chain in which the lower always strives for and is attracted by the higher, which never turns back but aspires upward in its turn. This process continues up to the deity, which itself does not love, but represents the eternally unmoving and unifying goal of all these aspirations of love. Too little attention has been given to the peculiar relation between this idea of love and the principle of the "agon," the ambitious contest for the goal, which dominated Greek life in all its aspects—from the Gymnasium and the games to dialectics and the political life of the Greek city states. Even the objects try to surpass each other in a race for victory, in a cosmic "agon" for the deity. Here the prize that will crown the victor is extreme: it is a participation in the essence, knowledge, and abundance of "being." Love is only the dynamic principle, immanent in the universe, which sets in motion this great "agon" of all things for the deity.

    Let us compare this with the Christian conception. In that conception there takes place what might be called a reversal in the move-

ment of love. The Christian view boldly denies the Greek axiom that
love is an aspiration of the lower toward the higher. On the contrary,
now the criterion of love is that the nobler stoops to the vulgar, the
healthy to the sick, the rich to the poor, the handsome to the ugly, the
good and saintly to the bad and common, the Messiah to the sinners
and publicans. The Christian is not afraid, like the ancient, that he
might lose something by doing so, that he might impair his own nobility. He acts in the peculiarly pious conviction that through this "self-
renunciation" he gains the highest good and becomes equal to God.
The change in the notion of God and his fundamental relation to man
and the world is not the cause, but the consequence of this reversal in
the movement of love. God is no longer the eternal unmoving goal—
like a star—for the love of all things, moving the world as "the beloved
moves the lover." Now the very essence of God is to love and serve.
Creating, willing, and acting are derived from these original qualities.
The eternal "first mover" of the world is replaced by the "creator" who
created it "out of love." An event that is monstrous for the man of
antiquity, that is absolutely paradoxical according to his axioms, is
supposed to have taken place in Galilee: God spontaneously
"descended" to man, became a servant, and died the bad servant's
death on the cross! Now the precept of loving good and hating evil,
loving one's friend and hating one's enemy, becomes meaningless.
There is no longer any "highest good" independent of and beyond the
act and movement of love! Love itself is the highest of all goods! The
summum bonum is no longer the value of a thing, but of an act, the
value of love itself as love—not for its results and achievements.
Indeed, the achievements of love are only symbols and proofs of its
presence in the person. And thus God himself becomes a "person"
who has no "idea of the good," no "form and order," no λόγος above
him, but only below him—through his deed of love. He becomes a
God who loves—for the man of antiquity something like a square circle, an "imperfect perfection!" How strongly did Neo-Platonic criticism stress that love is a form of "need" and "aspiration" which indicates "imperfection," and that it is false, presumptuous, and sinful to
attribute it to the deity! But there is another great innovation: in the
Christian view, love is a non-sensuous act of the spirit (not a mere state
of feeling, as for the moderns), but it is nevertheless not a striving and
desiring, and even less a need. These acts consume themselves in the
realization of the desired goal. Love, however, grows in action. And
there are no longer any rational principles, any rules or justice, higher
than love, independent of it and preceding it, which should guide its
action and its distribution among men according to their value. All are

worthy of love—friends and enemies, the good and the evil, the noble and the common. Whenever I see badness in another, I must feel partly guilty, for I must say to myself: "Would that man be bad if you had loved him enough?" In the Christian view, sensuous sympathy—together with its root in our most powerful impulse—is not the source, but the partial blockage of love. Therefore not only positive wrong-doing, but even the failure to love is "guilt." Indeed, it is the guilt at the bottom of all guiltness.

Thus the picture has shifted immensely. This is no longer a band of men and things that surpass each other in striving up to the deity. It is a band in which every member looks back toward those who are further removed from God and comes to resemble the deity by helping and serving them—for this great urge to love, to serve, to bend down, is God's own essence.

I do not here analyze the constructive forms which this emotional reversal has taken in dogma, theology, and religious worship, though the task is tempting—especially in the cases of Paul and Augustine. Confining myself to the essential, I ask: whence this reversal? Is res-sentiment really its mainspring?

The more I reflected on this question, the more clearly I realized that the root of Christian love is entirely free of ressentiment, but that ressentiment can very easily use it for its own purposes by simulating an emotion which corresponds to this idea. This simulation is often so perfect that even the sharpest observer can no longer distinguish real love from ressentiment which poses as love.

There are two fundamentally different ways for the strong to bend down to the weak, for the rich to help the poor, for the more perfect life to help the "less perfect." This action can be motivated by a pow-erful feeling of security, strength, and inner salvation, of the invincible fullness of one's own life and existence. All this unites into the clear awareness that one is rich enough to share one's being and possessions. Love, sacrifice, help, the descent to the small and the weak, here spring from a spontaneous overflow of force, accompanied by bliss and deep inner calm. Compared to this natural readiness for love and sacrifice, all specific "egoism," the concern for oneself and one's interest, and even the instinct of "self-preservation" are signs of a blocked and weakened life. Life is essentially expansion, development, growth in plenitude, and not "self-preservation," as a false doctrine has it. Devel-opment, expansion, and growth are not epiphenomena of mere pre-servative forces and cannot be reduced to the preservation of the "bet-ter adapted." We do believe that life itself can be sacrificed for values higher than life, but this does not mean that all sacrifice runs counter to life and its advancement. There is a form of sacrifice which is a free renunciation of one's own vital abundance, a beautiful and natural overflow of one's forces. Every living being has a natural instinct of sympathy for other living beings, which increases with their proximity and similarity to himself. Thus we sacrifice ourselves for beings with whom we feel united and solidary, in contrast to everything "dead." This sacrificial impulse is by no means a later acquisition of life, derived from originally egoistic urges. It is an original component of life and precedes all those particular "aims" and "goals" which calculation, intelligence, and reflection impose upon it later. We have an urge to sacrifice before we ever know why, for what, and for whom! Jesus' view of nature and life, which sometimes shines through his speeches and parables in fragments and hidden allusions, shows quite clearly that he understood this fact. When he tells us not to worry about eating and drinking, it is not because he is indifferent to life and its preservation, but because he sees also a vital weakness in all "worrying" about the next day, in all concentration on one's own physical well-being. The ravens with neither storehouse nor barn, the lilies which do not toil and spin and which God still arrays more gloriously than Solomon (Lk 12:24 and 27)—they are symbols of that profound total impression he has of life: all voluntary concentration on one's own bodily well-being, all worry and anxiety, hampers rather than furthers the creative force which instinctively and beneficently governs all life. "And which of you with taking thought can add to his stature one cubit?" (Lk 12:25). This kind of indifference to the external means of life (food, clothing, etc.) is not a sign of indifference to life and its value, but rather of a profound and secret confidence in life's own vigor and of an inner security from the mechanical accidents which may befall it. A gay, light, bold, knightly indifference to external circumstances, drawn from the depth of life itself—that is the feeling which inspires these words! Egoism and fear of death are signs of a declining, sick, and broken life. Let us remember that the fear of death was so widespread in antiquity that some schools of philosophy, that of the Epicureans among others, see the aim of philosophy in freeing man from it. The periods of greatest vitality were indifferent to life and its end. Such indifference is itself a state of mind which has vital value.

This kind of love and sacrifice for the weaker, the sick, and the small springs from inner security and vital plenitude. In addition to this vital security, there is that other feeling of bliss and security, that awareness of safety in the fortress of ultimate being itself (Jesus calls it "kingdom" of God). The deeper and more central it is, the more man can and may be almost playfully "indifferent" to his "fate" in the

peripheral zones of his existence—indifferent to whatever is still accessible to "happiness" and "suffering," "pleasure" and "displeasure,"
"joy" and "pain."

When a person's spontaneous impulse of love and sacrifice finds
a specific goal, an opportunity for applying itself, he does not welcome
it as a chance to plunge into such phenomena as poverty, sickness, or
ugliness. He does not help this struggling life because of those negative
values, but despite them—he helps in order to develop whatever may
still be sound and positive. He does not love such life because it is sick,
poor, small, and ugly, and he does not passively dwell upon these attributes. The positive vital values (and even more, of course, the spiritual
personal values of that individual) are completely independent of
these defects and lie much deeper. Therefore his own fullness of life
can (and therefore "should") overcome his natural reaction of fearing
and fleeing them, and his love should helpfully develop whatever is
positive in the poor or sick man. He does not love sickness and poverty, but what is behind them, and his help is directed against these
evils. When Francis of Assisi kisses festering wounds and does not
even kill the bugs that bite him, but leaves his body to them as a hos-
pitable home, these acts (if seen from the outside) could be signs of
perverted instincts and of a perverted valuation. But that is not
actually the case. It is not a lack of nausea or a delight in the pus which
makes St. Francis act in this way. He has overcome his nausea through
a deeper feeling of life and vigor! This attitude is completely different
from that of recent modern realism in art and literature, the exposure
of social misery, the description of little people, the wallowing in the
morbid—a typical ressentiment phenomenon. Those people saw
something bug-like in everything that lives, whereas Francis sees the
holiness of "life" even in the bug.

In the ancient notion of love, on the other hand, there is an element of anxiety. The noble fears the descent to the less noble, is afraid
of being infected and pulled down. The "sage" of antiquity does not
have the same firmness, the same inner certainty of himself and his
own value, as the genius and hero of Christian love.

A further characteristic! Love in Jesus' sense helps energetically.
But it does not consist in the desire to help, or even in "benevolence."
Such love is, as it were, immersed in positive value, and helping and
benevolence are only its consequences. The fake love of ressentiment
man offers no real help, since for his perverted sense of values, evils
like "sickness" and "poverty" have become goods. He believes, after
all, that "God giveth grace to the humble" (1 Pet 5:5), so that raising

the small or curing the sick would mean removing them from their salvation. But this does not mean that the value of love in the genuine Christian sense lies in the usefulness of its helping deed. The usefulness may be great with little love or none at all, and it may be small while love is great. The widow's mites (Mk 12:42-44) are more to God than the gifts of the rich—not because they are only "mites" or because the giver is only a "poor widow," but because her action reveals more love. Thus the increase in value originally always lies on the side of him who loves, not on the side of him who is helped. Love is no spiritual "institution of charity" and is not in contrast to one's bliss. In the very act of self-renunciation, the person eternally wins himself. He is blissful in loving and giving, for "it is more blessed to give than to receive" (Acts 20:35). Love is not valuable and does not bestow distinction on the lover because it is just one of the countless forces which further human or social welfare. No, the value is love itself, its penetration of the whole person—the higher, firmer, and richer life and existence of which its movement is the sign and the gem. The important thing is not the amount of welfare, it is that there should be a maximum of love among men. The act of helping is the direct and adequate expression of love, not its meaning or "purpose." Its meaning lies in itself, in its illumination of the soul, in the nobility of the loving soul in the act of love. Therefore nothing can be further removed from this genuine concept of Christian love than all kinds of "socialism," "social feeling," "altruism," and other subaltern modern things. When the rich youth is told to divest himself of his riches and give them to the poor, it is really not in order to help the "poor" and to effect a better distribution of property in the interest of general welfare. Nor is it because poverty as such is supposed to be better than wealth. The order is given because the act of giving away, and the spiritual freedom and abundance of love which manifest themselves in this act, ennoble the youth and make him even "richer" than he is.

This element is also present in the metaphysico-religious conceptions of man's relation to God. The old covenant between God and man, which is the root of all "legality," is replaced by the love between God and his children. And even the love "for God" is not to be founded on his works alone, in gratitude for his constant gifts, his care and maintenance. All these experiences of God's actions and works are only means to make us look up to "eternal love" and to the infinite abundance of value of which these works are but the proof. They should be admired and loved only because they are works of love!

D. Fear and Trembling

Soren Kierkegaard

An old proverb fetched from the outward and visible world says: "Only the man that works gets the bread." Strangely enough this proverb does not aptly apply in that world to which it expressly belongs. For the outward world is subjected to the law of imperfection, and again and again the experience is repeated that he too who does not work gets the bread, and that he who sleeps gets it more abundantly than the man who works. In the outward world everything is made payable to the bearer, this world is in bondage to the law of indifference, and to him who has the ring, the spirit of the ring is obedient, whether he be Noureddin or Aladdin, and he who has the world's treasure, has it, however he got it. It is different in the world of spirit. Here an eternal divine order prevails, here it does not rain both upon the just and upon the unjust, here the sun does not shine both upon the good and upon the evil, here it holds good that only he who works gets the bread, only he who was in anguish finds repose, only he who descends into the underworld rescues the beloved, only he who draws the knife gets Isaac. He who will not work does not get the bread but remains deluded, as the gods deluded Orpheus with an airy figure in place of the loved one, deluded him because he was effeminate, not courageous, because he was a cithara-player, not a man. Here it is of no use to have Abraham for one's father, nor to have seventeen ancestors—he who will not work must take note of what is written about the maidens of Israel, for he gives birth to wind, but he who is willing to work gives birth to his own father.

There is a knowledge which would presumptuously introduce into the world of spirit the same law of indifference under which the external world sighs. It counts it enough to think the great—other work is not necessary. But therefore it doesn't get the bread, it perishes of hunger, while everything is transformed into gold. And what does it really know? There were many thousands of Greek contemporaries, and countless numbers in subsequent generations, who knew all the triumphs of Miltiades, but only one was made sleepless by them. There were countless generations which knew by rote, word for word, the story of Abraham—how many were made sleepless by it?

Now the story of Abraham has the remarkable property that it is always glorious, however poorly one may understand it; yet here again the proverb applies, that all depends upon whether one is willing to labor and be heavy laden. But they will not labor, and yet they would understand the story. They exalt Abraham—but how? They express the whole thing in perfectly general terms: "The great thing was that he loved God so much that he was willing to sacrifice to Him the best." That is very true, but "the best" is an indefinite expression. In the course of thought, as the tongue wags on, Issac and "the best" are confidently identified, and he who meditates can very well smoke his pipe during the meditation, and the auditor can very well stretch out his legs in comfort. In case that rich young man whom Christ encountered on the road had sold all his goods and given to the poor, we should extol him, as we do all that is great, though without labor we would not understand him—and yet he would not have become an Abraham, in spite of the fact that he offered his best. What they leave out of Abraham's history is dread; for to money I have no ethical obligation, but to the son the father has the highest and most sacred obligation. Dread, however, is a perilous thing for effeminate natures, hence they forget it, and in spite of that they want to talk about Abraham. So they talk—in the course of the oration they use indifferently the two terms, Isaac and "the best." All goes famously. However, if it chanced that among the auditors there was one who suffered from insomnia—then the most dreadful, the profoundest tragic and comic misunderstanding lies very close. He went home, he would do as Abraham did, for the son is indeed "the best."

If the orator got to know of it, he perhaps went to him, he summoned all his clerical dignity, he shouted, "O abominable man, offscouring of society, what devil possessed thee to want to murder thy son?" And the parson, who had not been conscious of warmth or perspiration in preaching about Abraham, is astonished at himself, at the earnest wrath which he thundered down upon that poor man. He was delighted with himself, for he had never spoken with such verve and unction. He said to himself and to his wife, "I am an orator. What I lacked was the occasion. When I talked about Abraham on Sunday I did not feel moved in the least." In case the same orator had a little superabundance of reason which might be lost, I think he would have lost it if the sinner were to say calmly and with dignity, "That in fact is what you yourself preached on Sunday." How could the parson be able to get into his head such a consequence? And yet it was so, and the mistake was merely that he didn't know what he was saying. Would there were a poet who might resolve to prefer such situations, rather than the stuff and nonsense with which comedies and novels are filled! The comic and the tragic here touch one another at the absolute point of infinity. The parson's speech was perhaps in itself ludicrous enough, but it became infinitely ludicrous by its effect, and yet this consequence was quite natural. Or if the sinner, without raising any objection, were to be converted by the parson's severe lecture, if the zealous clergyman were to go joyfully home, rejoicing in the consciousness that he not only was effective in the pulpit, but above all by his irresistible power as a pastor of souls, who on Sunday roused the congregation to enthusiasm, and on Monday like a cherub with a flaming sword placed himself before the man who by his action wanted to put to shame the old proverb, that "things don't go on in the world as the parson preaches."

If on the other hand the sinner was not convinced, his situation is pretty tragic. Presumably he would be executed or sent to the lunatic asylum, in short, he would have become unhappy in relation to so-called reality—in another sense I can well think that Abraham made him happy, for he that labors does not perish.

How is one to explain the contradiction illustrated by that orator? Is it because Abraham had a prescriptive right to be a great man, so that what he did is great, and when another does the same it is sin, a heinous sin? In that case I do not wish to participate in such thoughtless eulogy. If faith does not make it a holy act to be willing to murder one's son, then let the same condemnation be pronounced upon Abraham as upon every other man. If a man perhaps lacks courage to carry his thought through, and to say that Abraham was a murderer, then it is surely better to acquire this courage, rather than waste time upon undeserved eulogies. The ethical expression for what Abraham did is, that he would murder Isaac; the religion expression is that he would sacrifice Isaac; but precisely in this contradiction consists the dread which can well make a man sleepless, and yet Abraham is not what he is without this dread. Or perhaps he did not do at all what is related, but something altogether different, which is accounted for by the circumstances of his times—then let us forget him, for it is not worth while to remember *that* past which cannot become a present. Or had perhaps that orator forgotten something which corresponds to the ethical forgetfulness of the fact that Isaac was the son? For when faith is eliminated by becoming null or nothing, then there only remains the crude fact that Abraham wanted to murder Isaac—which is easy enough for anyone to imitate who has not faith, the faith, that is to say, which makes it hard for him.

For my part I do not lack the courage to think a thought whole. Hitherto there has been no thought I have been afraid of; if I should run across such a thought, I hope that I have at least the sincerity to say, "I am afraid of this thought, it stirs up something else in me, and therefore I will not think it. If in this I do wrong, the punishment will not fail to follow." If I had recognized that it was the verdict of truth that Abraham was a murderer, I do not know whether I would have been able to silence my pious veneration for him. However, if I had thought that, I presumably would have kept silent about it, for one should not initiate others into such thoughts. But Abraham is no dazzling illusion, he did not sleep into renown, it was not a whim of fate.

Can one then speak plainly about Abraham without incurring the danger that an individual might in bewilderment go ahead and do likewise? If I do not dare to speak freely, I will be completely silent about Abraham, above all I will not disparage him in such a way that precisely thereby he becomes a pitfall for the weak. For if one makes faith everything, that is, makes it what it is, then, according to my way of thinking, one may speak of it without danger to our age, which hardly extravagates in the matter of faith, and it is only by faith one attains likeness to Abraham, not by murder. If one makes love a transitory mood, a voluptuous emotion in a man, then one only lays pitfalls for the weak when one would talk about the exploits of love. Transient emotions every man surely has, but if as a consequence of such emotions one would do the terrible thing which love has sanctified as an immortal exploit, then all is lost, including the exploit and the bewildered doer of it.

So one surely can talk about Abraham, for the great can never do harm when it is apprehended in its greatness; it is like a two-edged sword which slays and saves. If it should fall to my lot to talk on the subject, I would begin by showing what a pious and God-fearing man Abraham was, worthy to be called God's elect. Only upon such a man is imposed such a test. But where is there such a man? Next I would describe how Abraham loved Isaac. To this end I would pray all good spirits to come to my aid, that my speech might be as glowing as paternal love is. I hope that I should be able to describe it in such a way that there would not be many a father in the realms and territories of the King who would dare to affirm that he loved his son in such a way. But if he does not love like Abraham, then every thought of offering Isaac would be not a trial but a base temptation [*Anfechtung*]. On this theme one could talk for several Sundays, one need be in no haste. The consequence would be that, if one spoke rightly, some few of the fathers would not require to hear more, but for the time being they would be joyful if they really succeeded in loving their sons as Abraham loved. If there was one who, after having heard about the greatness, but also about the dreadfulness of Abraham's deed, ventured to go forth upon that road, I would saddle my horse and ride with him. At every stopping place till we came to Mount Moriah I would explain to him that he still could turn back, could repent the misunderstanding that he was called to be tried in such a conflict, that he could confess his lack of courage, so that God Himself must take Isaac, if He would have him. It is my conviction that such a man is not repudiated but may become blessed like all the others. But in time he does not become blessed. Would they not, even in the great ages of faith, have passed this judgment upon such a man? I knew a person who on one occasion could have saved my life if he had been magnanimous. He said, "I see well enough what I could do, but I do not dare to. I am afraid that later I might lack strength and that I should regret it." He was not magnanimous, but who for this cause would not continue to love him?

Having spoken thus and moved the audience so that at least they had sensed the dialectical conflict of faith and its gigantic passion, I would not give rise to the error on the part of the audience that "he then has faith in such a high degree that it is enough for us to hold on to his skirts." For I would add, "I have no faith at all, I am by nature a shrewd pate, and every such person always has great difficulty in making the movements of faith—not that I attach, however, in and for itself, *any value to this difficulty which through the overcoming of it brought the clever head further than the point which the simplest and most ordinary man reaches more easily.*"

After all, in the poets love has its priests, and sometimes one hears a voice which knows how to defend it; but of faith one hears never a word. Who speaks in honor of this passion? Philosophy goes further. Theology sits rouged at the window and courts its favor, offering to sell her charms to philosophy. It is supposed to be difficult to understand Hegel, but to understand Abraham is a trifle. To go beyond Hegel is a miracle, but to get beyond Abraham is the easiest thing of all. I for my part have devoted a good deal of time to the understanding of the Hegelian philosophy, I believe also that I understand it tolerably well, but when in spite of the trouble I have taken there are certain passages I cannot understand, I am foolhardy enough to think that he himself has not been quite clear. All this I do easily and naturally, my head does not suffer from it. But on the other hand when I have to think of Abraham, I am as though annihilated. I catch sight every moment of that enormous paradox which is the substance of Abraham's life, every moment I am repelled, and my thought in spite of all its passion cannot get a hairs-breadth further. I strain every muscle to get a view of it—that very instant I am paralyzed.

I am not unacquainted with what has been admired as great and noble in the world, my soul feels affinity with it, being convinced in all humility that it was in my cause the hero contended, and the instant I contemplate his deed I cry out to myself, *jam tua res agitur.* I *think* myself *into* the hero, but into Abraham I cannot think myself; when I reach the height I fall down, for what I encounter there is the paradox. I do not however mean in any sense to say that faith is something lowly, but on the contrary that it is the highest thing, and that it is dishonest of philosophy to give something else instead of it and to make light of faith. Philosophy cannot and should not give faith, but it should understand itself and know what it has to offer and take nothing away, and least of all should fool people out of something as if it were nothing. I am not unacquainted with the perplexities and dangers of life, I do not fear them, and I encounter them buoyantly. I am not unacquainted with the dreadful, my memory is a faithful wife, and my imagination is (as I myself am not) a diligent little maiden who all day sits quietly at her work, and in the evening knows how to chat to me about it so prettily that I must look at it, though not always, I must say, is it landscapes, or flowers, or pastoral idyls she paints. I have seen the dreadful before my own eyes, I do not flee from it timorously, but I know very well that, although I advance to meet it, my courage is not the courage of faith, nor anything comparable to it. I am unable to make the movements of faith, I cannot shut my eyes and plunge confidently into the absurd, for me that is an impossibility . . . but I do not boast of it. I am convinced that God is love, this thought has for me a primitive lyrical validity. When it is present to me, I am unspeakably blissful, when it is absent, I long for it more vehemently than does the lover for his object; but I do not believe, this courage I lack. For me the love of God is, both in a direct and in an inverse sense, incommensurable with the whole of reality. I am not cowardly enough to whimper and complain, but neither am I deceitful enough to deny that faith is something much higher. I can well endure living in my way, I am joyful and content, but my joy is not that of faith, and in comparison with that it is unhappy. I do not trouble God with my petty sorrows, the particular does not trouble me, I gaze only at my love, and I keep its virginal flame pure and clear. Faith is convinced that God is concerned about the least things. I am content in this life with being married to the left hand, faith is humble enough to demand the right hand—for that this is humility I do not deny and shall never deny.

But really is everyone in my generation capable of making the movements of faith, I wonder? Unless I am very much mistaken, this generation is rather inclined to be proud of making what they do not even believe I am capable of making, viz. incomplete movements. It is repugnant to me to do as so often is done, namely, to speak inhumanly about a great deed, as though some thousands of years were an immense distance; I would rather speak humanly about it, as though it had occurred yesterday, letting only the greatness be the distance, which either exalts or condemns. So if (*in the quality of a tragic hero,* for I can get no higher) I had been summoned to undertake such a royal progress to Mount Moriah, I know well what I would have done. I would not have been cowardly enough to stay at home, neither would I have laid down or sauntered along the way, nor have forgotten the knife, so that there might be a little delay—I am pretty well convinced that I would have been there on the stroke of the clock and would have had everything in order, perhaps I would have arrived too early in order to get through with it sooner. But I also know what else I would have done. The very instant I mounted the horse I would have said to myself, "Now all is lost. God requires Isaac, I sacrifice him, and with him my joy—yet God is love and continues to be that for me; for in the temporal world God and I cannot talk together, we have no language in common." Perhaps one or another in our age will be foolish enough, or envious enough of the great, to want to make himself and me believe that if I really had done this, I would have done even a greater deed than Abraham; for my prodigious resignation was far more ideal and poetic than Abraham's narrow-mindedness. And yet this is the greatest falsehood, for my prodigious resignation was the surrogate for faith, nor could I do more than make the infinite movement, in order to find myself and again repose in myself. In that case I would not have loved Isaac as Abraham loved. That I was resolute in making the movement might prove my courage, humanly speaking; that I loved him with all my soul is the presumption apart from which the whole thing becomes a crime, but yet I did not love like Abraham, for in that case I would have held back even at the last minute, though not for this would I have arrived too late at Mount Moriah. Besides, by my behavior I would have spoiled the whole story; for if I had got Isaac back again, I would have been in embarrassment. What Abraham found easiest, I would have found hard, namely to be joyful again with Isaac; for he who with all the infinity of his soul, *proprio motu et proprii auspiciis* [by his own power and on his own responsibilty], has performed the infinite movement [of resignation] and cannot do more, only retains Isaac with pain.

But what did Abraham do? He arrived neither too soon nor too late. He mounted the ass, he rode slowly along the way. All that time he believed—he believed that God would not require Isaac of him, whereas he was willing nevertheless to sacrifice him if it was required. He believed by virtue of the absurd; for there could be no question of human calculation, and it was indeed the absurd that God who required it of him should the next instant recall the requirement. He climbed the mountain, even at the instant when the knife glittered he believed . . . that God would not require Isaac. He was indeed astonished at the outcome, but by a double-movement he had reached his first position, and therefore he received Isaac more gladly than the first time. Let us go further. We let Isaac be really sacrificed. Abraham believed. He did not believe that some day he would be blessed in the beyond, but that he would be happy here in the world. God could give him a new Isaac, could recall to life him who had been sacrificed. He believed by virtue of the absurd; for all human reckoning had long since ceased to function. That sorrow can derange a man's mind, that we see, and it is sad enough. That there is such a thing as strength of will which is able to haul up so exceedingly close to the wind that it saves a man's reason, even though he remains a little queer, that too one sees. I have no intention of disparaging this; but to be able to lose one's reason, and therefore the whole finiteness of which reason is the broker, and then by virtue of the absurd to gain precisely the same finiteness—that appalls my soul, but I do not for this cause say that it is something lowly, since on the contrary it is the only prodigy. Generally people are of the opinion that what faith produces is not a work of art, that it is coarse and common work, only for the more clumsy natures; but in fact this is far from the truth. The dialectic of faith is the finest and most remarkable of all; it possesses an elevation, of which indeed I can form a conception, but nothing more. I am able to make from the springboard the great leap whereby I pass into infinity, my back is like that of a tight-rope dancer, having been twisted in my childhood, hence I find this easy; with a one-two-three! I can walk about existence on my head; but the next thing I cannot do, for I cannot perform the miraculous, but can only be astonished by it. Yes, if Abraham the instant he swung his leg over the ass's back had said to himself, "Now, since Isaac is lost, I might just as well sacrifice him here at home, rather than ride the long way to Moriah"—then I should have no need of Abraham, whereas now I bow seven times before his name and seventy times before his deed. For this indeed he did not do, as I can prove by the fact that he was glad at receiving Isaac, heartily glad, that he needed no preparation, no time to concentrate upon the finite and its joy. If this had not been the case with Abraham, then perhaps he might have loved God but not believed; for he who loves God without faith reflects upon himself, he who loves God believingly reflects upon God.

Upon this pinnacle stands Abraham. The last stage he loses sight of is the infinite resignation. He really goes further, and reaches faith; for all these caricatures of faith, the miserable lukewarm indolence which thinks, "There surely is no instant need, it is not worth while sorrowing before the time," the pitiful hope which says, "One cannot know what is going to happen . . . it might possibly be after all"—these caricatures of faith are part and parcel of life's wretchedness, and the infinite resignation has already consigned them to infinite contempt.

Abraham I cannot understand, in a certain sense there is nothing I can learn from him but astonishment. If people fancy that by considering the outcome of this story they might let themselves be moved to believe, they deceive themselves and want to swindle God out of the first movement of faith, the infinite resignation. They would suck worldly wisdom out of the paradox. Perhaps one or another may succeed in that, for our age is not willing to stop with faith, with its miracle of turning water into wine, it goes further, it turns wine into water.

Would it not be better to stop with faith, and is it not revolting that everybody wants to go further? When in our age (as indeed is proclaimed in various ways) they will not stop with love, where then are they going? To earthy wisdom, to petty calculation, to paltriness and wretchedness, to everything which can make man's divine origin doubtful. Would it not be better that they should stand still at faith, and that he who stands should take heed lest he fall? For the movements of faith must constantly be made by virtue of the absurd, yet in such a way, be it observed, that one does not lose the finite but gains it every inch. For my part I can well describe the movements of faith, but I cannot make them. When one would learn to make the motions of swimming one can let oneself be hung by a swimming-belt from the ceiling and go through the motions (describe them, so to speak, as we speak of describing a circle), but one is not swimming. In that way I can describe the movements of faith, but when I am thrown into the water, I swim, it is true (for I don't belong to the beach-waders), but I make other movements, I make the movements of infinity, whereas faith does the opposite: after having made the movements of infinity, it makes those of finiteness. Hail to him who can make those movements, he performs the marvellous, and I shall never grow tired of admiring him, whether he be Abraham or a slave in Abraham's house; whether he be a professor of philosophy or a servant-girl, I look only at the movements. But at them I do look, and do not let myself be fooled, either by myself or by any other man. The knights of the infinite resignation are easily recognized: their gait is gliding and assured. Those on the other hand who carry the jewel of faith are likely to be delusive, because their outward appearance bears a striking resemblance to that which both the infinite resignation and faith profoundly despise . . . to Philistinism.

IV

THE
IDEAL
SELF

A. Reason in History

G. W. F. Hegel

The question of the *means* whereby Freedom develops itself into a world leads us directly to the phenomenon of history. Although Freedom as such is primarily an internal idea, the means it uses are the external phenomena which in history present themselves directly before our eyes. The first glance at history convinces us that the actions of men spring from their needs, their passions, their interests, their characters, and their talents. Indeed, it appears as if in this drama of activities these needs, passions, and interests are the sole springs of action and the main efficient cause. It is true that this drama involves also universal purposes, benevolence, or noble patriotism. But such virtues and aims are insignificant on the broad canvas of history. We may, perhaps, see the ideal of Reason actualized in those who adopt such aims and in the spheres of their influence; but their number is small in proportion to the mass of the human race and their influence accordingly limited. Passions, private aims, and the satisfaction of selfish desires are, on the contrary, tremendous springs of action. Their power lies in the fact that they respect none of the limitations which law and morality would impose on them; and that these natural impulses are closer to the core of human nature than the artificial and troublesome discipline that tends toward order, self-restraint, law, and morality.

When we contemplate this display of passions and the consequences of their violence, the unreason which is associated not only with them, but even—rather we might say *especially*—with *good* designs and righteous aims; when we see arising therefrom the evil, the vice, the ruin that has befallen the most flourishing kingdoms which the mind of man ever created, we can hardly avoid being filled with sorrow at this universal taint of corruption. And since this decay is not the work of mere nature, but of human will, our reflections may well lead us to a moral sadness, a revolt of the good will (spirit)—if indeed it has a place within us. Without rhetorical exaggeration, a simple, truthful account of the miseries that have overwhelmed the noblest of nations and polities and the finest-exemplars of private virtue forms a most fearful picture and excites emotions of the profoundest and most hopeless sadness, counter-balanced by no consoling result. We can endure it and strengthen ourselves against it only by thinking that this is the way it had to be—it is fate; nothing can be done. And at last, out of the boredom with which this sorrowful reflection threatens us, we draw back into the vitality of the present, into our aims and interests of the moment; we retreat, in short, into the selfishness that stands on the quiet shore and thence enjoys in safety the distant spectacle of wreckage and confusion.

But in contemplating history as the slaughter-bench at which the happiness of peoples, the wisdom of states, and the virtue of individuals have been sacrificed, a question necessarily arises: To what principle, to what final purpose, have these monstrous sacrifices been offered?

From here one usually proceeds to the starting point of our investigation: the events which make up this picture of gloomy emotion and thoughtful reflection are only the means for realizing the essential destiny, the absolute and final purpose, or, what amounts to the same thing, the true result of world history. We have all along purposely eschewed that method of reflection which ascends from this scene of particulars to general principles. Besides, it is not in the interest of such sentimental reflections really to rise above these depressing emotions and to solve the mysteries of Providence presented in such contemplations. It is rather their nature to dwell melancholically on the empty and fruitless sublimities of their negative result. For this reason we return to our original point of view. What we shall have to say about it will also answer the questions put to us by this panorama of history.

The first thing we notice—something which has been stressed more than once before but which cannot be repeated too often, for it belongs to the central point of our inquiry—is the merely general and abstract nature of what we call principle, final purpose, destiny, or the nature and concept of Spirit. A principle, a law is something implicit, which as such, however true in itself, is not completely real (actual). Purposes, principles, and the like, are at first in our thoughts, our inner intention. They are not yet in reality. That which is in itself is a possibility, a faculty. It has not yet emerged out of its implicitness into existence. A second element must be added for it to become reality, namely, activity, actualization. The principle of this is the will, man's activity in general. It is only through this activity that the concept and its implicit ("being-in-themselves") determinations can be realized, actualized; for of themselves they have no immediate efficacy. The activity which puts them in operation and in existence is the need, the instinct, the inclination, and passion of man. When I have an idea I am greatly interested in transforming it into action, into actuality. In its realization through my participation I want to find my own satisfaction. A purpose for which I shall be active must in some way be my purpose; I must thereby satisfy my own desires, even though it may have ever so many aspects which do not concern me. This is the infinite right of the individual to find itself satisfied in its activity and labor. If men are to be interested in anything they must have "their heart" in it. Their feelings of self-importance must be satisfied. But here a misunderstanding must be avoided. To say that an individual "has an interest" in something is justly regarded as a reproach or blame; we imply that he seeks only his private advantage. Indeed, the blame implies not only his disregard of the common interest, but his taking advantage of it and even his sacrificing it to his own interest. Yet, he who is active for a cause is not simply "interested," but "interested *in it*." Language faithfully expresses this distinction. Nothing therefore happens, nothing is accomplished, unless those concerned with an issue find their own satisfaction in it. They are particular individuals; they have their special needs, instincts, and interests. They have their own particular desires and volitions, their own insight and conviction, or at least their own attitude and opinion, once the aspirations to reflect, understand, and reason have been awakened. Therefore people demand that a cause for which they should be active accord with their ideas. And they expect their opinion—concerning its goodness, justice, advantage, profit—to be taken into account. This is of particular importance today when people are moved to support a cause not by faith in other people's authority, but rather on the basis of their own independent judgment and conviction.

We assert then that nothing has been accomplished without an interest on the part of those who brought it about. And if "interest" be called "passion"—because the whole individuality is concentrating all its desires and powers, with every fiber of volition, to the neglect of all other actual or possible interests and aims, on one object—we may then affirm without qualification that *nothing great in the world* has been accomplished without passion.

Two elements therefore enter into our investigation: first, the Idea, secondly, the complex of human passions; the one the warp, the other the woof of the vast tapestry of world history. Their contact and concrete union constitutes moral liberty in the state. We have already spoken of the Idea of freedom as the essence of Spirit and absolutely final purpose of history. Passion is regarded as something wrong, something more or less evil; man is not supposed to have passions. "Passion," it is true, is not quite the right word for what I wish to express. I mean here nothing more than human activity resulting from private interest, from special or, if you will, self-seeking designs—with this qualification: that the whole energy of will and character is devoted to the attainment of one aim and that other interests or possible aims, indeed everything else, is sacrificed to this aim. This particular objective is so bound up with the person's will that it alone and entirely determines its direction and is inseparable from it. It is that which makes the person what he is. For a person is a specific existence. He is not man in general—such a thing does not exist—but a particular human being. The term "character" also expresses this uniqueness of will and intelligence. But character comprises all individual features whatever—the way in which a person conducts himself in his private and other relations. It does not connote this individuality itself in its practical and active phase. I shall therefore use the term "passion" to mean the particularity of a character insofar as its individual volitions not only have a particular content but also supply the impelling and actuating force for deeds of universal scope. Passion is thus the subjective and therefore the formal aspect of energy, will, and activity, whose content and aim are at this point still undetermined. And a similar relation exists between individual conviction, insight, and conscience, on the one hand, and their content, on the other. If someone wants to decide whether my conviction and passion are true and substantial, he must consider the *content* of my conviction and the *aim* of my passion. Conversely, if they are true and substantial, they cannot help but attain actual existence.

From this comment on the second essential element in the historical embodiment of an aim, we infer—considering for a moment the institution of the state—that a state is then well constituted and internally vigorous when the private interest of its citizens is one with the common interest of the state, and the one finds gratification and realization in the other—a most important proposition. But in a state many institutions are necessary—inventions, appropriate arrangements, accompanied by long intellectual struggles in order to find out what is really appropriate, as well as struggles with private interests and passions, which must be harmonized in difficult and tedious discipline. When a state reaches this harmony, it has reached the period of its bloom, its excellence, its power and prosperity. But world history does not begin with any conscious aim, as do the *particular* circles of men. Already the simple instinct of living together contains the conscious purpose of securing life and property; once this primal society has been established, the purpose expands. But world history begins its *general* aim—to realize the idea of Spirit—only in an implicit form *(an sich),* namely, as Nature—as an innermost, unconscious instinct. And the whole business of history, as already observed, is to bring it into consciousness. Thus, appearing in the form of nature, of natural will, what we have called the subjective side is immediate, actual existence *(für sich)*: need, instinct, passion, private interest, even opinion and subjective representation. These vast congeries of volitions, interests, and activities constitute the tools and means of the World Spirit for attaining its purpose, bringing it to consciousness, and realizing it. And this purpose is none other than finding itself—coming to itself—and contemplating itself in concrete actuality. But one may indeed question whether those manifestations of vitality on the part of individuals and peoples in which they seek and satisfy their own purposes are, at the same time, the means and tools of a higher and broader purpose of which they know nothing, which they realize unconsciously. This purpose has been questioned, and in every variety of form denied, decried, and denounced as mere dreaming and "philosophy." On this point, however, I announced my view at the very outset, and asserted our hypothesis—which eventually will appear as the result of our investigation—namely, that Reason governs the world and has consequently governed its history. In relation to this Reason, which is universal and substantial, in and for itself, all else is subordinate, subservient, and the means for its actualization. Moreover, this Reason is immanent in historical existence and reaches its own perfection in and through this existence. The union of the abstract universal, existing in and for itself, with the particular or subjective, and the fact that this union alone constitutes truth are a matter of speculative philosophy which, in this general form, is treated in logic. But in its historical development [*the subjective side, consciousness, is not yet able to know what is*] the abstract final aim of history, the idea of Spirit, for it is then itself in process and incomplete. The idea of Spirit is not yet its distinct object of desire and interest. Thus desire is still unconscious of its purpose; yet it already exists in the particular purposes and realizes itself through them. The problem concerning the union of the general and the subjective may also be raised under the form of the union of freedom and necessity. We consider the immanent development of the Spirit, existing in and for itself, as necessary, while we refer to freedom the interests contained in men's conscious volitions. Since, as was said, the speculative, that is, the conceptual aspect of this connection belongs to logic, it would be out of place to analyze it here. But the chief and cardinal points may be mentioned.

In philosophy we show that the Idea proceeds to its infinite antithesis.... [*The Idea has within itself the determination of its self-consciousness, of activity. Thus it is God's own eternal life, as it was, so to speak, before the creation of the world, (the) logical connection (of all things). It still lacks at this point the form of being which is actuality. It still is the universal, the immanent, the represented. The second stage begins when the Idea satisifies the contrast which originally is only ideally in it and posits the difference between itself in its free universal mode, in which it remains within itself, and itself as purely abstract reflection in itself. In thus stepping over to one side (in order to be object of reflection) the Idea sets the other side as formal actuality (Fürsichsein), as formal freedom, as abstract unity of self-consciousness, as infinite reflection in itself, and as infinite negativity (antithesis). Thus it becomes Ego, which, as an atom (indivisible), opposes itself to all content and thus is the most complete antithesis—the antithesis, namely, of the whole plenitude of the Idea. The absolute Idea is thus, on the one hand, substantial fullness of content and, on the other hand, abstract free volition. God and universe have separated, and set each other as opposites. Consciousness, the Ego, has a being such that the other (everything else) is for it (its object). In developing this train of thought one arrives at the creation of free spirits, the world, and so on. The absolute antithesis, the atom (i.e., the Ego), which at the same time is a manifold (of contents of consciousness), is finiteness itself. It is for itself (in actuality) merely exclusion of its antithesis (the absolute Idea). It is its limit and barrier. Thus it is the Absolute itself become finite. Reflection in itself, individual self-consciousness, is the antithesis of the absolute Idea and hence the Idea in absolute finiteness. This finitude, the acme of freedom, this formal knowledge—when referred to the glory of God as to the absolute Idea which recognizes what ought to be—is the soil on which the spiritual element of knowledge as such is falling; thus it constitutes the absolute aspect of its actuality, though it remains merely formal.]*

To comprehend the absolute connection of this opposition is the profound task of metaphysics. [*The Divine, and hence religion, exists for the Ego, and likewise also the world in general, that is, the universal totality of finite existence, exists for the Ego. The Ego, in this relation, is itself its own finiteness and comprehends itself as finite. Thus it is the viewpoint of finite purposes, of mere appearance. (At the same time it is particularity of consciousness.) Consciousness in itself, freedom abstractly considered, is the formal aspect of the activity of the absolute Idea. This self-consciousness, first of all, wills itself in general and, secondly, wills itself in every particular. This self-knowing subjectivity projects itself into all objectivity. This constitutes the Ego's certainty of its own existence. Inasmuch as this subjectivity has no other content, it must be called the rational desire—just as piety is nothing but the desire for the subject's salvation. The Ego thus wills itself primarily not as con-*

scious but as finite in its immediacy. This is the sphere of its phenomenality. It wills itself in its particularity. At this point we find the passions, where individuality realizes *its particularity. If it succeeds in thus realizing its finiteness, it doubles itself (its potential finiteness becomes actual finiteness). Through this reconciliation of the atom and its othernesses individuals are what we call happy, for happy is he who is in harmony with himself. One may contemplate history from the point of view of happiness.*] But actually history is not the soil of happiness. The periods of happiness are blank pages in it. [*There is, it is true, satisfaction in world history. But it is not the kind that is called happiness, for it is satisfaction of purposes that are above particular interests. Purposes that are relevant for world history must be grasped in abstract volition and with energy. The world-historical individuals who have pursued such purposes have satisified themselves, it is true, but they did not want to be happy.*

This element of abstract action] is to be regarded as the bond, the middle term, between the universal Idea, which reposes in the inner recesses of Spirit, and the external world. [*It is that which carries the Idea from its immanence into its external state. Universality, in being externalized, is at the same time made particular. The immanent by itself would be dead, abstract. Through action it becomes existent. Conversely, activity elevates (the) empty objectivity (of nature) to be the appearance of the essence which is in and for itself.*]

B. One-Dimensional Man

Herbert Marcuse

Having discussed the political integration of advanced industrial society, an achievement rendered possible by growing technological productivity and the expanding conquest of man and nature, we will now turn to a corresponding integration in the realm of culture. In this chapter, certain key notions and images of literature and their fate will illustrate how the progress of technological rationality is liquidating the oppositional and transcending elements in the "higher culture." They succumb in fact to the process of *desublimation* which prevails in the advanced regions of contemporary society.

The achievements and the failures of this society invalidate its higher culture. The celebration of the autonomous personality, of humanism, of tragic and romantic love appears to be the ideal of a backward stage of the development. What is happening now is not the deterioration of higher culture into mass culture but the refutation of this culture by the reality. The reality surpasses its culture. Man today can do *more* than the culture heroes and half-gods; he has solved many insoluble problems. But he has also betrayed the hope and destroyed the truth which were preserved in the sublimations of higher culture. To be sure, the higher culture was always in contradiction with social reality, and only a privileged minority enjoyed its blessings and represented its ideals. The two antagonistic spheres of society have always coexisted; the higher culture has always been accommodating, while the reality was rarely disturbed by its ideals and its truth.

Today's novel feature is the flattening out of the antagonism between culture and social reality through the obliteration of the oppositional, alien, and transcendent elements in the higher culture by virtue of which it constituted *another dimension* of reality. This liquidation of *two-dimensional* culture takes place not through the denial and rejection of the "cultural values," but through their wholesale incorporation into the established order, through their reproduction and display on a massive scale.

In fact, they serve as instruments of social cohesion. The greatness of a free literature and art, the ideals of humanism, the sorrows and joys of the individual, the fulfillment of the personality are important

items in the competitive struggle between East and West. They speak
heavily against the present forms of communism, and they are daily
administered and sold. The fact that they contradict the society which
sells them does not count. Just as people know or feel that advertise-
ments and political platforms must not be necessarily true or right, and
yet hear and read them and even let themselves be guided by them, so
they accept the traditional values and make them part of their mental
equipment. If mass communications blend together harmoniously,
and often unnoticeably, art, politics, religion, and philosophy with
commercials, they bring these realms of culture to their common
denominator—the commodity form. The music of the soul is also the
music of salesmanship. Exchange value, not truth value counts. On it
centers the rationality of the status quo, and all alien rationality is bent
to it.

As the great words of freedom and fulfillment are pronounced by
campaigning leaders and politicians, on the screens and radios and
stages, they turn into meaningless sounds which obtain meaning only
in the context of propaganda, business, discipline, and relaxation. This
assimilation of the ideal with reality testifies to the extent to which the
ideal has been surpassed. It is brought down from the sublimated
realm of the soul or the spirit or the inner man, and translated into
operational terms and problems. Here are the progressive elements of
mass culture. The perversion is indicative of the fact that advanced
industrial society is confronted with the possibility of a materialization
of ideals. The capabilities of this society are progressively reducing the
sublimated realm in which the condition of man was represented,
idealized, and indicated. Higher culture becomes part of the material
culture. In this transformation, it loses the greater part of its truth.

The higher culture of the West—whose moral, aesthetic, and intellectual values industrial society still professes—was a pre-technological culture in a functional as well as chronological sense. Its validity
was derived from the experience of a world which no longer exists and
which cannot be recaptured because it is in a strict sense invalidated
by technological society. Moreover, it remained to a large degree a feudal culture, even when the bourgeois period gave it some of its most
lasting formulations. It was feudal not only because of its confinement
to privileged minorities, not only because of its inherent romantic element (which will be discussed presently), but also because its authentic
works expressed a conscious, methodical alienation from the entire

sphere of business and industry, and from its calculable and profitable order.

While this bourgeois order found its rich—and even affirmative—representation in art and literature (as in the Dutch painters of the seventeenth century, in Goethe's *Wilhelm Meister,* in the English novel of the nineteenth century, in Thomas Mann), it remained an order which was overshadowed, broken, refuted by another dimension which was irreconcilably antagonistic to the order of business, indicting it and denying it. And in the literature, this other dimension is represented *not* by the religious, spiritual, moral heroes (who often sustain the established order) but rather by such disruptive characters as the artist, the prostitute, the adulteress, the great criminal and outcast, the warrior, the rebel-poet, the devil, the fool—those who don't earn a living, at least not in an orderly and normal way.

To be sure, these characters have not disappeared from the literature of advanced industrial society, but they survive essentially transformed. The vamp, the national hero, the beatnik, the neurotic housewife, the gangster, the star, the charismatic tycoon perform a function very different from and even contrary to that of their cultural predecessors. They are no longer images of another way of life but rather freaks or types of the same life, serving as an affirmation rather than negation of the established order.

Surely, the world of their predecessors was a backward, pre-technological world, a world with the good conscience of inequality and toil, in which labor was still a fated misfortune; but a world in which man and nature were not yet organized as things and instrumentalities. With its code of forms and manners, with the style and vocabulary of its literature and philosophy, this past culture expressed the rhythm and content of a universe in which valleys and forests, villages and inns, nobles and villains, salons and courts were a part of the experienced reality. In the verse and prose of this pre-technological culture is the rhythm of those who wander or ride in carriages, who have the time and the pleasure to think, contemplate, feel and narrate.

It is an outdated and surpassed culture, and only dreams and childlike regressions can recapture it. But this culture is, in some of its decisive elements, also a *post*-technological one. Its most advanced images and positions seem to survive their absorption into administered comforts and stimuli; they continue to haunt the consciousness with the possibility of their rebirth in the consummation of technical progress. They are the expression of that free and conscious alienation from the established forms of life with which literature and the arts opposed these forms even where they adorned them.

In contrast to the Marxian concept, which denotes man's relation to himself and to his work in capitalist society, the *artistic alienation* is the conscious transcendence of the alienated existence—a "higher level" or mediated alienation. The conflict with the world of progress, the negation of the order of business, the anti-bourgeois elements in bourgeois literature and art are neither due to the aesthetic lowliness of this order nor to romantic reaction—nostalgic consecration of a disappearing stage of civilization. "Romantic" is a term of condescending defamation which is easily applied to disparaging avant-garde positions, just as the term "decadent" far more often denounces the genuinely progressive traits of a dying culture than the real factors of decay. The traditional images of artistic alienation are indeed romantic in as much as they are in aesthetic incompatibility with the developing society. This incompatibility is the token of their truth. What they recall and preserve in memory pertains to the future: images of a gratification that would dissolve the society which suppresses it. The great surrealist art and literature of the 'Twenties and 'Thirties has still recaptured them in their subversive and liberating function. Random examples from the basic literary vocabulary may indicate the range and the kinship of these images, and the dimension which they reveal: Soul and Spirit and Heart; *la recherche de l'absolu, Les Fleurs du mal, la femme-enfant;* the Kingdom by the Sea; *Le Bateau ivre* and the Long-legged Bait; *Ferne* and *Heimat;* but also demon rum, demon machine, and demon money; Don Juan and Romeo; the Master Builder and When We Dead Awake.

Their mere enumeration shows that they belong to a lost dimension. They are invalidated not because of their literary obsolescence. Some of these images pertain to contemporary literature and survive in its most advanced creations. What has been invalidated is their subversive force, their destructive content—their truth. In this transformation, they find their home in everyday living. The alien and alienating oeuvres of intellectual culture become familiar goods and services. Is their massive reproduction and consumption only a change in quantity, namely, growing appreciation and understanding, democratization of culture?

The truth of literature and art has always been granted (if it was granted at all) as one of a "higher" order, which should not and indeed did not disturb the order of business. What has changed in the contemporary period is the difference between the two orders and their truths.

The absorbent power of society depletes the artistic dimension by assimilating its antagonistic contents. In the realm of culture, the new totalitarianism manifests itself precisely in a harmonizing pluralism, where the most contradictory works and truths peacefully coexist in indifference.

Prior to the advent of this cultural reconciliation, literature and art were essentially alienation, sustaining and protecting the contradiction—the unhappy consciousness of the divided world, the defeated possibilities, the hopes unfulfilled, and the promises betrayed. They were a rational, cognitive force, revealing a dimension of man and nature which was repressed and repelled in reality. Their truth was in the illusion evoked, in the insistence on creating a world in which the terror of life was called up and suspended—mastered by recognition. This is the miracle of the *chef-d'oeuvre;* it is the tragedy, sustained to the last, and the end of tragedy—its impossible solution. To live one's love and hatred, to live that which one *is* means defeat, resignation, and death. The crimes of society, the hell that man has made for man become unconquerable cosmic forces.

The tension between the actual and the possible is transfigured into an insoluble conflict, in which reconciliation is by grace of the oeuvre as *form:* beauty as the "promesse de bonheur." In the form of the oeuvre, the actual circumstances are placed in another dimension where the given reality shows itself as that which it is. Thus it tells the truth about itself; its language ceases to be that of deception, ignorance, and submission. Fiction calls the facts by their name and their reign collapses; fiction subverts everyday experience and shows it to be mutilated and false. But art has this magic power only as the power of negation. It can speak its own language only as long as the images are alive which refuse and refute the established order.

Flaubert's *Madame Bovary* is distinguished from equally sad love stories of contemporary literature by the fact that the humble vocabulary of her real-life counterpart still contained the heroine's images, or she read stories still containing such images. Her anxiety was fatal because there was no psychoanalyst, and there was no psychoanalyst because, in her world, he would not have been capable of curing her. She would have rejected him as part of the order of Yonville which destroyed her. Her story was "tragic" because the society in which it occurred was a backward one, with a sexual morality not yet liberalized, and a psychology not yet institutionalized. The society that was still to come has "solved" her problem by suppressing it. Certainly it would be nonsense to say that her tragedy or that of Romeo and Juliet is solved in modern democracy, but it would also be nonsense to deny the historical essence of the tragedy. The devleoping technological reality undermines not only the traditional forms but the very basis of the artistic alienation—that is, it tends to invalidate not only certain "styles" but also the very substance of art.

To be sure, alienation is not the sole characteristic of art. An analysis, and even a statement of the problem is outside the scope of this work, but some suggestions may be offered for clarification. Throughout whole periods of civilization, art appears to be entirely integrated into its society. Egyptian, Greek, and Gothic art are familiar examples; Bach and Mozart are usually also cited as testifying to the "positive" side of art. The place of the work of art in a pre-technological and two-dimensional culture is very different from that in a one-dimensional civilization, but alienation characterizes affirmative as well as negative art.

The decisive distinction is not the psychological one between art created in joy and art created in sorrow, between sanity and neurosis, but that between the artistic and the societal reality. The rupture with the latter, the magic or rational transgression, is an essential quality of even the most affirmative art; it is alienated also from the very public to which it is addressed. No matter how close and familiar the temple or cathedral were to the people who lived around them, they remained in terrifying or elevating contrast to the daily life of the slave, the peasant, and the artisan—and perhaps even to that of their masters.

Whether ritualized or not, art contains the rationality of negation. In its advanced positions, it is the Great Refusal—the protest against that which is. The modes in which man and things are made to appear, to sing and sound and speak, are modes of refuting, breaking, and recreating their factual existence. But these modes of negation pay tribute to the antagonistic society to which they are linked. Separated from the sphere of labor where society reproduces itself and its misery, the world of art which they create remains, with all its truth, a privilege and an illusion.

In this form it continues, in spite of all democratization and popularization, through the nineteenth and into the twentieth century. The "high culture" in which this alienation is celebrated has its own rites and its own style. The salon, the concert, opera, theater are designed to create and invoke another dimension of reality. Their attendance requires festive-like preparation; they cut off and transcend everyday experience.

Now this essential gap between the arts and the order of the day, kept open in the artistic alienation, is progressively closed by the advancing technological society. And with its closing, the Great Refusal is in turn refused; the "other dimension" is absorbed into the prevailing state of affairs. The works of alienation are themselves incorporated into this society and circulate as part and parcel of the equipment which adorns and psychoanalyzes the prevailing state of affairs. Thus they become commercials—they sell, comfort, or excite.

The neo-conservative critics of leftist critics of mass culture ridicule the protest against Bach as background music in the kitchen, against Plato and Hegel, Shelley and Baudelaire, Marx and Freud in the drugstore. Instead, they insist on recognition of the fact that the classics have left the mausoleum and come to life again, that people are just so much more educated. True, but coming to life as classics, they come to life as other than themselves; they are deprived of their antagonistic force, of the estrangement which was the very dimension of their truth. The intent and function of these works have thus fundamentally changed. If they once stood in contradiction to the status quo, this contradiction is now flattened out.

But such assimilation is historically premature; it establishes cultural equality while preserving domination. Society is eliminating the prerogatives and privileges of feudal-aristocratic culture together with its content. The fact that the transcending truths of the fine arts, the aesthetics of life and thought, were accessible only to the few wealthy and educated was the fault of a repressive society. But this fault is not corrected by paperbacks, general education, long-playing records, and the abolition of formal dress in the theater and concert hall. The cultural privileges expressed the injustice of freedom, the contradiction between ideology and reality, the separation of intellectual from material productivity; but they also provided a protected realm in which the tabooed truths could survive in abstract integrity—remote from the society which suppressed them.

Now this remoteness has been removed—and with it the transgression and the indictment. The text and the tone are still there, but the distance is conquered which made them *Luft von anderen Planeten*. The artistic alienation has become as functional as the architecture of the new theaters and concert halls in which it is performed. And here too, the rational and the evil are inseparable. Unquestionably the new architecture is better, i.e., more beautiful and more practical than the monstrosities of the Victorian era. But is is also more "integrated"—the cultural center is becoming a fitting part of the shopping center, or municipal center, or government center. Domination has its own aesthetics, and democratic domination has its democratic aesthetics. It is good that almost everyone can now have the fine arts at his fingertips, by just turning a knob on his set, or by just stepping into his drugstore. In this diffusion, however, they become cogs in a culture-machine which remakes their content.

Artistic alienation succumbs, together with other modes of negation, to the process of technological rationality. The change reveals its depth and the degree of its irreversibility if it is seen as a result of technical progress. The present stage redefines the possibilities of man and nature in accordance with the new means available for their realization and, in their light, the pre-technological images are losing their power.

C. Thus Spoke Zarathustra

Friedrich Nietzsche

When Zarathustra was thirty years of age he left his home and the lake-side where he dwelt and went into the mountains. There he possessed his spirit in solitude and for ten years wearied not thereof. But at length his heart changed,—on a day he arose with the dawn, stood before the presence of the Sun, and spake thus unto him:

Thou great star! Where were thy happiness, without those for whom thou shinest!

Ten years hast thou climbed hither to my cave: thou wouldst have wearied of thy light and of this pathway were it not for me, mine Eagle and my Serpent.

But we awaited thee each morning and took of thy superabundance and blessed thee therefor.

Lo! I am weary of my wisdom, as the bee that hath gathered overmuch honey; I need hands outstretched to take it.

Fain would I bestow and distribute until the wise amongst men rejoice again in their folly, and the poor in their riches.

To that end must I descend into the deeps: even as thou dost at nightfall, when thou sinkest behind the sea, and bringest light to the underworld, thou most bounteous star!

Like thee, I must *go down,* as say the men to whom I would descend.

Bless me, then, thou tranquil eye that canst look without envy even upon too great a happiness!

Bless the cup that is about to overflow, so that its waters may be a golden flood, carrying everywhere the reflected splendour of thy bliss!

Lo! This cup must again become empty, and Zarathustra must again become a man.

Thus began Zarathustra's down-going.

Zarathustra went down the mountain-side alone, and no man met with him. But when he reached the woods, suddenly there stood before him an Aged Man that had left his hermitage to seek roots in the forest. And thus spake the Aged Man to Zarathustra:

No stranger to me is this Wanderer: many years since passed he by. Zarathustra was his name; but he is changed.

Then thou didst bear thine ashes into the mountains: wilt thou to-day bear thy fire into the valleys? Dost thou not fear the incendiary's doom?

Yea, I know thee that thou art Zarathustra! Clear is his eye, nor lurketh any loathing about his mouth. Goeth he not his way like a dancer?

Zarathustra is changed: Zarathustra became as a child: Zarathustra is awakened: what wilt thou amongst the sleepers?

Thou dwelledst in solitude as in a sea, and the sea hath sustained thee. Alas, wilt thou now go upon land? Alas, wilt thou drag again the burden of thy body?

Zarathustra answered: I love mankind.

Wherefore, said the Saint, went I to the forest and the desert? Was it not because I loved mankind inordinately?

Now love I God: mankind I love not. Man for me is a thing far too imperfect. Love of mankind would destroy me.

Zarathustra answered: What said I of love! I bring mankind a gift.

Give them naught, said the Saint. Rather take something from them and bear it with them—that will do them best service: may it but serve thee also!

Yet if thou wilt give them aught, give them no more than an alms, and let them beg even for that.

Nay, said Zarathustra, I do not give alms. I am not poor enough for that.

The Saint laughed at Zarathustra and spake thus: Then see to it that they accept thy treasures! They are mistrustful of hermits and will not believe that we come in order to give.

In their ears our step hath too solitary a sound in the streets. Even as when at night from their beds they hear one pass long ere sunrise, they ask: Whither goeth the thief?

Go not to men, but tarry in the forest! Go rather to the beasts! Why wilt thou not be as I am—a bear among bears, a bird among birds?

And what doth the Saint in the forest? asked Zarathustra.

The Saint answered: I make songs and sing them, and making songs I laugh, weep, and chant: thus I praise God.

Singing, weeping, laughing, and chanting I praise that God which is my God. But what gift is it thou bringest us?

When Zarathustra had heard these words he saluted the Saint and said: What could I have to give thee! But let me depart quickly, lest I take aught from thee.—And thus they took their leave, the old man and the other, like two laughing boys.

But when Zarathustra was alone he spake thus within his heart: Can it indeed be possible! This old Saint in his forest hath not yet heard that *God is dead*!—

When Zarathustra reached that city which lieth nighest to the forest, he found there many folk assembled in the marketplace: for it was said they should see a Rope-dancer. And Zarathustra spake thus unto the people:

'I teach you the Superman. Man is a thing to be surmounted. What have ye done to surmount him?

All beings hitherto have created something above themselves: will ye be the ebb of this great tide and rather revert to the beast than surmount man?

What is the ape to man? A jest or a thing of shame. So shall man be to Superman—a jest or a thing of shame.

Ye have trod the way from worm to man, and much in you is yet worm. Once were ye apes, and even yet man is more ape than any ape.

But he that is wisest amongst you is but a discord, a hybrid of plant and ghost. But do I bid you become either ghosts or plants?

Behold, I teach you the Superman!

The Superman is the meaning of the earth. Let your will say: the Superman *shall be* the meaning of the earth.

I conjure you, my brethren, *remain true to the earth* and believe them not which speak to you of superterrestrial hopes! Poisoners are they, whether or not they know it.

Contemners of life are they, moribund and themselves poisoned, of whom the earth is weary: away with them!

Once blasphemy against God was the greatest of blasphemies, but God died, so that these blasphemies died also. Now the most terrible of sins is to blaspheme against the earth and to rate the bowels of the Unknowable One higher than the meaning of the earth!

Once the soul looked contemptuously upon the body: in those days was this contempt the highest ideal:—the soul would have the body meagre, ugly, and starved. Thus the soul thought to escape the body and the earth.

Oh, that soul was itself meagre, hideous, and famished: and in cruelty was that soul's delight!

But ye also, my brethren, tell me: What saith your body of your soul? Is not your soul full of poverty and uncleanness and despicable ease?

Verily, a polluted stream is man. One must be a very ocean to be able to receive a polluted stream without becoming unclean.

Behold, I teach you the Superman: he is that ocean, in him can your great contempt be o'erwhelmed.

What is the greatest thing ye can experience? It is the hour of great contempt. The hour in which even your happiness is loathsome to you, and your reason and your virtue likewise.

The hour in which ye say: What is my happiness worth! It is poverty and uncleanness and despicable ease. Yet my happiness should justify Being itself!

The hour in which ye say: What is my reason worth! Desireth it knowledge as the lion his prey? It is poverty and uncleanness and despicable ease.

The hour in which ye say: What is my virtue worth! Not yet hath it roused me to fury. How I weary of my good and mine evil! It is all naught but poverty and uncleanness and despicable ease!

The hour in which ye say: What is my righteousness worth! I perceive not that I am flame and fuel. Yet the righteous man is flame and fuel!

The hour in which ye say: What is my pity worth! Is not pity the cross upon which he is nailed that loveth mankind? But my pity is no crucifixion.

Spake ye ever thus? Cried ye ever thus? Ah, that I had heard you cry thus!

Not your sin, but your sufficiency crieth unto heaven, your niggardliness even in sin crieth unto heaven!

Where is the lightning to lick you with its tongue? Where is the frenzy with which ye must be infected?

Behold! I teach you the Superman: he is this lightning, he is this frenzy!'

When Zarathustra had thus spoken, one of the people cried: We have *heard* enough about this Rope-dancer; now let us *see* him! And all the people laughed at Zarathustra. The Rope-dancer, however, thought that he was called for, and set himself to his work.

But Zarathustra looking on the people wondered. Then he spake thus:

Man is a rope stretched betwixt beast and Superman—a rope over an abyss.

Perilous is the crossing, perilous the way, perilous the backward look, perilous all trembling and halting by the way.

Man is great in that he is a bridge and not a goal: man can be loved in that he is a transition and a perishing.

I love them which live not save as under-goers, for they are the over-goers.

I love them which greatly scorn because they also greatly adore; they are arrows of longing for the farther shore.

I love them which seek no reason beyond the stars wherefore they should perish, wherefore they should be sacrificed, but which sacrifice themselves to the earth that the earth hereafter may be the Superman's.

I love him which liveth that he may know, and which seeketh knowledge that hereafter the Superman may live: for thus he willeth his own down-going.

I love him which worketh and deviseth to build an house for the Superman, to prepare for him earth, beast, and plant; for thus he willeth his own down-going.

I love him which loveth his virtue: for virtue is the will to down-going, and an arrow of longing.

I love him which reserveth no share of spirit for himself, but willeth to be wholly the spirit of his virtue: thus in spirit he crosseth over the bridge.

I love him which maketh of his virtue his inclination and his destiny: for thus for his virtue's sake he willeth either to live on or to cease to live.

I love him which desireth not too many virtues. One virtue is more virtue than two, because it is so much the more a knot on which destiny hangs.

I love him whose soul lavisheth itself, that neither requireth nor returneth thanks: for he giveth ever and keepeth naught for himself.

I love him which is ashamed when the dice fall in his favour and asketh: Am I a cheating player?—for he desireth to perish.

I love him which streweth golden words before his deeds and performeth yet more than he promiseth: for he seeketh his own down-going.

I love him which justifieth future generations and redeemeth past generations: for he willeth to perish by the present generation.

I love him which chastiseth his God because he loveth his God: for he must perish by the wrath of his God.

I love him whose soul is deep even for wounding and whom a slight matter may destroy: for he gladly goeth over the bridge.

I love him whose soul is over-full so that he forgetteth himself, and all things are within him: thus all things become his downfall.

I love him which is of a free mind and of a free heart: for his head is but the bowels of his heart, but his heart driveth him to destruction.

I love all them which are as heavy rain-drops falling one by one from the dark cloud that lowereth over mankind: they herald the coming of the lightning, and they perish as heralds.

Behold, I am an herald of the lightning and an heavy raindrop from the clouds: but that lightning is named *Superman.*—

When he had spoken these words Zarathustra looked again on the people and was silent. There they stand, he said within his heart, they laugh: they understand me not: I am not the mouth for these ears.

Must needs their ears be battered that they may learn to hear with their eyes? Must a man clamour like a kettle-drum or like a Lenten preacher? Or will they believe only the stammerer?

They have a thing whereof they are proud. How call they that whereof they are proud? Culture they call it which distinguisheth them from the goatherds.

Wherefore they love not to hear words of contempt used of themselves. I will speak therefore to their pride.

I will speak therefore to them of the most contemptible of all things: and that is the *Last Man.*

And thus Zarathustra spake to the people:

'It is time for Man to mark his goal. It is time for man to sow the seed of his highest hope.

His soil is yet rich enough therefor. But the day cometh when that soil shall be impoverished and effete, and no tall tree shall any longer be able to grow therefrom.

Alas! the day cometh when man shall no longer shoot the arrow of his desire beyond man, when his bowstring shall have forgotten its use!

I say unto you: a man must have chaos yet within him to be able to give birth to a dancing star. I say unto you: ye have chaos yet within you.

Alas! the day cometh when man shall give birth to no more stars! Alas! the day cometh of that most contemptible man which can no longer contemn himself.

Behold! I show you the *Last Man.*

What is love? What is creation? What is desire? What is a star? asketh the Last Man, and he blinketh!

Then will earth have grown small, and upon it shall hop the Last Man which maketh all things small. His kind is inexterminable like the ground-flea; the Last Man liveth longest.

'We have discovered happiness,'—say the Last Men, and they blink.

They have left the regions where it was hard to live, for one must have warmth. Man still loveth his neighbour and rubbeth himself against him; for one must have warmth.

Sickness and mistrust they hold sinful. They go warily. A fool is he that yet stumbleth either over stones or men!

A little poison now and then: for that causeth pleasant dreams. And much poison at the last for an easy death.

They still work, for work is a pastime. But they take heed, lest the pastime harm them.

They grow no longer poor nor rich; it is too troublesome to do either. Who desireth to rule? Who to obey? Both are too troublesome.

No shepherd and but one flock! All men will alike, all are alike; he that feeleth otherwise goeth voluntarily to a madhouse.

'Once all the world was mad,' say these most refined ones, and they blink.

They are clever and know all that hath come to pass, so that there is no end of mockery. They quarrel yet, but are soon reconciled—lest their stomachs turn.

They have little lusts for the day and little lusts for the night: but they have regard for health.

We have discovered happiness, say the Last Men, and they blink.'—

And here ended Zarathustra's first discourse, which is also called 'the Prologue', for at this point the clamour and mirth of the people interrupted him. Give us these Last Men, O Zarathustra, they cried, make us as these Last Men. Thou mayest keep thy Superman! And all the people cheered and clicked their tongues. But Zarathustra grieved, and said within his heart:

They understand me not: I am not the mouth for these ears.

Too long, perchance, have I dwelt in the mountains, listened too long to brooks and trees: now my speech is to them as that of goatherds.

My soul is still and bright like the mountains ere midday. But they deem me cold and a mocker whose jests are terrible.

How they look on me and laugh: and while they laugh they hate me. There is ice in their laughter.

Then that came to pass which silenced every mouth and fixed every eye. For in the meantime the Rope-dancer had begun his task: he had stepped forth from a little door and walked upon the rope which was stretched between two towers so that it spanned the market-place and the people. When he was now midway the little door again opened and a gaily-dressed fellow like a Clown leaped out and went with quick steps after the first. On with you, lame-leg, he cried in a terrible voice, on with you, lazybones, cheat, sallow-face!—lest I tickle thee with my heel! What dost thou here between the towers? Thy place is *in* the tower. Thou shouldst be jailed, for thou barrest free way to thy better!—And at each word the clown drew nearer and nearer: but when he was but one step behind, there happened that terrible thing which silenced every mouth and fixed every eye: for uttering a cry like a devil, he leaped over him that barred his way, who, seeing his rival's triumph, lost both his head and his footing on the rope, threw aside his wand, and himself shot down yet faster with arms and legs whirling. The market-place and the crowd became as a storm-tossed sea: every man fled stumbling over his neighbour, and chiefly there where the body was about to strike the ground.

Zarathustra, however, kept his place, and the body fell close beside him, badly disfigured and broken, but not yet dead. After a while consciousness returned to the injured man, and he saw Zarathustra kneeling beside him. What dost thou there? he asked at last, I knew long since that the devil would trip me. Now he draggeth me into hell: wilt thou prevent him?

By mine honour, friend, answered Zarathustra, that of which thou speakest doth not exist: there is no devil and no hell. Thy soul will be dead even sooner than thy body: henceforward fear nothing more.

The man looked up distrustfully: If thou speakest truth, he said, losing my life I lose naught. I am little more than a beast, taught to dance by blows and titbits.

Not so, said Zarathustra; thou hast made danger thy calling, there is naught contemptible in that. Now thou diest by thy calling: therefore will I bury thee with mine own hands.

When Zarathustra had spoken thus the dying man made no answer, but moved his hand as though he sought Zarathustra's, to thank him.

In the meantime evening fell, and the market-place was shrouded in darkness: the people dispersed, for even curiosity and terror grow weary. Zarathustra, however, sat on the ground beside the dead man, absorbed in thought, forgetful of the time. But at length it was night, and a cold wind blew over the Solitary. Then Zarathustra, rising, said within his heart:

Verily, fine fishing was Zarathustra's to-day! He caught no man, but a corpse!

Man's life is a strange matter and ever full of unreason: a buffoon may be fatal to it.

I will teach men the meaning of their being—Superman, which is the lightning from the dark cloud, Man.

But I am yet far from them and my mind speaketh not to their minds. To men I am as yet a thing half fool, half corpse.

Dark is the night and dark the ways of Zarathustra. Come, thou cold and stiff companion! I will bear thee to a place where I shall bury thee with mine own hands.

When Zarathustra had spoken thus within his heart he took the corpse upon his back and went his way. And ere he had yet gone an hundred paces, one stole upon him and whispered in his ear—and lo! it was the Clown from the tower. Depart from this city, O Zarathustra, he said; too many hate thee here. The Good and Righteous hate thee, and call thee enemy and despiser. The orthodox faithful hate thee, and call thee a danger to the multitude. It was thy good fortune to be laughed at: and, verily, thou spakest like a buffoon. It was thy good fortune to associate with this dead dog; in thus humiliating thyself thou hast saved thyself this day. But depart from this city—or to-morrow I shall leap over thee—a living man over a dead one. And when he had said thus, the man vanished; but Zarathustra went on his way through the dark alleys.

At the gate of the city he met with the grave-diggers. They held their torches to his face, and knowing Zarathustra, mocked him sorely. Zarathustra bears away the dead dog! It is well that Zarathustra hath turned grave-digger! For our hands are too clean for this carrion. Will Zarathustra steal from the Devil his morsel? Well, then, blessings on the repast! If only the Devil do not out-thieve Zarathustra!—steal both and eat both! And they laughed and put their heads together.

Zarathustra answered no word and went his way. When he had journeyed two hours through forest and marsh he heard the hungry howling of wolves and himself felt hunger. So he stayed before a lonely house wherein a light burned.

Hunger hath overtaken me, said Zarathustra, like a robber. Amidst forests and marshes in the depth of the night mine hunger is fallen upon me.

Mine hunger hath strange humours. Often it cometh only after the repast, and to-day it came not all day: where was it?

Thereupon Zarathustra knocked at the door of the house. An Aged Man came. He bore a light and asked: Who cometh to me and to mine evil sleep?

A living man and a dead one, replied Zarathustra. Give me to eat and to drink, I forgot it in the day-time. He that feedeth the hungry refresheth his own soul; thus saith wisdom.

The Aged Man departed and returned immediately, and offered Zarathustra bread and wine. This is an ill place for the hungry, said he; therefore I dwell here. Beast and man come to me, the hermit. But bid also thy companion eat and drink; he is more weary than thou art. Zarathustra answered: My companion is dead; I shall scarcely persuade him to do so. That concerns not me, said the Aged Man sullenly; he that knocketh at my house must take whatever I offer him. Eat and fare ye weil!

Then Zarathustra went yet another two hours and trusted to the path and the light of the stars: for he was accustomed to walk by night and loved to look upon the sleeping face of all things. But when morning dawned, Zarathustra found himself in a deep forest and saw no path more. Then he laid the dead man in an hollow tree near his own head—for he would defend him from the wolves—and himself upon the mossy ground. And immediately he fell asleep, tired in body, but with tranquil soul.

Long slept Zarathustra, and not the dawn only passed over his head, but the morning also. But at length his eyes opened: astonished, Zarathustra looked upon the forest and the stillness, astonished he looked within himself. Then he arose with speed like a mariner that on a sudden seeth land, and he exulted: for he saw a new truth. And thus he spake within his heart:

A light hath dawned on me. I need companions—living ones, not dead companions and corpses which I may carry with me where I will.

But I need living companions which follow me because they desire to follow themselves—and to go to that place whither I wish to go.

A light hath dawned on me: let not Zarathustra speak to the people, but to companions! Zarathustra shall not be shepherd and sheep-dog to a herd!

To entice many away from the herd—to that end I came. The people and the herd will be angry: Zarathustra shall be called a robber by the shepherds.

Shepherds I say, but they call themselves the Good and the Righteous. Herdsmen I say, but they call themselves the Orthodox Faithful.

Lo, the Good and Righteous! Whom hate they most? Him that breaketh in pieces their tables of values—the breaker, the law-breaker. But *he* is the creator.

Lo, the faithful of all creeds! Whom hate they most? Him that breaketh in pieces their tables of values—the breaker, the law-breaker. But *he* is the creator.

The creator seeketh companions, not corpses, neither herds nor believers. The creator seeketh such as will be creators with him, such as write new values on new tables.

The creator seeketh companions, and such as will reap with him: for to him all things are ripe unto harvest. But he lacketh the hundred sickles, so that he teareth up the ears and is wroth.

The creator seeketh companions, and such as know how to whet their sickles. Destroyers shall they be called and despisers of good and evil. But they are reapers and harvesters.

Zarathustra seeketh such as will be creators with him, such as will reap with him and rejoice with him: what hath he to do with herds and shepherds and corpses!

And thou, my first companion, fare thee well! Well have I buried thee in thy hollow tree, well have I hidden thee from the wolves.

But now I take leave of thee, for the time is past. Betwixt dawn and dawn a new truth was revealed to me.

I must be neither shepherd nor grave-digger. I must speak no more to the people. I have spoken for the last time to a dead man.

The creators, the reapers, the rejoicers shall be my companions. I will show them the rainbow and the ladder to the Superman.

I will sing my song to hermits which dwell singly or in pairs. And whosoever hath yet ears for unheard-of things his heart will I over-charge with my bliss.

I will find my goal, I will follow my course, I will o'erleap them that loiter and delay. Let my on-going be their down-going!

Zarathustra had said thus within his heart when the sun stood at noontide: then suddenly gazed he upwards, wondering—for he heard above him the sharp cry of a bird. And lo! an Eagle swept in wide circles through the air, and from it hung a Serpent, not as prey but as friend, for it lay coiled about the Eagle's neck.

These are my beasts, said Zarathustra, and rejoiced in his heart.

The proudest creature beneath the sun, and the wisest creature beneath the sun—they have come to spy out the land.

They have desired to know whether Zarathustra yet liveth. Verily, do I yet live?

More perils found I amongst men than amongst beasts. In dangerous paths goeth Zarathustra. May my beasts guide me!

When Zarathustra had so said he thought on the words of the Saint in the forest and sighing he spake thus within his heart:

Would I were wiser! Would I were altogether wise like my Serpent!

But I ask the impossible. Therefore I ask my pride to go ever with my wisdom.

And should my wisdom ever forsake me—alas! it loveth to flee away!—may my pride then fly with my folly!

Thus began Zarathustra's down-going.

D. The Life of Reason

George Santayana

It is a remarkable fact, which may easily be misinterpreted, that while all the benefits and pleasures of life seem to be associated with external things, and all certain knowledge seems to describe material laws, yet a defined nature has generally inspired a religion of melancholy. Why has man's conscience in the end invariably rebelled against naturalism and reverted in some form or other to a cultus of the unseen?

We may answer in the words of Saint Paul: because things seen are temporal and things not seen are eternal. And we may add, remembering our analysis of the objects inhabiting the mind, that the eternal is the truly human, that which is akin to the first indispensable products of intelligences, which arise by the fusion of successive images in discourse, and transcend the particular in time, peopling the mind with permanent and recognisable objects, and strengthening it with a synthetic, dramatic apprehension of itself and its own experience. Concretion in existence, on the contrary, yields essentially detached and empirical unities, foreign to mind in spite of their order, and unintelligible in spite of their clearness. Reason fails to assimilate in them precisely that which makes them real, namely, their presence here and now, in this order and number. The form and quality of them we can retain, domesticate, and weave into the texture of reflection, but their existence and individuality remain a datum of sense, needing to be verified anew at every moment and actually receiving continual verification or disproof while we live in this world.

"This world" we call it, not without justifiable pathos, for many other worlds are conceivable and if discovered might prove more rational and intelligible and more akin to the soul than this strange universe which man has hitherto always looked upon with increasing astonishment. When an empirical philosophy, therefore, calls us back from the irresponsible flights of imagination to the shock of sense and tries to remind us that in this alone we touch existence and come upon fact, we feel dispossessed of our nature and cramped in our life. The dependence upon sense, which are reduced to when we consider the world of existences, becomes a too plain hint of our essential impotence and mortality, while the play of logical fancy, though it remain inevitable, is saddened by a consciousness of its own insignificance.

177

That dignity, then, which inheres in logical ideas and their affinity to moral enthusiasm, springs from their congruity with the primary habits of intelligence and idealisation. The soul or self or personality, which in sophisticated social life is so much the centre of passion and concern, is itself an idea, a concretion in discourse; and the level at which it swims comes to be, by association and affinity, the region of all the more vivid and massive human interests. The pleasures which lie beneath it are despised, and the ideals which lie above it are not perceived. Aversion to an empirical or naturalistic philosophy accordingly expresses a sort of logical patriotism and attachment to homespun ideas. The actual is too remote and unfriendly to the dreamer; to understand it he has to learn a foreign tongue, which his native prejudice imagines to be unmeaning and unpoetical. The truth is, however, that nature's language is too rich for man; and the discomfort he feels when he is compelled to use it merely marks his lack of education. There is nothing cheaper than idealism. It can be had by merely not observing the ineptitude of our chance prejudices, and by declaring that the first rhymes that have struck our ear are the eternal and necessary harmonies of the world.

The thinker's bias is naturally favourable to logical ideas. The man of reflection will attribute, as far as possible, validity and reality to these alone. Platonism remains the classic instance of this way of thinking. Living in an age of rhetoric, with an education that dealt with nothing but ideal entities, verbal, moral, or mathematical, Plato saw in concretions in discourse the true elements of being. Definable meanings, being the terms of thought, must also, he fancied, be the constituents of reality. And with that directness and audacity which was possible to the ancient, and of which Pythagoreans and Eleatics had already given brilliant examples, he set up these terms of discourse, like the Pythagorean numbers, for absolute and eternal entities, existing before all things, revealed in all things, giving the cosmic artificer his models and the creature his goal. By some inexplicable necessity the creation had taken place. The ideas had multiplied themselves in a flux of innumerable images which could be recognised by their resemblance to their originals, but were at once canceled and expunged by virtue of their essential inadequacy. What sounds are to words and words to thoughts, that was a thing to its idea.

Plato, however, retained the moral and significant essence of his ideas, and while he made them ideal absolutes, fixed meanings antecedent to their changing expressions, never dreamed that they could be natural existences, or psychological beings. In an original thinker, in one who really thinks and does not merely argue, to call a thing supernatural, or spiritual, or intelligible is to declare that it is no *thing* at all, no existence actual or possible, but a value, a term of thought, a merely ideal principle; and the more its reality in such a sense is insisted on the more its incommensurability with brute existence is asserted. To express this ideal reality myth is the natural vehicle; a vehicle Plato could avail himself of all the more freely that he inherited a religion still plastic and conscious of its poetic essence, and did not have to struggle, like his modern disciples, with the arrested childishness of minds that for a hundred generations have learned their metaphysics in the cradle. His ideas, although their natural basis was ignored, were accordingly always ideal, they always represented meanings and functions and were never degraded from the moral to the physical sphere. The counterpart of this genuine ideality was that the theory retained its moral forces and did not degenerate into a bewildered and idolatrous pantheism. Plato conceived the soul's destiny to be her emancipation from those material things which in this illogical apparition were so alien to her essence. She should return, after her baffling and stupefying intercourse with the world of sense and accident, into the native heaven of her ideas. For animal desires were no less illusory, and yet no less significant, than sensuous perceptions. They engaged man in the pursuit of the good and taught him, through disappointment, to look for it only in those satisfactions which can be permanent and perfect. Love, like intelligence, must rise from appearance to reality, and rest in that divine world which is the fulfilment of the human.

A geometrician does a good service when he declares and explicates the nature of the triangle, an object suggested by many casual and recurring sensations. His service is not less real, even if less obvious, when he arrests some fundamental concretion in discourse, and formulates the first principles of logic. Mastering such definitions, sinking into the dry life of such forms, he may spin out and develop indefinitely, in the freedom of his irresponsible logic, their implications and congruous extensions, opening by his demonstration a depth of knowledge which we should otherwise never have discovered in ourselves. But if the geometer had a fanatical zeal and forbade us to consider space and the triangles it contains otherwise than as his own ideal science considers them: forbade us, for instance, to inquire how we came to perceive those triangles or that space; what organs and senses conspired in furnishing the idea of them; what material objects show that character, and how they came to offer themselves to our observation— then surely the geometer would qualify his service with a distinct injury and while he opened our eyes to one fascinating vista would tend to blind them to others no less tempting and beautiful. For the naturalist and psychologist have also their rights and can tell us things well worth knowing; nor will any theory they may possibly propose concerning the origin of spatial ideas and their material embodiments ever invalidate the demonstrations of geometry. These, in their hypothetical sphere, are perfectly autonomous and self-generating, and their applicability to experience will hold so long as the initial images they are applied to continue to abound in perception.

If we awoke to-morrow in a world containing nothing but music, geometry would indeed lose its relevance to our future experience; but it would keep its ideal cogency, and become again a living language if any spatial objects should ever reappear in sense.

The history of such reappearances—natural history—is meantime a good subject for observation and experiment. Chronicler and critic can always approach reality with a method complementary to the deductive methods pursued in mathematics and logic: instead of developing the import of a definition, the prophet develops the import of his trance, and the theologian the import of the prophecy: which prevents not the historian from coming later and showing the origin, the growth, and the possible function of that maniacal sort of wisdom. True, the theologian commonly dreads a critic more than does the geometer, but this happens only because the theologian has probably not developed the import of his facts with any austerity or clearness, but has distorted that ideal interpretation with all sorts of concessions and side-glances at other tenets to which he is already pledged, so that he justly fears, when his methods are exposed, that the religious heart will be alienated from him and his conclusions be left with no foothold in human nature. If he had not been guilty of such misrepresentation, no history or criticism that reviewed his construction would do anything but recommend it to all those who found in themselves the primary religious facts and religious faculties which that construction had faithfully interpreted in its ideal deductions and extensions. All who perceived the facts would thus learn their import; and theology would reveal to the soul her natural religion.

The most legitimate constructions of reasons soon become merely speculative, soon pass, I mean, beyond the sphere of practical application; and the man of affairs, adjusting himself at every turn to the opaque brutality of fact, loses his respect for the higher reaches of logic and forgets that his recognition of facts themselves is an application of logical principles. In his youth, perhaps, he pursued metaphysics, which are the love-affairs of the understanding; now he is wedded to convention and seeks in the passion he calls business or in the habit he calls duty some substitute for natural happiness. He fears to question the value of his life, having found that such questioning adds nothing to his powers; and he thinks the mariner would die of old age in port who should wait for reason to justify his voyage. Reason is indeed like the sad Iphigenia whom her royal father, the Will, must sacrifice before any wind can fill his sails. The emanation of all things from the One involves not only the incarnation but the crucifixion of the Logos. Reason must be eclipsed by its supposed expressions, and can only shine in a darkness which does not comprehend it. For reason is essentially hypothetical and subsidiary, and can never constitute what it expresses in man, nor what it recognises in nature. The idea of nature remains true after psychology has analysed its origin, and not only true, but beautiful and beneficent. For unlike many negligible products of speculative fancy it is woven out of recurrent perceptions into a hypothetical cause from which further perceptions can be deduced as they are actually experienced.

Such a naturalism once discovered confirms itself at every breath we draw, and surrounds every object in history and nature with infinite and true suggestions, making it doubly interesting, fruitful, and potent over the mind. The naturalist accordingly welcomes criticism because his constructions, though no less hypothetical and speculative than the idealist's dreams, are such legitimate and fruitful fictions that they are obvious truths. For truth, at the intelligible level where it arises, means not sensible fact, but valid ideation, verified hypothesis, and inevitable, stable inference.

If idealism is intrenched in the very structure of human reason, empiricism represents all those energies of the external universe which, as Spinoza says, must infinitely exceed the energies of man. If meditation breeds science, wisdom comes by disillusion, even on the subject of science itself. Docility to the facts makes the sanity of science. Reason is only half grown and not really distinguishable from imagination so long as she cannot check and recast her own processes wherever they render the moulds of thought unfit for their subject-matter. Docility is, as we have seen, the deepest condition of reason's existence; for if a form of mental synthesis were by chance developed which was incapable of appropriating the data of sense, logical thoughts would play idly, like so many parasites in the mind, and ultimately languish and die of inanition. To be nourished and employed, intelligence must have developed such structure and habits as will enable it to assimilate what food comes in its way; so that the persistence of any intellectual habit is a proof that it has some applicability, however partial, to the facts of sentience. This applicability, the prerequisite of significant thought, is also its eventual test; and the gathering of new experiences, the consciousness of more and more facts crowding into the memory and demanding co-ordination, is at once the presentation to reason of her legitimate problem and a proof that she is already at work. It is a presentation of her problem, because reason is not a faculty of dreams but the art of living.

Reason's function is to embody the good, but the test of excellence is itself ideal; therefore before we can assure ourselves that reason has been manifested in any given case we must make out the reasonableness of the ideal that inspires us. And in general, before we can convince ourselves that a Life of Reason, or behaviour guided by science and directed toward spiritual goods, is at all worth having, we must make out the possibility and character of its ultimate end. Yet each ideal is its own justification; so that the only sense in which an ultimate end can be established and become a test of general progress is this: that a harmony and cooperation of impulses should be conceived, leading to the maximum satisfaction possible in the whole community of spirits affected by our action. Now, without considering for the present any concrete Utopia, such, for instance, as Plato's Republic or the heavenly beatitude described by theologians, we may inquire what formal qualities are imposed on the ideal by its nature and function and by the relation it bears to experience and to desire.

The rational ideal has the same relation to given demands that the reality has to given perceptions. In the face of the ideal, particular demands forfeit their authority and the goods to which a particular being may aspire cease to be absolute; nay, the satisfaction of desire comes to appear an indifferent or unholy thing when compared or opposed to the ideal to be realised. So, precisely, in perception, flying impressions come to be regarded as illusory when contrasted with a stable conception of reality. Yet of course flying impressions are the only material out of which that conception can be formed. Life itself is a flying impression, and had we no personal and instant experience, importuning us at each successive moment, we should have no occasion to ask for a reality at all, and no materials out of which to construct so gratuitous an idea. In the same way present demands are the only materials and occasions for any ideal: without demands the ideal would have no *locus standi* or foothold in the world, no power, no charm, and no prerogative. If the ideal can confront particular desires and put them to shame, that happens only because the ideal is the object of a more profound and voluminous desire and embodies the good which they blindly and perhaps deviously pursue. Otherwise each demand would render its object a detached, absolute, and unimpeachable good. But when each desire in turn has singed its wings and retired before some disillusion, reflection may set in to suggest residual satisfactions that may still be possible, or some shifting of the ground by which much of what was hoped for may yet be attained.

The force for this new trial is but the old impulse renewed; this new hope is a justified remnant of the old optimism. Each passion, in this second compaign, takes the field conscious that it has indomitable enemies and ready to sign a reasonable peace, and even to capitulate before superior forces. Such tameness may be at first merely a consequence of exhaustion and prudence; but a mortal will, though absolute in its deliverances, is very far from constant, and its sacrifices soon constitute a habit, its exile a new home. The old ambition, now proved to be unrealisable, begins to seem capricious and extravagant; the circle of possible satisfactions becomes the field of conventional happiness. Experience, which brings about this humbler and more prosaic state of mind, has its own imaginative fruits. Among those forces which compelled each particular impulse to abate its pretensions, the most conspicuous were other impulses, other interests active in oneself and in one's neighbours. When the power of these alien demands is recognised they begin, in a physical way, to be respected; when an adjustment to them is sought they begin to be understood, for it is only by studying their expression and tendency that the degree of their hostility can be measured. But to understand is more than to forgive, it is almost to adopt; and the passion that thought merely to withdraw into a sullen and maimed self-indulgence can feel itself expanded by sympathies which in its primal vehemence it would have excluded. Experience, in bringing humility, brings intelligence also. Personal interests begin to seem relative, factors only in a general voluminous welfare secured by many common institutions and arts, moulds for whatever is communicable or rational in every passion. Each original impulse, when trimmed down more or less according to its degree of savageness, can then inhabit the state, and every good, when sufficiently transfigured, can be found again in the general ideal. The factors may indeed often be unrecognisable in the result, so much does the process of domestication transform them; but the interests that animated them survive this discipline and the new purpose is really esteemed; else the ideal would have no moral force. As an absolute reality would be indescribable and without a function in the elucidation of phenomena, so a supreme good which was good for nobody would be without conceivable value. Respect for such an idol is a dialectical superstition; and if zeal for that shibboleth should actually begin to inhibit the exercise of intelligent choice or the development of appreciation for natural pleasures, it would constitute a reversal of the Life of Reason.

No less important, however, than this basis which the ideal must have in extant demands, is the harmony with which reason must endow it. If without the one the ideal loses its value, without the other it loses its finality. Human nature is fluid and imperfect; its demands are based on incidental desires, elicited by a variety of objects which perhaps cannot coexist in the world. If we merely transcribe these miscellaneous demands or allow these floating desires to dictate to us the elements of the ideal, we shall never come to a Whole or to an End.

The picture of life as an eternal war for illusory ends was drawn at first by satirists, unhappily with too much justification in the facts. Some grosser minds, too undisciplined to have ever pursued a good either truly attainable or truly satisfactory, then proceeded to mistake that satire on human folly for a sober account of the whole universe; and finally others were not ashamed to represent it as the ideal itself— so soon is the dyer's hand subdued to what it works in. A barbarous mind cannot conceive life, like health, as a harmony continually preserved or restored, and containing those natural and ideal activities which disease merely interrupts. Such a mind, never having tasted order, cannot conceive it, and identifies progress with new conflicts and life with continual death. Its deification of unreason, instability, and strife comes partly from piety and partly from inexperience. There is piety in saluting nature in her perpetual flux and in thinking that since no equilibrium is maintained for ever none, perhaps, deserves to be. There is inexperience in not considering that wherever interests and judgments exist, the natural flux has fallen, so to speak, into a vortex, and created a natural good, a cumulative life, and an ideal purpose. Art, science, government, human nature itself, are self-defining and self-preserving: by partly fixing a structure they fix an ideal. But the barbarian can hardly regard such things, for to have distinguished and fostered them would be to have founded a civilisation.

The aim prescribed by reason differs from the prescription of conscience, in that conscience is often the spokesman of one interest or of a group of interests in opposition to other primary impulses which it would annul altogether; while reason and the ideal are not active forces nor embodiments of passion at all, but merely a method by which objects of desire are compared in reflection. The goodness of an end is felt inwardly by conscience; by reason it can be only taken upon trust and registered as a fact. For conscience the object of an opposed will is an evil, for reason it is a good on the same ground as any other good, because it is pursued by a natural impulse and can bring a real satisfaction. Conscience, in fine, is a party to moral strife, reason an observer of it who, however, plays the most important and beneficent part in the outcome by suggesting the terms of peace. This suggested peace, inspired by sympathy and by knowledge of the world, is the ideal, which borrows its value and practical force from the irrational impulses which it embodies, and borrows its final authority from the truth with which it recognises them all and the necessity by which it imposes on each such sacrifices as are requisite to a general harmony.

Reason as such represents or rather constitutes a single formal interest, the interest in harmony. When two interests are simultaneous and fall within one act of apprehension the desirability of harmonising them is involved in the very effort to realise them together. If attention and imagination are steady enough to face this implication and not to allow impulse to oscillate between irreconcilable tendencies, reason comes into being. Henceforth things actual and things desired are confronted by an ideal which has both pertinence and authority.

V

THE
TRANSCENDENT
SELF

A. The Phaedo

Plato

Now then, I want to give the proof at once, to you as my judges, why I think it likely that one who has spent his life in philosophy should be confident when he is going to die, and have good hopes that he will win the greatest blessings in the next world when he has ended: so Simmias and Cebes my judges, I will try to show how this could be true.

"The fact is, those who tackle philosophy aright are simply and solely practising dying, practising death, all the time, but nobody sees it. If this is true, then it would surely be unreasonable that they should earnestly do this and nothing else all their lives, yet when death comes they should object to what they had been so long earnestly practising."

Simmias laughed at this, and said, "I don't feel like laughing just now, Socrates, but you have made me laugh. I think the many if they heard that would say, 'That's a good one for the philosophers!' And other people in my city would heartily agree that philosophers are really suffering from a wish to die, and now they have found them out, that they richly deserve it!"

"That would be true, Simmias," said Socrates, "except the words 'found out.' For they have not found out in what sense the real philosophers wish to die and deserve to die, and what kind of death it is. Let us say good-bye to them," he went on, "and ask ourselves: Do we think there is such a thing as death?"

"Certainly," Simmias put in.

"Is it anything more than the separation of the soul from the body?" said Socrates. "Death is, that the body separates from the soul, and remains by itself apart from the soul, and the soul, separated from the body, exists by itself apart from the body. Is death anything but that?"

"No," he said, "that is what death is."

"Then consider, my good friend, if you agree with me here, for I think this is the best way to understand the question we are examining. Do you think it the part of a philosopher to be earnestly concerned with what are called pleasures, such as these—eating and drinking, for example?"

"Not at all," said Simmias.

"The pleasures of love, then?"

"Oh no."

"Well, do you suppose a man like that regards the other bodily indulgences as precious? Getting fine clothes and shoes and other bodily adornments—ought he to price them high or low, beyond whatever share of them it is absolutely necessary to have?"

"Low, I think," he said, "if he is a true philosopher."

"Then in general," he said, "do you think that such a man's concern is not for the body, but as far as he can he stands aloof from that and turns towards the soul?"

"I do."

"Then firstly, is it not clear that in such things the philosopher as much as possible sets free the soul from communion with the body, more than other men?"

"So it appears."

"And I suppose, Simmias, it must seem to most men that he who has no pleasure in such things and takes no share in them does not deserve to live, but he is getting pretty close to death if he does not care about pleasures which he has by means of the body."

"Quite true, indeed."

"Well then, what about the actual getting of wisdom? Is the body in the way or not, if a man takes it with him as companion in the search? I mean, for example, is there any truth for men in their sight and hearing? Or as poets are forever dinning into our ears, do we hear nothing and see nothing exactly? Yet if these of our bodily senses are not exact and clear, the others will hardly be, for they are all inferior to these, don't you think so?"

"Certainly," he said.

"Then," said he, "when does the soul get hold of the truth? For whenever the soul tries to examine anything in company with the body, it is plain that it is deceived by it."

"Quite true."

"Then is it not clear that in reasoning, if anywhere, something of the realities becomes visible to it?"

"Yes."

"And I suppose it reasons best when none of these senses disturbs it, hearing or sight, or pain, or pleasure indeed, but when it is completely by itself and says good-bye to the body, and so far as possible has no dealings with it, when it reaches out and grasps that which really is."

"That is true."

"And is it not then that the philosopher's soul chiefly holds the body cheap and escapes from it, while it seeks to be by itself?"

"So it seems."

"Let us pass on, Simmias. Do we say there is such a thing as justice by itself, or not?"

"We do say so, certainly!"

"Such a thing as the good and beautiful?"

"Of course!"

"And did you ever see one of them with your eyes?"

"Never," said he.

"By any other sense of those the body has did you ever grasp them? I mean all such things, greatness, health, strength, in short everything that really is the nature of things whatever they are: Is it through the body that the real truth is perceived? Or is this better—whoever of us prepares himself most completely and most exactly to comprehend each thing which he examines would come nearest to knowing each one?"

"Certainly."

"And would he do that most purely who should approach each with his intelligence alone, not adding sight to intelligence, or dragging in any other sense along with reasoning, but using the intelligence uncontaminated alone by itself, while he tries to hunt out each essence uncontaminated, keeping clear of eyes and ears and, one might say, of the whole body, because he thinks the body disturbs him and hinders the soul from getting possession of truth and wisdom when body and soul are companions—is not this the man, Simmias, if anyone, who will hit reality?"

"Nothing could be more true, Socrates," said Simmias.

"Then from all this," said Socrates, "genuine philosophers must come to some such opinion as follows, so as to make to one another statements such as these: 'A sort of direct path, so to speak, seems to take us to the conclusion that so long as we have the body with us in our enquiry, and our soul is mixed up with so great an evil, we shall never attain sufficiently what we desire, and that, we say, is the truth. For the body provides thousands of busy distractions because of its necessary food; besides, if diseases fall upon us, they hinder us from the pursuit of the real. With loves and desires and fears and all kinds of fancies and much rubbish, it infects us, and really and truly makes us, as they say, unable to think one little bit about anything at any time. Indeed, wars and factions and battles all come from the body and its desires, and from nothing else. For the desire of getting wealth causes all wars, and we are compelled to desire wealth by the body, being slaves to its culture; therefore we have no leisure for philosophy, from all these reasons. Chief of all is that if we do have some leisure, and turn away from the body to speculate on something, in our searches it is everywhere interfering, it causes confusion and disturbance, and dazzles us so that it will not let us see the truth; so in fact we see that if we are ever to know anything purely we must get rid of it, and examine the real things by the soul alone; and then, it seems, after we are dead, as the reasoning shows, not while we live, we shall possess that which we desire, lovers of which we say we are, namely wisdom. For if it is impossible in company with the body to know anything purely, one thing of two follows: either knowledge is possible nowhere, or only after death; for then alone the soul will be quite by itself apart from the body, but not before. And while we are alive, we shall be nearest to knowing, as it seems, if as far as possible we have no commerce or communion with the body which is not absolutely necessary, and if we are not infected with its nature, but keep ourselves pure from it, until God himself shall set us free. And so, pure and rid of the body's foolishness, we shall probably be in the company of those like ourselves, and shall know through our own selves complete incontamination, and that is perhaps the truth. But for the impure to grasp the pure is not, it seems, allowed.' So we must think, Simmias, and so we must say to one another, all who are rightly lovers of learning; don't you agree?"

"Assuredly, Socrates."

"Then," said Socrates, "if this is true, my comrade, there is great hope that when I arrive where I am traveling, there if anywhere I shall sufficiently possess that for which all our study has been pursued in this past life. So the journey which has been commanded for me is made with good hope, and the same for any other man who believes he has got his mind purified, as I may call it."

"Certainly," replied Simmias.

"And is not purification really that which has been mentioned so often in our discussion, to separate as far as possible the soul from the body, and to accustom it to collect itself together out of the body in every part, and to dwell alone by itself as far as it can, both at this present and in the future, being freed from the body as if from a prison?"

"By all means," said he.

"Then is not this called death—a freeing and separation of soul from body?"

"Not a doubt of that," said he.

"But to set it free, as we say, is the chief endeavour of those who rightly love wisdom, nay of those alone, and the very care and practice of the philosophers is nothing but the freeing and separation of soul from body, don't you think so?"

"It appears to be so."

"Then, as I said at first, it would be absurd for a man preparing himself in his life to be as near as possible to death, so to live, and then when death came, to object?"

"Of course."

"Then in fact, Simmias," he said, "those who rightly love wisdom are practising dying, and death to them is the least terrible thing in the world. Look at it in this way: If they are everywhere at enmity with the body, and desire the soul to be alone by itself, and if, when this very thing happens, they shall fear and object—would not that be wholly unreasonable? Should they not willingly go to a place where there is good hope of finding what they were in love with all through life (and they loved wisdom), and of ridding themselves of the companion which they hated? When human favourites and wives and sons have died, many have been willing to go down to the grave, drawn by the hope of seeing there those they used to desire, and of being with them; but one who is really in love with wisdom and holds firm to this same hope, that he will find it in the grave, and nowhere else worth speaking of—will he then fret at dying and not go thither rejoicing? We must surely think, my comrade, that he will go rejoicing, if he is really a philosopher; he will surely believe that he will find wisdom in its purity there and there alone. If this is true, would it not be most unreasonable, as I said just now, if such a one feared death?"

"Unreasonable, I do declare," said he.

"Then this is proof enough," he said, "that if you see a man fretting because he is to die, he was not really a philosopher, but a philosōma—not a wisdom-lover but a body-lover. And no doubt the same man is money-lover and honours-lover, one or both."

"It certainly is so, as you say," he replied.

"Then, Simmias," he said, "does not what is called courage belong specially to persons so disposed as philosophers are?"

"I have no doubt of it," said he.

"And the same with temperance, what the many call temperance, not to be agitated about desires but to hold them lightly and decently; does not this belong to those alone who hold the body lightly and live in philosophy?"

"That must be so," he said.

"You see," said he, "if you will consider the courage and temperance of others, you will think it strange."

"How so, Socrates?"

"You know," said he, "that everyone else thinks death one of the greatest evils?"

"Indeed I do," he said.

"Then is it not fear of greater evils which makes the brave endure death, when they do?"

"That is true."

"Then fear, and fearing, makes all men brave, except philosophers. Yet it is unreasonable to become brave by fear and cowardice!"

"Certainly."

"And what of the decent men? Are they not in the same case? A sort of intemperance makes them temperate! Although we say such a thing is impossible, nevertheless with that self-complacent temperance they are in a similar case; because they fear to be deprived of other pleasures, and because they desire them, they abstain from some because they are mastered by others. They say, of course, intemperance is 'to be ruled by pleasures'; yet what happens to them is, to master some pleasures and to be mastered by others, and this is much the same as what was said just now, that in a way intemperance has made them temperate."

"So it seems."

"Bless you, Simmias! This is hardly an honest deal in virtue—to trade pleasure for pleasure, and pain for pain, and fear for fear, and even greater for less, as if they were current coin; no, the only honest currency, for which all these must be traded, is wisdom, and all things are in truth to be bought with this and sold for this. And courage and temperance and justice and, in short, true virtue, depend on wisdom, whether pleasure and fear and all other such things are added or taken away. But when they are deprived of wisdom and exchanged one for another, virtue of that kind is no more than a make-believe, a thing in reality slavish and having no health or truth in it; and truth is in reality a cleansing from all such things, and temperance and justice and courage, and wisdom itself, are a means of purification. Indeed, it seems those who established our mystic rites were no fools; they in truth spoke with a hidden meaning long ago when they said that whoever is uninitiated and unconsecrated when he comes to the house of Hades will lie in mud, but the purified and consecrated when he goes there will dwell with gods. Indeed, as they say in the rites, 'Many are called but few are chosen', and these few are in my opinion no others than those who have loved wisdom in the right way. One of these I have tried to be by every effort in all my life, and I have left nothing undone according to my ability; if I have endeavoured in the right way, if we have succeeded at all, we shall know clearly when we get there; very soon, if God will, as I think. There is my defence before you gentlemen on the bench, Simmias and Cebes, showing that in leaving you and my masters here, I am reasonable in not fretting or being upset, because I believe that I shall find there good masters and good comrades. So if I am more convincing to you in my defence than I was to the Athenian judges, I should be satisfied."

B. Prolegomena

Immanuel Kant

We cannot indeed, beyond all possible experience, form a definite concept of what things in themselves may be. Yet we are not at liberty to abstain entirely from inquiring into them; for experience never satisfies reason fully but, in answering questions, refers us further and further back and leaves us dissatisfied with regard to their complete solution. This anyone may gather from the dialectic of pure reason, which therefore has its good subjective grounds. Having acquired, as regards the nature of our soul, a clear conception of the subject, and having come to the conviction that its manifestations cannot be explained materialistically, who can refrain from asking what the soul really is and, if no concept of experience suffices for the purpose, from accounting for it by a concept of reason (that of a simple immaterial being), though we cannot by any means prove its objective reality? Who can satisfy himself with mere empirical knowledge in all the cosmological questions of the duration and of the magnitude of the world, of freedom or of natural necessity, since every answer given on principles of experience begets a fresh question, which likewise requires its answer and thereby clearly shows the insufficiency of all physical modes of explanation to satisfy reason? Finally, who does not see in the thoroughgoing contingency and dependence of all his thoughts and assumptions on mere principles of experience the impossibility of stopping there? And who does not feel himself compelled, notwithstanding all interdictions against losing himself in transcendent Ideas, to seek rest and contentment, beyond all the concepts which he can vindicate by experience, in the concept of a Being the possibility of the Idea of which cannot be conceived but at the same time cannot be refuted, because it relates to a mere being of the understanding and without it reason must needs remain forever dissatisfied?

Bounds (in extended beings) always presuppose a space existing outside a certain definite place and inclosing it; limits do not require this, but are mere negations which affect a quantity so far as it is not absolutely complete. But our reason, as it were, sees in its surroundings a space for knowledge of things in themselves, though we can never have definite concepts of them and are limited to appearances only.

As long as the knowledge of reason is homogeneous, definite bounds to it are inconceivable. In mathematics and in natural philosophy, human reason admits of limits but not of bounds, namely, it admits that something indeed lies without it, at which it can never arrive, but not that it will at any point find completion in its internal progress. The enlarging of our views in mathematics and the possibility of new discoveries are infinite; and the same is the case with the discovery of new properties of nature, of new powers and laws, by continued experience and its rational combination. But limits cannot be mistaken here, for mathematics refers to appearances only, and what cannot be an object of sensuous intuition, such as the concepts of metaphysics and of morals, lies entirely without its sphere; it can never lead to them, but neither does it require them. There is, therefore, not a continual progress and approximation towards these sciences, and there is not, as it were, any point or line of contact. Natural science will never reveal to us the internal constitution of things, which, though not appearance, yet can serve as the ultimate ground for explaining appearances. Nor does that science require this for its physical explanations. Nay, even if such grounds should be offered from other sources (for instance, the influence of immaterial beings), they must be rejected and not used in the progress of its explanations. For these explanations must only be grounded upon that which as an object of sense can belong to experience, and be brought into connection with our actual perceptions and empirical laws.

But metaphysics leads us towards bounds in the dialectical attempts of pure reason (not undertaken arbitrarily or wantonly, but stimulated thereto by the nature of reason itself). And the transcendental Ideas, as they do not admit of evasion but are never capable of realization, serve to point out to us actually not only the bounds of the pure use of reason, but also the way to determine them. Such is the end and the use of this natural predisposition of our reason, which has brought forth metaphysics as its favorite child, whose generation, like every other in the world, is not to be ascribed to blind chance but to an original germ, wisely organized for great ends. For metaphysics, in its fundamental features, perhaps more than any other science, is placed in us by nature itself and cannot be considered the production of an arbitrary choice or a casual enlargement in the progress of experience from which it is quite disparate.

Reason through all its concepts and laws of the understanding which are sufficient to it for empirical use, that is, within the sensible world, finds in it no satisfaction, because ever-recurring questions deprive us of all hope of their complete solution. The transcendental

Ideas which have that completion in view are such problems of reason. But it sees clearly that the sensuous world cannot contain this completion; neither, consequently, can all the concepts which serve merely for understanding the world of sense, for example, space and time, and what we have adduced under the name of pure concepts of the understanding. The sensuous world is nothing but a chain of appearances connected according to universal laws; it has therefore no subsistence by itself; it is not the thing in itself, and consequently must point to that which contains the basis of this appearance, to beings which cannot be known merely as appearances, but as things in themselves. In the knowledge of them alone can reason hope to satisfy its desire for completeness in proceeding from the conditioned to its conditions.

We have above indicated the limits of reason with regard to all knowledge of mere beings of thought. Now, since the transcendental Ideas have made it necessary to approach them and thus have led us, as it were, to the spot where the occupied space (namely, experience) touches the void (that of which we can know nothing, namely, *noumena*), we can determine the bounds of pure reason. For in all bounds there is something positive (for example, a surface is the boundary of corporeal space, and is therefore itself a space; a line is a space, which is the boundary of the surface, a point the boundary of the line, but yet always a place in space), but limits contain mere negations. The limits pointed out in those paragraphs are not enough after we have discovered that beyond them there still lies something (though we can never know what it is in itself). For the question now is, What is the attitude of our reason in this connection of what we know with what we do not, and never shall, know? This is an actual connection of a known thing with one quite unknown (and which will always remain so), and though what is unknown should not become in the least more known—which we cannot even hope—yet the concept of this connection must be definite and capable of being rendered distinct.

We must therefore think an immaterial being, a world of understanding, and a Supreme Being (all mere *noumena*), because in them only, as things in themselves, reason finds that completion and satisfaction which it can never hope for in the derivation of appearances from their homogeneous grounds, and because these actually have reference to something distinct from them (and totally heterogeneous), as appearances always presuppose an object in itself and therefore suggest its existence whether we can know more of it or not.

C. The Transcendentalist

Ralph Waldo Emerson

The first thing we have to say respecting what are called *new views* here in New England, at the present time, is, that they are not new, but the very oldest of thoughts cast into the mould of these new times. The light is always identical in its composition, but it falls on a great variety of objects, and by so falling is first revealed to us, not in its own form, for it is formless, but in theirs; in like manner, thought only appears in the objects it classifies. What is popularly called Transcendentalism among us, is Idealism; Idealism as it appears in 1842. As thinkers, mankind have ever divided into two sects, Materialists and Idealists; the first class founding on experience, the second on consciousness; the first class beginning to think from the data of the senses, the second class perceive that the senses are not final, and say, The senses give us representations of things, but what are the things themselves, they cannot tell. The materialist insists on facts, on history, on the force of circumstances and the animal wants of man; the idealist on the power of Thought and of Will, on inspiration, on miracle, on individual culture. These two modes of thinking are both natural, but the idealist contends that his way of thinking is in higher nature. He concedes all that the other affirms, admits the impressions of sense, admits their coherency, their use and beauty, and then asks the materialist for his grounds of assurance that things are as his senses represent them. But I, he says, affirm facts not affected by the illusions of sense, facts which are of the same nature as the faculty which reports them, and not liable to doubt; facts which in their first appearance to us assume a native superiority to material facts, degrading these into a language by which the first are to be spoken; facts which it only needs a retirement from the senses to discern. Every materialist will be an idealist; but an idealist can never go backward to be a materialist.

The idealist, in speaking of events, sees them as spirits. He does not deny the sensuous fact: by no means; but he will not see that alone. He does not deny the presence of this table, this chair, and the walls of this room, but he looks at these things as the reverse side of the tapestry, as the *other end,* each being a sequel or completion of a spiritual fact which nearly concerns him. This manner of looking at things transfers every object in nature from an independent and anomalous position without there, into the consciousness. Even the materialist Condillac, perhaps the most logical expounder of materialism, was constrained to say, "Though we should soar into the heavens, though we should sink into the abyss, we never go out of ourselves; it is always our own thoughts that we perceive." What more could an idealist say?

The materialist, secure in the certainty of sensation, mocks at fine-spun theories, at star-gazers and dreams, and believes that his life is solid, that he at least takes nothing for granted, but knows where he stands, and what he does. Yet how easy it is to show him that he also is a phantom walking and working amid phantoms, and that he need only ask a question or two beyond his daily questions to find his solid universe growing dim and impalpable before his sense. The sturdy capitalist, no matter how deep and square on blocks of Quincy granite he lays the foundations of his banking-house or Exchange, must set it, at last, not on a cube corresponding to the angles of his structure, but on a mass of unknown materials and solidity, red-hot or white-hot perhaps at the core, which rounds off to an almost perfect sphericity, and lies floating in soft air, and goes spinning away, dragging bank and banker with it at a rate of thousands of miles the hour, he knows not whither—a bit of bullet, now glimmering, now darkling through a small cubic space on the edge of an unimaginable pit of emptiness. And this wild balloon, in which his whole venture is embarked, is a just symbol of his whole state and faculty. One thing at least, he says, is certain, and does not give me the headache, that figures do not lie; the multiplication table has been hitherto found unimpeachable truth; and, moreover, if I put a gold eagle in my safe, I find it again to-morrow; but for these thoughts, I know not whence they are. They change and pass away. But ask him why he believes that an uniform experience will continue uniform, or on what grounds he founds his faith in his figures, and he will perceive that his mental fabric is built up on just as strange and quaking foundations as his proud edifice of stone.

In the order of thought, the materialist takes his departure from the external world, and esteems a man as one product of that. The idealist takes his departure from his consciousness, and reckons the world an appearance. The materialist respects sensible masses, Society, Government, social art and luxury, every establishment, every mass, whether majority of numbers, or extent of space, or amount of objects, every social action. The idealist has another measure, which is metaphysical, namely the *rank* which things themselves take in his consciousness; not at all the size or appearance. Mind is the only reality, of which men and all other natures are better or worse reflectors. Nature, literature, history, are only subjective phenomena. Although in his action overpowered by the laws of action, and so, warmly co-operating with men, even preferring them to himself, yet when he speaks scientifically, or after the order of thought, he is constrained to degrade persons into representatives of truths. He does not respect labor, or the products of labor, namely property, otherwise than as a manifold symbol, illustrating with wonderful fidelity of details the laws of being; he does not respect government, except as far as it reiterates the law of his mind; nor the church, nor charities, nor arts, themselves; but hears, as at a vast distance, what they say, as if his consciousness would speak to him through a pantomimic scene. His thought—that is the Universe. His experience inclines him to behold the procession of facts you call the world, as flowing perpetually outward from an invisible, unsounded centre in himself, centre alike of him and of them, and necessitating him to regard all things as having a subjective or relative existence, relative to that aforesaid Unknown Centre of him.

From this transfer of the world into the consciousness, this beholding of all things in the mind, follow easily his whole ethics. It is simpler to be self-dependent. The height, the deity of man is to be self-sustained, to need no gift, no foreign force. Society is good when it does not violate me, but best when it is likest to solitude. Everything real is self-existent. Everything divine shares the self-existence of Deity. All that you call the world is the shadow of that substance which you are, the perpetual creation of the powers of thought, of those that are dependent and of those that are independent of your will. Do not cumber yourself with fruitless pains to mend and remedy remote effects; let the soul be erect, and all things will go well. You think me the child of my circumstances: I make my circumstances. Let any thought or motive of mine be different from that they are, the difference will transform my condition and economy. I—this thought which is called I—is the mould into which the world is poured like melted wax. The mould is invisible, but the world betrays the shape of the mould. You call it the power of circumstance, but it is the power of me. Am I in harmony with myself? my position will seem to you just and commanding. Am I vicious and insane? my fortunes will seem to you obscure and descending. As I am, so shall I associate, and so shall I act; Caesar's history will paint out Caesar. Jesus acted so, because he thought so. I do not wish to overlook or to gainsay any reality: I say I make my circumstance; but if you ask me, Whence am I? I feel like other men my relation to that Fact which cannot be spoken, or defined, nor even thought, but which exists, and will exist.

The Transcendentalist adopts the whole connection of spiritual doctrine. He believes in miracle, in the perpetual openness of the human mind to new influx of light and power; he believes in inspiration, and in ecstasy. He wishes that the spiritual principle should be suffered to demonstrate itself to the end, in all possible applications to the state of man, without the admission of anything unspiritual; that is, anything positive, dogmatic, personal. Thus the spiritual measure of inspiration is the depth of the thought, and never, who said it? And so he resists all attempts to palm other rules and measures on the spirit than its own.

In action he easily incurs the charge of anti-nomianism by his avowal that he, who has the Law-giver, may with safety not only neglect, but even contravene every written commandment. In the play of Othello, the expiring Desdemona absolves her husband of the murder, to her attendant Emilia. Afterwards, when Emilia charges him with the crime, Othello exclaims,

"You heard her say herself it was not I."

Emilia replies

"The more angel she, and thou the blacker devil."

Of this fine incident, Jacobi, the Transcendental moralist, makes use, with other parallel instances, in his reply to Fichte. Jacobi, refusing all measure of right and wrong except the determinations of the private spirit, remarks that there is no crime but has sometimes been a virtue. "I," he says, "am that atheist, that godless person who, in opposition to an imaginary doctrine of calculation, would lie as the dying Desdemona lied; would lie and deceive, as Pylades when he personated Orestes; would assassinate like Timoleon; would perjure myself like Epaminondas and John de Witt; I would resolve on suicide like Cato; I would commit sacrilege with David; yea, and pluck ears of corn on the Sabbath, for no other reason than that I was fainting for lack of food. For I have assurance in myself that in pardoning these faults according to the letter, man exerts the sovereign right which the majesty of his being confers on him; he sets the seal of his divine nature to the grace he accords."

In like manner, if there is anything grand and daring in human thought or virtue, any reliance on the vast, the unknown; any presentiment, any extravagance of faith, the spiritualist adopts it as most in nature. The oriental mind has always tended to this largeness. Buddhism is an expression of it. The Buddhist, who thanks no man, who says, "Do not flatter your benefactors," but who, in his conviction that every good deed can by no possibility escape its reward, will not deceive the benefactor by pretending that he has done more than he should, is a Transcendentalist.

You will see by this sketch that there is no such thing as a Transcendental *party;* that there is no pure Transcendentalist; that we know of none but prophets and heralds of such a philosophy; that all who by strong bias of nature have leaned to the spiritual side in doctrine, have stopped short of their goal. We have had many harbingers and forerunners; but of a purely spiritual life, history has afforded no example. I mean we have yet no man who has leaned entirely on his character, and eaten angels' food; who, trusting to his sentiments, found life made of miracles; who, working for universal aims, found himself fed, he knew not how; clothed, sheltered, and weaponed, he knew not how, and yet it was done by his own hands. Only in the instinct of the lower animals we find the suggestion of the methods of it, and something higher than our understanding. The squirrel hoards nuts and the bee gathers honey, without knowing what they do, and they are thus provided for without selfishness or disgrace.

Shall we say then that Transcendentalism is the Saturnalia or excess of Faith; the presentiment of a faith proper to man in his integrity, excessive only when his imperfect obedience hinders the satisfaction of his wish? Nature is transcendental, exists primarily, necessarily, ever works and advances, yet takes no thought for the morrow. Man owns the dignity of the life which throbs around him, in chemistry, and tree, and animal, and in the involuntary functions of his own body; yet he is balked when he tries to fling himself into this enchanted circle, where all is done without degradation. Yet genius and virtue predict in man the same absence of private ends and of condescension to circumstances, united with every trait and talent of beauty and power.

This way of thinking, falling on Roman times, made Stoic philosophers; falling on despotic times, made patriot Catos and Brutuses; falling on superstitious times, made prophets and apostles; on popish times, made protestants and ascetic monks, preachers of Faith against the preachers of Works; on prelatical times, made Puritans and Quakers; and falling on Unitarian and commercial times, makes the peculiar shades of Idealism which we know.

It is well known to most of my audience that the Idealism of the present day acquired the name of Transcendental from the use of that term by Immanuel Kant, of Königsberg, who replied to the skeptical philosophy of Locke, which insisted that there was nothing in the intellect which was not previously in the experience of the senses, by showing that there was a very important class of ideas or imperative forms, which did not come by experience, but through which experience was acquired; that these were intuitions of the mind itself; and he denominated them *Transcendental* forms. The extraordinary profoundness and precision of that man's thinking have given vogue to his nomenclature, in Europe and America, to that extent that whatever belongs to the class of intuitive thought is popularly called at the present day *Transcendental.*

Although, as we have said, there is no pure Transcendentalist, yet the tendency to respect the intuitions and to give them, at least in our creed, all authority over our experience, has deeply colored the conversation and poetry of the present day; and the history of genius and of religion in these times, though impure, and as yet not incarnated in any powerful individual, will be the history of this tendency.

It is a sign of our times, conspicuous to the coarsest observer, that many intelligent and religious persons withdraw themselves from the common labors and competitions of the market and the caucus, and betake themselves to a certain solitary and critical way of living, from which no solid fruit has yet appeared to justify their separation. They hold themselves aloof: they feel the disproportion between their faculties and the work offered them, and they prefer to ramble in the country and perish of ennui, to the degradation of such charities and such ambitions as the city can propose to them. They are striking work, and crying out for somewhat worthy to do! What they do is done only because they are overpowered by the humanities that speak on all sides; and they consent to such labor as is open to them, though to their lofty dream the writing of Iliads or Hamlets, or the building of cities or empires seems drudgery.

Now every one must do after his kind, be he asp or angel, and these must. The question which a wise man and a student of modern history will ask, is, what that kind is? And truly, as in ecclesiastical history we take so much pains to know what the Gnostics, what the Essenes, what the Manichees, and what the Reformers believed, it would not misbecome us to inquire nearer home, what these companions and contemporaries of ours think and do, at least so far as these thoughts and actions appear to be not accidental and personal, but common to many, and the inevitable flower of the Tree of Time. Our American literature and spiritual history are, we confess in the optative mood; but whoso knows these seething brains, these admirable radicals, these unsocial worshippers, these talkers who talk the sun and moon away, will believe that this heresy cannot pass away without leaving its mark.

They are lonely; the spirit of their writing and conversation is lonely; they repel influences; they shun general society; they incline to shut themselves in their chamber in the house, to live in the country rather than in the town, and to find their tasks and amusements in solitude. Society, to be sure, does not like this very well; it saith, Whoso goes to walk alone, accuses the whole world; he declares all to be unfit to be his companions; it is very uncivil, nay, insulting; Society will retaliate. Meantime, this retirement does not proceed from any whim on the part of these separators; but if any one will take pains to talk with them, he will find that this part is chosen both from temperament and from principle; with some unwillingness too, and as a choice of the less of two evils; for these persons are not by nature melancholy, sour, and unsocial—they are not stockish or brute—but joyous, susceptible, affectionate; they have even more than others a great wish to be loved. Like the young Mozart, they are rather ready to cry ten times a day, "But are you sure you love me?" Nay, if they tell you their whole thought, they will own that love seems to them the last and highest gift of nature; that there are persons whom in their hearts they daily thank for existing—persons whose faces are perhaps unknown to them, but whose fame and spirit have penetrated their solitude—and for whose sake they wish to exist. To behold the beauty of another character, which inspires a new interest in our own; to behold the beauty lodged in a human being, with such vivacity of apprehension that I am instantly forced home to inquire if I am not deformity itself; to behold in another the expression of a love so high that it assures itself—assures itself also to me against every possible casualty except my unworthiness; these are degrees on the scale of human happiness to which they have ascended; and it is a fidelity to this sentiment which has made common association distasteful to them. They wish a just and even fellowship, or none. They cannot gossip with you, and they do not wish, as they are sincere and religious, to gratify any mere curiosity which you may entertain. Like fairies, they do not wish to be spoken of. Love me, they say, but do not ask who is my cousin and my uncle. If you do not need to hear my thought, because you can read it in my face and behavior, then I will tell it you from sunrise to sunset. If you cannot divine it, you would not understand what I say. I will not molest myself for you. I do not wish to be profaned.

And yet, it seems as if this loneliness, and not this love, would prevail in their circumstances, because of the extravagant demand they make on human nature. That, indeed, constitutes a new feature in their portrait, that they are the most exacting and extortionate critics. Their quarrel with every man they meet is not with his kind, but with his degree. There is not enough of him—that is the only fault. They prolong their privilege of childhood in this wise; of doing nothing, but making immense demands on all the gladiators in the lists of action and fame. They make us feel the strange disappointment which overcasts every human youth. So many promising youths, and never a finished man! The profound nature will have a savage rudeness; the delicate one will be shallow, or the victim of sensibility; the richly accomplished will have some capital absurdity; and so every piece has a crack. 'T is strange, but this masterpiece is the result of such an extreme delicacy that the most unobserved flaw in the boy will neutralize the most aspiring genius, and spoil the work. Talk with a seaman of the hazards to life in his profession and he will ask you, 'Where are the old sailors? Do you not see that all are young men?' And we, on this sea of human thought, in like manner inquire, Where are the old idealists? where are they who represented to the last generation that extravagant hope which a few happy aspirants suggest to ours? In looking at the class of counsel, and power, and wealth, and at the matronage of the land, amidst all the prudence and all the triviality, one asks, Where are they who represented genius, virtue, the invisible and heavenly world, to these? Are they dead—taken in early ripeness to the gods—as ancient wisdom foretold their fate? Or did the high idea die out of them, and leave their unperfumed body as its tomb and tablet, announcing to all that the celestial inhabitant, who once gave them beauty, had departed? Will it be better with the new generation? We easily predict a fair future to each new candidate who enters the lists, but we are frivolous and volatile, and by low aims and ill example do what we can to defeat this hope. Then these youths bring us a rough but effectual aid. By their unconcealed dissatisfaction they expose our poverty and the insignificance of man to man. A man is a poor limitary benefactor. He ought to be a shower of benefits—a great influence, which should never let his brother go, but should refresh old merits continually with new ones; so that though absent he should never be out of my mind, his name never far from my lips; but if the earth should open at my side, or my last hour were come, his name should be the prayer I should utter to the Universe. But in our experience, man is cheap and friendship wants its deep sense. We affect to dwell with our friends in their absence, but we do not; when deed, word, or letter comes not, they let us go. These exacting children advertise us of our wants. There is no compliment, no smooth speech with them; they pay you only this one compliment, of insatiable expectation; they aspire, they severely exact, and if they only stand fast in this watch tower, and persist in demanding unto the end, and without end, then are they terrible friends, whereof poet and priest cannot choose but stand in awe; and what if they eat clouds, and drink wind, they have not been without service to the race of man.

With this passion for what is great and extraordinary, it cannot be wondered at that they are repelled by vulgarity and frivolity in people. They say to themselves, It is better to be alone than in bad company. And it is really a wish to be met—the wish to find society for their hope and religion—which prompts them to shun what is called society. They feel that they are never so fit for friendship as when they have quitted mankind and taken themselves to friend. A picture, a book, a favorite spot in the hills or the woods which they can people with the fair and worthy creation of the fancy, can give them often forms so vivid that these for the time shall seem real, and society the illusion.

But their solitary and fastidious manners not only withdraw them from the conversation, but from the labors of the world; they are not good citizens, not good members of society; unwillingly they bear their part of the public and private burdens; they do not willingly share in the public charities, in the public religious rites, in the enterprises of education, of missions foreign and domestic, in the abolition of the slave-trade, or in the temperance society. They do not even like to vote. The philanthropists inquire whether Transcendentalism does not mean sloth: they had as lief hear that their friend is dead, as that he is a Transcendentalist; for then is he paralyzed, and can never do anything for humanity. What right, cries the good world, has the man of genius to retreat from work, and indulge himself? The popular literary creed seems to be, 'I am a sublime genius; I ought not therefore to labor.' But genius is the power to labor better and more availably. Deserve thy genius: exalt it. The good, the illuminated, sit apart from the rest, censuring their dulness and vices, as if they thought that by sitting very grand in their chairs, the very brokers, attorneys, and congressmen would see the error of their ways, and flock to them. But the good and wise must learn to act, and carry salvation to the combatants and demagogues in the dusty arena below.

On the part of these children it is replied that life and their faculty seem to them gifts too rich to be squandered on such trifles as you propose to them. What you call your fundamental institutions, your great and holy causes, seem to them great abuses, and, when nearly seen, paltry matters. Each 'cause' as it is called—say Abolition, Temperance, say Calvinism, or Unitarianism—becomes speedily a little shop, where the article, let it have been at first never so subtle and ethereal, is now made up into portable and convenient cakes, and retailed in small quantities to suit purchasers. You make very free use of these words 'great' and 'holy,' but few things appear to them such. Few persons have any magnificence of nature to inspire enthusiasm, and the philanthropies and charities have a certain air of quackery. As to the general course of living, and the daily employments of men, they cannot see much virtue in these, since they are parts of this vicious circle; and as no great ends are answered by the men, there is nothing noble in the arts by which they are maintained. Nay, they have made the experiment and found that from the liberal professions to the coarsest manual labor, and from the courtesies of the academy and the college to the conventions of the cotillon-room and the morning call, there is a spirit of cowardly compromise and seeming which intimates a frightful skepticism, a life without love, and an activity without an aim.

Unless the action is necessary, unless it is adequate, I do not wish to perform it. I do not wish to do one thing but once. I do not love routine. Once possessed of the principle, it is equally easy to make four or forty thousand applications of it. A great man will be content to have indicated in any the slightest manner his perception of the reigning Idea of his time, and will leave to those who like it the multiplication of examples. When he has hit the white, the rest may shatter the target. Everything admonishes us how needlessly long life is. Every moment of a hero so raises and cheers us that a twelvemonth is an age. All that the brave Xanthus brings home from his wars is the recollection that at the storming of Samos, "in the heat of the battle, Pericles smiled on me, and passed on to another detachment." It is the quality of the moment, not the number of days, of events, or of actors, but imports.

New, we confess, and by no means happy, is our condition: if you want the aid of our labor, we ourselves stand in greater want of the labor. We are miserable with inaction. We perish of rest and rust: but we do not like your work.

'Then,' says the world, 'show me your own.'

'We have none.'

'What will you do, then?' cries the world.

'We will wait.'

'How long?'

'Until the Universe beckons and calls us to work.'

'But whilst you wait, you grow old and useless.'

'Be it so: I can sit in a corner and *perish* (as you call it), but I will not move until I have the highest command. If no call should come for years, for centuries, then I know that the want of the Universe is the attestation of faith by my abstinence. Your virtuous projects, so called, do not cheer me. I know that which shall come will cheer me. If I cannot work, at least I need not lie. All that is clearly due today is not to lie. In other places other men have encountered sharp trials, and have behaved themselves well. The martyrs were sawn asunder, or hung alive on meat-hooks. Cannot we screw our courage to patience and truth, and without complaint, or even with good-humor, await our turn of action in the Infinite Counsels?'

But to come a little closer to the secret of these persons, we must say that to them it seems a very easy matter to answer the objections of the man of the world, but not so easy to dispose of the doubts and objections that occur to themselves. They are exercised in their own spirit with queries which acquaint them with all adversity, and with the trials of the bravest heroes. When I asked them concerning their private experience, they answered somewhat in this wise: It is not to be denied that there must be some wide difference between my faith and other faith; and mine is a certain brief experience, which surprised me in the highway or in the market, in some place, at some time— whether in the body or out of the body. God knoweth—and made me aware that I had played the fool with fools all this time, but that law existed for me and for all; that to me belonged trust, a child's trust and obedience, and the worship of ideas, and I should never be fool more. Well, in the space of an hour probably, I was let down from this height; I was at my old tricks, the selfish member of a selfish society. My life is superficial, takes no root in the deep world; I ask, When shall I die and be relieved of the responsibility of seeing a Universe I do not use? I wish to exchange this flash-of-lightning faith for continuous daylight, this fever-glow for a benign climate.

These two states of thought diverge every moment, and stand in wild contrast. To him who looks at his life from these moments of illumination, it will seem that he skulks and plays a mean, shiftless and subaltern part in the world. That is to be done which he has not skill to do, or to be said which others can say better, and he lies by, or occupies his hands with some plaything, until his hour comes again. Much of our reading, much of our labor, seems mere waiting; it was not that we were born for. Any other could do it as well or better. So little skill enters into these works, so little do they mix with the divine life, that it really signifies little what we do, whether we turn a grindstone, or ride, or run, or make fortunes, or govern the state. The worst feature of this double consciousness is, that the two lives, of the understanding and of the soul, which we lead, really show very little relation to each other; never meet and measure each other; one prevails now, all buzz and din; and the other prevails then, all infinitude and paradise; and, with the progress of life, the two discover no greater disposition to reconcile themselves. Yet, what is my faith? What am I? What but a thought of serenity and independence, an abode in the deep blue sky? Presently the clouds shut down again; yet we retain the belief that this pretty web we weave will at last be overshot and reticulated with veins of the blue, and that the moments will characterize the days. Patience, then, is for us, is it not? Patience, and still patience. When we pass, as presently we shall, into some new infinitude, out of this Iceland of negations, it will please us to reflect that though we had few virtues or consolations, we bore with our indigence, nor once strove to repair it with hypocrisy or false heat of any kind.

But this class are not sufficiently characterized if we omit to add that they are lovers and worshippers of Beauty. In the eternal trinity of Truth, Goodness, and Beauty, each in its perfection including the three, they prefer to make Beauty the sign and head. Something of the same taste is observable in all the moral movements of the time, in the religious and benevolent enterprises. They have a liberal, even an aesthetic spirit. A reference to Beauty in action sounds, to be sure, a little hollow and ridiculous in the ears of the old church. In politics, it has often sufficed, when they treated of justice, if they kept the bounds of selfish calculation. If they granted restitution, it was prudence which granted it. But the justice which is now claimed for the black, and the pauper, and the drunkard, is for Beauty—if for a necessity to the soul of the agent, not of the beneficiary. I say this is the tendency, not yet the realization. Our virtue totters and trips, does not yet walk firmly. Its representatives are austere; they preach and denounce; their rectitude is not yet a grace. They are still liable to that slight taint of burlesque which in our strange world attaches to the zealot. A saint should be as dear as the apple of the eye. Yet we are tempted to smile, and we flee from the working to the speculative reformer, to escape that same slight ridicule. Alas for these days of derision and criticism! We call the Beautiful the highest, because it appears to us the golden mean, escaping the dowdiness of the good and the heartlessness of the true. They are lovers of nature also, and find an indemnity in the inviolable order of the world for the violated order and grace of man.

There is, no doubt, a great deal of well-founded objection to be spoken or felt against the sayings and doings of this class, some of whose traits we have selected; no doubt they will lay themselves open to criticism and to lampoons, and as ridiculous stories will be to be told of them as of any. There will be cant and pretension; there will be subtilty and moonshine. These persons are of unequal strength, and do not all prosper. They complain that everything around them must be denied; and if feeble, it takes all their strength to deny, before they can begin to lead their own life. Grave seniors insist on their respect to this institution and that usage; to an obsolete history; to some vocation, or college, or etiquette, or beneficiary, or charity, or morning or evening call, which they resist as what does not concern them. But it costs such sleepless nights, alienations and misgivings—they have so many moods about it; these old guardians never change *their* minds; they have but one mood on the subject, namely, that Antony is very perverse—that it is quite as much as Antony can do to assert his rights, abstain from what he thinks foolish, and keep his temper. He cannot help the reaction of this injustice in his own mind. He is braced-up and stilted; all freedom and flowing genius, all sallies of wit and frolic nature are quite out of the question; it is well if he can keep from lying, injustice, and suicide. This is no time for gaiety and grace. His strength and spirits are wasted in rejection. But the strong spirits overpower those around them without effort. Their thought and emotion comes in like a flood, quite withdraws them from all notice of these carping critics; they surrender themselves with glad heart to the heavenly guide, and only by implication reject the clamorous nonsense of the hour. Grave seniors talk to the deaf—church and old book mumble and ritualize to an unheeding, preoccupied and advancing mind, and thus they by happiness of greater momentum lose no time, but take the right road at first.

But all these of whom I speak are not proficients; they are novices; they only show the road in which man should travel, when the soul has greater health and prowess. Yet let them feel the dignity of their charge, and deserve a larger power. Their heart is the ark in which the fire is concealed which shall burn in the broader and universal flame. Let them obey the Genius then most when his impulse is wildest; then most when he seems to lead to uninhabitable deserts of thought and life; for the path which the hero travels alone is the highway of health and benefit to mankind. What is the privilege and nobility of our nature but its persistency, through its power to attach itself to what is permanent?

Society also has its duties in reference to this class, and must behold them with what charity it can. Possibly some benefit may yet accrue from them to the state. In our Mechanics' Fair, there must be not only bridges, ploughs, carpenters' planes, and baking troughs, but also some few finer instruments—rain-gauges, thermometers, and telescopes; and in society, besides farmers, sailors, and weavers, there must be a few persons of purer fire kept specially as gauges and meters of character; persons of a fine, detecting instinct, who note the smallest accumulations of wit and feeling in the bystander. Perhaps too there might be room for the exciters and monitors; collectors of the heavenly spark, with power to convey the electricity to others. Or, as the storm-tossed vessel at sea speaks the frigate or 'line packet' to learn its longitude, so it may not be without its advantage that we should now and then encounter rare and gifted men, to compare the points of our spiritual compass, and verify our bearings from superior chronometers.

Amidst the downward tendency and proneness of things, when every voice is raised for a new road or another statute or a subscription of stock; for an improvement in dress, or in dentistry; for a new house or a larger business; for a political party, or the division of an estate; will you not tolerate one or two solitary voices in the land, speaking for thoughts and principles not marketable or perishable? Soon these improvements and mechanical inventions will be superseded; these modes of living lost out of memory; these cities rotted, ruined by war, by new inventions, by new seats of trade, or the geologic changes: all gone, like the shells which sprinkle the sea-beach with a white colony to-day, forever renewed to be forever destroyed. But the thoughts which these few hermits strove to proclaim by silence as well as by speech, not only by what they did, but by what they forbore to do, shall abide in beauty and strength, to reorganize themselves in nature, to invest themselves anew in other, perhaps higher endowed and happier mixed clay than ours, in fuller union with the surrounding system.

D. Ideas

Edmund Husserl

THE WORLD OF THE NATURAL STANDPOINT:
I AND MY WORLD ABOUT ME

Our first outlook upon life is that of natural human beings, imaging, judging, feeling, willing, *"from the natural standpoint"*. Let us make clear to ourselves what this means in the form of simple meditations which we can best carry on in the first person.

I am aware of a world, spread out in space endlessly, and in time becoming and become, without end. I am aware of it, that means, first of all, I discover it immediately, intuitively, I experience it. Through sight, touch, hearing, etc., in the different ways of sensory perception, corporeal things somehow spatially distributed are *for me simply there,* in verbal or figurative sense "present", whether or not I pay them special attention by busying myself with them, considering, thinking, feeling, willing. Animal beings also, perhaps men, are immediately there for me; I look up, I see them, I hear them coming towards me, I grasp them by the hand; speaking with them, I understand immediately what they are sensing and thinking, the feelings that stir them, what they wish or will. They too are present as realities in my field of intuition, even when I pay them no attention. But it is not necessary that they and other objects likewise should be present precisely in my *field of perception*. For me real objects are there, definite, more or less familiar, agreeing with what is actually perceived without being themselves perceived or even intuitively present. I can let my attention wander from the writing-table I have just seen and observed, through the unseen portions of the room behind my back to the verandah, into the garden, to the children in the summer-house, and so forth, to all the objects concerning which I precisely "know" that they are there and yonder in my immediate co-perceived surroundings—a knowledge which has nothing of conceptual thinking in it, and first changes into clear intuiting with the bestowing of attention, and even then only partially and for the most part very imperfectly.

But not even with the added reach of this intuitively clear or dark, distinct or indistinct *co-present* margin, which forms a continuous ring

around the actual field of perception, does that world exhaust itself
which in every waking moment is in some conscious measure "present" before me. It reaches rather in a fixed order of being into the limitless beyond. What is actually perceived, and what is more or less
clearly co-present and determinate (to some extent at least), is partly
pervaded, partly girt about with a *dimly apprehended depth or fringe
of indeterminate reality*. I can pierce it with rays from the illuminating
focus of attention with varying success. Determining representations,
dim at first, then livelier, fetch me something out, a chain of such rec-
ollections takes shape, the circle of determinacy extends ever farther,
and eventually so far that the connexion with the actual field of perception as the *immediate* environment is established. But in general
the issue is a different one: an empty mist of dim indeterminacy gets
studded over with intuitive possibilities or presumptions, and only the
"form" of the world as "world" is foretokened. Moreover, the zone of
indeterminacy is infinite. The misty horizon that can never be completely outlined remains necessarily there.

As it is with the world in its ordered being as a spatial present—
the aspect I have so far been considering—so likewise is it with the
world in respect to its *ordered being in the succession of time*. This
world now present to me, and in every waking 'now' obviously so, has
its temporal horizon, infinite in both directions, its known and
unknown, its intimately alive and its unalive past and future. Moving
freely within the moment of experience which brings what is present
into my intuitional grasp, I can follow up these connexions of the reality which immediately surrounds me. I can shift my standpoint in
space and time, look this way and that, turn temporally forwards and
backwards; I can provide for myself constantly new and more or less
clear and meaningful perceptions and representations, and images also
more or less clear, in which I make intuitable to myself whatever can
possibly exist really or supposedly in the steadfast order of space and
time.

In this way, when consciously awake, I find myself at all times,
and without my ever being able to change this, set in relation to a
world which, through its constant changes, remains one and ever the
same. It is continually "present" for me, and I myself am a member
of it. Therefore this world is not there for me as a mere *world of facts
and affairs,* but, with the same immediacy, as a *world of values, a world
of goods, a practical world*. Without further effort on my part I find the
things before me furnished not only with the qualities that befit their
positive nature, but with value-characters such as beautiful or ugly,
agreeable or disagreeable, pleasant or unpleasant, and so forth. Things

in their immediacy stand there as objects to be used, the "table" with its "books", the "glass to drink from", the "vase", the "piano", and so forth. These values and practicalities, they too belong to *the constitution of the "actually present" objects as such,* irrespective of my turning or not turning to consider them or indeed any other objects. The same considerations apply of course just as well to the men and beasts in my surroundings as to "mere things". They are my "friends" or my "foes", my "servants" or "superiors", "strangers" or "relatives", and so forth.

THE "COGITO". MY NATURAL WORLD-ABOUT-ME AND THE IDEAL WORLDS-ABOUT-ME

It is then to this world, *the world in which I find myself and which is also my world-about-me,* that the complex forms of my manifold and shifting *spontaneities* of consciousness stand related: observing in the interest of research the bringing of meaning into conceptual form through description; comparing and distinguishing, collecting and counting, presupposing and inferring, the theorizing activity of consciousness, in short, in its different forms and stages. Related to it likewise are the diverse acts and states of sentiment and will: approval and disapproval, joy and sorrow, desire and aversion, hope and fear, decision and action. All these, together with the sheer acts of the Ego, in which I become acquainted with the world as *immediately* given me, through spontaneous tendencies to turn towards it and to grasp it, are included under the one Cartesian expression: *Cogito.* In the natural urge of life I live continually in *this fundamental form of all "wakeful" living,* whether in addition I do or do not assert the *cogito,* and whether I am or am not "reflectively" concerned with the Ego and the *cogitare.* If am so concerned, a new *cogito* has become livingly active, which for its part is not reflected upon, and so not objective for me.

I am present to myself continually as someone who perceives, represents, thinks, feels, desires, and so forth; and *for the most part* herein I find myself related in present experience to the fact-world which is constantly about me. But I am not always so related, not every *cogito* in which I love has for its *cogitatum* things, men, objects or contents of one kind or another. Perhaps I am busied with pure numbers and the laws they symbolize: nothing of this sort is present in the world about me, this world of "real fact". And yet the world of numbers also is there for me, as the field of objects with which I am arithmetically-busied; while I am thus occupied some numbers or constructions of a numerical kind will be at the focus of vision, girt by an arithmetical horizon partly defined, partly not; but obviously this being-there-for-me, like the being there at all, is something very different from this. *The arithmetical world is there for me only when and so long as I occupy the arithmetical standpoint.* But the *natural* world, the world in the ordinary sense of the word, is *constantly there for me,* so long as I live naturally and look in its direction. I am then at the *"natural stand-point",* which is just another way of stating the same thing. And there is no need to modify these conclusions when I proceed to appropriate to myself the arithmetical world, and other similar "worlds", by adopting the corresponding standpoint. The natural world *still remains "present",* I am at the natural standpoint after as well as before, and in this respect *undisturbed by the adoption of new standpoints.* If my *cogito* is active *only* in the world proper to the new standpoints, the natural world remains unconsidered; it is now the background for my consciousness as act, but it is *not the encircling sphere within which an arithmetical world finds its true and proper place.* The two worlds are present together but *disconnected,* apart, that is, from their relation to the Ego, in virtue of which I can freely direct my glance or my acts to the one or to the other.

THE "OTHER" EGO-SUBJECT AND THE INTERSUBJECTIVE NATURAL WORLD-ABOUT-ME

Whatever holds good for me personally, also holds good, as I know, for all other men whom I find present in my world-about-me. Experiencing them as men, I understand and take them as Ego-subjects, units like myself, and related to their natural surroundings. But this in such wise that I apprehend the world-about-them and the world-about-me objectively as one and the same world, which differs in each case only through affecting consciousness differently. Each has his place whence he sees the things that are present, and each enjoys accordingly different appearances of the things. For each, again, the fields of perception and memory actually present are different, quite apart from the fact that even that which is here intersubjectively known in common is known in different ways, is differently apprehended, shows different grades of clearness, and so forth. Despite all this, we come to understandings with our neighbours, and set up in common an objective spatio-temporal fact-world *as the world about us that is there for us all, and to which we ourselves none the less belong.*

THE GENERAL THESIS OF THE NATURAL STANDPOINT

That which we have submitted towards the characterization of what is given to us from the natural standpoint, and thereby of the natural standpoint itself, was a piece of pure description *prior to all "theory"*. In these studies we stand bodily aloof from all theories, and by 'theories' we here mean anticipatory ideas of every kind. Only as facts of our environment, not as agencies for uniting facts validly together, do theories concern us at all. But we do not set ourselves the task of continuing the pure description and raising it to a systematically inclusive and exhaustive characterization of the data, in their full length and breadth, discoverable from the natural standpoint (or from any standpoint, we might add, that can be knit up with the same in a common consent). A task such as this can and must—as scientific— be undertaken, and it is one of extraordinary importance, although so far scarcely noticed. Here it is not ours to attempt. For us who are striving towards the entrance-gate of phenomenology all the necessary work in this direction has already been carried out; the few features pertaining to the natural standpoint which we need are of a quite general character, and have already figured in our descriptions, and been sufficiently *and fully clarified*. We even made a special point of securing this full measure of clearness.

We emphasize a most important point once again in the sentences that follow: I find continually present and standing over against me the one spatio-temporal fact-world to which I myself belong, as do all other men found in it and related in the same way to it. This "fact-world", as the word already tells us, I find to *be out there,* and also *take it just as it gives itself to me as something that exists out there.* All doubting and rejecting of the data of the natural world leaves standing the *general thesis of the natural standpoint.* "The" world is as fact-world always there; at the most it is at odd points "other" than I supposed, this or that under such names as "illusion", "hallucination", and the like, must be struck *out of it,* so to speak; but the "it" remains ever, in the sense of the general thesis, a world that has its being out there. To know it more comprehensively, more trustworthily, more perfectly than the naive lore of experience is able to do, and to solve all the problems of scientific knowledge which offer themselves upon its ground, that is the goal of the *sciences of the natural standpoint.*

RADICAL ALTERATION OF THE
NATURAL THESIS "DISCONNEXION", "BRACKETING"

Instead now of remaining at this standpoint, we propose to alter it radically. Our aim must be to convince ourselves of the possibility of this alteration on grounds of principle.

The General Thesis according to which the real world about me is at all times known not merely in a general way as something apprehended, but as a fact-world *that has its being out there,* does *not* consist of course *in an act proper,* in an articulated judgment *about* existence. It is and remains something all the time the standpoint is adopted, that is, it endures persistently during the whole course of our life of natural endeavour. What has been at any time perceived clearly, or obscurely made present, in short everything out of the world of nature known through experience and prior to any thinking, bears in its totality and in all its articulated sections the character "present" "out there", a character which can function essentially as the ground of support for an explicit (predicative) existential judgment which is in agreement with the character it is grounded upon. If we express that same judgment, we know quite well that in so doing we have simply put into the form of a statement grasped as a predication what already lay somehow in the original experience, or lay there as the character of something "present to one's hand".

We can treat the potential and unexpressed thesis exactly as we do the thesis of the explicit judgment. A procedure of this sort, *possible at any time,* is, for instance, *the attempt to doubt everything* which *Descartes,* with an entirely different end in view, with the purpose of setting up an absolutely indubitable sphere of Being, undertook to carry through. We link on here, but add directly and emphatically that this attempt to doubt everything should serve us *only as a device of method,* helping us to stress certain points which by its means, as though secluded in its essence, must be brought clearly to light.

The attempt to doubt everything has its place in the realm of our *perfect freedom.* We can *attempt to doubt* anything and everything, however convinced we may be concerning what we doubt, even though the evidence which seals our assurance is completely adequate.

Let us consider what is essentially involved in an act of this kind. He who attempts to doubt is attempting to doubt "Being" of some form or other, or it may be Being expanded into such predicative forms as "It is", "It is this or thus", and the like. The attempt does not affect the form of Being itself. He who doubts, for instance, whether an object, whose Being he does not doubt, is constituted in such and such a way, doubts *the way it is constituted.* We can obviously transfer this way of speaking from the doubting to the *attempt* at doubting. It is clear that we cannot doubt the Being of anything, and in the same act of consciousness (under the unifying form of simultaneity) bring what is substantive to this Being under the terms of the Natural Thesis, and so confer upon it the character of "being actually there" *(vorhanden).* Or to put the same in another way: we cannot at once doubt and hold for certain one and the same quality of Being. It is likewise clear that the *attempt* to doubt any object of awareness in respect of its *being actually there necessarily conditions a certain suspension (Aufhebung) of the thesis;* and it is precisely this that interests us. It is not a transformation of the thesis into its antithesis, of positive into negative; it is also not a transformation into presumption, suggestion, indecision, doubt (in one or another sense of the word); such shifting indeed is not at our free pleasure. *Rather is it something quite unique. We do not abandon the thesis we have adopted, we make no change in our conviction,* which remains in itself what it is so long as we do not introduce new motives of judgment, which we precisely refrain from doing. And yet the thesis undergoes a modification—whilst remaining in itself what it is, *we set it as it were "out of action", we "disconnect it", "bracket it".* It still remains there like the bracketed in the bracket, like the disconnected outside the connexional system. We can also say: The thesis is experience as lived *(Erlebnis), but we make "no use" of it,* and by that, of course, we do not indicate privation (as when we say of the ignorant that he makes no use of a certain thesis); in this case rather, as with all parallel expressions, we are dealing with indicators that point to a definite but *unique form of consciousness,* which clamps on to the original simple thesis (whether it actually or even predicatively *posits* existence or not), and transvalues it in a quite peculiar way. *This transvaluing is a concern of our full freedom, and is opposed to all cognitive attitudes* that would set themselves up as co-ordinate with *the thesis,* and yet within the unity of "simultaneity" remain incompatible with it, as indeed it is in general with all attitudes whatsoever in the strict sense of the word.

In *the attempt to doubt* applied to a thesis which, as we presuppose, is certain and tenaciously held, the "disconnexion" takes place in and with a modification of the antithesis, namely, with the *"supposition" (Ansetzung) of Non-Being,* which is thus the partial basis of the attempt to doubt. With Descartes this is so markedly the case that one can say that his universal attempt at doubt is just an attempt at universal denial. We disregard this possibility here, we are not interested in every analytic component of the attempt to doubt, nor therefore in its exact and completely sufficing analysis. *We extract only the phenomenon of "bracketing" or "disconnecting",* which is obviously not limited to that of the attempt to doubt, although it can be detached from it with special ease, but can appear *in other contexts also,* and with no less ease *independently.* In relation to *every* thesis and wholly uncoerced we can use this *peculiar ἐποχή, a certain refraining from judgment which is compatible with the unshaken and unshakable because self-evidencing conviction of Truth.* The thesis is "put out of action", bracketed, it passes off into the modified status of a "bracketed thesis", and the judgment *simpliciter* into *"bracketed judgment".*

Naturally one should not simply identify this consciousness with that of "mere supposal", that nymphs, for instance, are dancing in a ring; for thereby *no disconnecting* of a living conviction that goes on living takes place, although from another side the close relation of the two forms of consciousness lies clear. Again, we are not concerned here with supposal in the sense of *"assuming"* or *taking for granted,* which in the equivocal speech of current usage may also be expressed in the words: "I suppose (I make the assumption) that it is so and so."

Let us add further that nothing hinders us *from speaking of bracketing correlatively* also, in respect of *an objectivity to be posited,* whatever be the region or category to which it belongs. What is meant in this case is that *every thesis related to this objectivity* must be *disconnected* and changed into its bracketed counterpart. On closer view, moreover, the 'bracketing' image is from the outset better suited to the sphere of the object, just as the expression 'to put out of action' better suits the sphere of the Act or of Consciousness.

THE PHENOMENOLOGICAL ἐποχή

We can now let the universal ἐποχή in the sharply defined and novel sense we have given to it step into the place of the Cartesian attempt at universal doubt. But on good grounds we *limit* the universality of this ἐποχή. For were it as inclusive as it is in general capable of being, then since every thesis and every judgment can be modified freely to any extent, and every objectivity that we can judge or criticize can be bracketed, no field would be left over for unmodified judgments, to say nothing of a science. But our design is just to discover a new scientific domain, such as might be won precisely *through the method of bracketing,* though only through a definitely limited form of it.

The limiting consideration can be indicated in a word.

We put out of action the general thesis which belongs to the essence of the natural standpoint, we place in brackets whatever it includes respecting the nature of Being: *this entire natural world therefore* which is continually "there for us", "present to our hand", and will ever remain there, is a "fact-world" of which we continue to be conscious, even though it pleases us to put it in brackets.

If I do this, as I am fully free to do, I do *not* then *deny* this "world", as though I were a sophist, *I do not doubt that it is there* as though I were a sceptic; but I use the "phenomenological" ἐποχή, which *completely bars* me *from using any judgment that concerns spatio-temporal existence (Dasein).*

Thus *all sciences which relate to this natural world,* though they stand never so firm to me, though they fill me with wondering admiration, though I am far from any thought of objecting to them in the least degree, *I disconnect them* all, *I make absolutely no use of their standards, I do not appropriate a single one of the propositions that enter into their systems, even though their evidential value is perfect, I take none of them, no one of them serves me for a foundation*—so long, that is, as it is understood, in the way these sciences themselves understand it, as a truth *concerning the realities* of this world. *I may accept it only after I have placed it in the bracket.* That means: only in the modified consciousness of the judgment as it appears in disconnexion, and *not as it figures within the science as its proposition, a proposition which claims to be valid and whose validity I recognize and make use of.*

The ἐποχή here in question will not be confused with that which positivism demands, and against which, as we were compelled to admit, it is itself an offender. We are not concerned at present with removing the preconceptions which trouble the pure positivity *(Sachlichkeit)* of research, with the constituting of a science "free from theory" and "free from metaphysics" by bringing all the grounding back to the immediate data, nor with the means of reaching such ends, concerning whose value there is indeed no question. What *we* demand lies along another line. The whole world as placed within the nature-setting and presented in experience as real, taken completely "free from all theory", just as it is in reality experienced, and made clearly manifest in and through the linkings of our experiences, has now no validity for us, it must be set in brackets, untested indeed but also uncontested.

Similarly all theories and sciences, positivistic or otherwise, which relate to this world, however good they may be, succumb to the same fate.

INTIMATION CONCERNING "PURE" OR "TRANSCENDENTAL CONSCIOUSNESS" AS PHENOMENOLOGICAL RESIDUUM

We have learnt to understand the meaning of the phenomenological ἐποχή, but we are still quite in the dark as to its serviceability. In the first place it is not clear to what extent the limitation of the total field of the ἐποχή, as discussed in the previous pages, involves a real narrowing of its general scope. *For what can remain over when the whole world is bracketed, including ourselves and all our thinking (cogitare)?*

Since the reader already knows that the interest which governs these 'Meditations' concerns a new eidetic science, he will indeed at first expect the world as fact to succumb to the disconnexion, but not *the world as Eidos*, nor any other sphere of Essential Being. The disconnecting of the world does not as a matter of fact mean the disconnecting of the number series, for instance, and the arithmetic relative to it.

However, we do not take this path, nor does our goal lie in its direction. That goal we could also refer to as *the winning of a new region of Being, the distinctive character of which has not yet been defined*, a region of *individual* Being, like every genuine region. We must leave the sequel to teach us what that more precisely means.

We proceed in the first instance by showing up simply and directly what we see; and since the Being to be thus shown up is neither more nor less than that which we refer to on essential grounds as "pure experiences (*Erlebnisse*)", "pure consciousness" with its pure "correlates of consciousness", and on the other side its "pure Ego", we observe that it is from *the* Ego, *the* consciousness, *the* experience as given to us from the natural standpoint, that we take our start.

I, the real human being, am a real object like others in the natural world. I carry out *cogitationes*, "acts of consciousness" in both a narrower and a wider sense, and these acts, as belonging to this human subject, are events of the same natural world. And all my remaining experiences *(Erlebnisse)* likewise, out of whose changing stream the specific acts of the Ego shine forth in so distinctive a way, glide into one another, enter into combinations, and are being incessantly modified. Now in its *widest connotation* the expression *"consciousness"* (then indeed less suited for its purpose) includes *all* experiences *(Erlebnisse),* and entrenched in the natural standpoint as we are even in our scientific thinking, grounded there in habits that are most firmly established since they have never misled us, we take all these data of psychological reflexion as real world-events, as the experiences *(Erlebnisse)* of animal beings. So natural is it to us to see them only in this light that, though acquainted already with the possibility of a change of standpoint, and on the search for the new domain of objects, we fail to notice that it is from out these centres of experience *(Erlebnisse)* themselves that through the adoption of the new standpoint the new domain emerges. Connected with this is the fact that instead of keeping our eyes turned towards these centres of experience, we turned them away and sought the new objects in the ontological realms of arithmetic, geometry, and the like, whereby indeed nothing truly new was to be won.

Thus we fix our eyes steadily upon the sphere of Consciousness and study what it is that we find immanent in *it*. At first, without having yet carried out the phenomenological suspensions of the element of judgment, we subject this sphere of Consciousness in its essential nature to a systematic though in no sense exhaustive analysis. What we lack above all is a certain general insight into the essence of *consciousness in general,* and quite specially also of consciousness, so far as in and through its essential Being, the "natural" fact-world comes to be known. In these studies we go so far as is needed to furnish the full insight at which we have been aiming, to wit, *that Consciousness in itself has a being of its own which in its absolute uniqueness of nature remains unaffected by the phenomenological disconnexion.* It therefore remains over as a *"phenomenological residuum",* as a region of Being which is in principle unique, and can become in fact the field of a new science—the science of Phenomenology.

Through this insight the "phenomenological" ἐποχή will for the first time deserve its name; to exercise it in full consciousness of its import will turn out to be the necessary operation which *renders "pure" consciousness accessible to us, and subsequently the whole phenomenological region.* And thus we shall be able to understand why this region and the new science attached to it was fated to remain unknown. From the natural standpoint nothing can be seen except the natural world. So long as the possibility of the phenomenological standpoint was not grasped, and the method of relating the objectivities which emerge therewith to a primordial form of apprehension had not been devised, the phenomenological world must needs have remained unknown, and indeed barely divined at all.

We would add yet the following to our terminology: Important motives which have their ground in epistemological requirements justify us in referring to "pure" consciousness, of which much is yet to be said, also as *transcendental consciousness,* and the operation through which it is acquired as *transcendental ἐποχή.* On grounds of method this operation will split up into different steps of "disconnexion" or "bracketing", and thus our method will assume the character of a graded reduction. For this reason we propose to speak, and even preponderatingly, of *phenomenological reductions* (though, in respect of their unity as a whole, we would speak in unitary form of *the* phenomenological reduction). From the epistemological viewpoint we would also speak of transcendental reductions. Moreover, these and *all* our terms must be understood exclusively in accordance with the sense which *our* presentations indicate for them, but not in any other one which history or the terminological habits of the reader may favour.

VI

THE COSMIC SELF

A. The World as Will and Representation

Arthur Schopenhauer

The will, as the thing-in-itself, constitutes the inner, true, and indestructible nature of man; yet in itself it is without consciousness. For consciousness is conditioned by the intellect, and the intellect is a mere accident of our being, for it is a function of the brain. The brain, together with the nerves and spinal cord attached to it, is a mere fruit, a product, in fact a parasite, of the rest of the organism, in so far as it is not directly geared to the organism's inner working, but serves the purpose of self-preservation by regulating its relations with the external world. On the other hand, the organism itself is the visibility, the objectivity, of the individual will, its image, as this image presents itself in that very brain (which in the first book we learned to recognize as the condition of the objective world in general). Therefore, this image is brought about by the brain's forms of knowledge, namely space, time, and causality; consequently it presents itself as something extended, successively acting, and material, in other words, operative or effective. The parts of the body are both directly felt and perceived by means of the senses only in the brain. In consequence of this, it can be said that the intellect is the secondary phenomenon, the organism the primary, that is, the immediate phenomenal appearance of the will; the will is metaphysical, the intellect physical; the intellect, like its objects, is mere phenomenon, the will alone is thing-in-itself. Then, in a more and more *figurative* sense, and so by way of comparison, it can be said that the will is the substance of man, the intellect the accident; the will is the matter, the intellect the form; the will is heat, the intellect light.

We will now first of all verify, and at the same time elucidate, this thesis by the following facts appertaining to the inner life of man. Perhaps, on this occasion, more will be gained for knowledge of the inner man than is to be found in many systematic psychologies.

1. Not only the consciousness of other things, i.e., the apprehension of the external world, but also *self-consciousness,* as already mentioned, contains a knower and a known, otherwise it would not be a *consciousness.* For *consciousness* consists in knowing, but knowing requires a knower and a known. Therefore self-consciousness could not exist if there were not in it a known opposed to the knower and different therefrom. Thus, just as there can be no object without a sub-

239

ject, so there can be no subject without an object, in other words, no knower without something different from this that is known. Therefore, a consciousness that was through and through pure intelligence would be impossible. The intelligence is like the sun that does not illuminate space unless an object exists by which its rays are reflected. The knower himself, precisely as such, cannot be known, otherwise he would be the *known* of another knower. But as the *known* in self-consciousness we find exclusively the *will*. For not only willing and deciding in the narrowest sense, but also all striving, wishing, shunning, hoping, fearing, loving, hating, in short all that directly constitutes our own weal and woe, desire and disinclination, is obviously only affection of the will, is a stirring, a modification, of willing and not-willing, is just that which, when it operates outwards, exhibits itself as an act of will proper. But in all knowledge the known, not the knower, is the first and essential thing, inasmuch as the former is the $\pi\rho\omega\tau\acute{o}\tau\upsilon\pi\sigma$, the latter the $\acute{\epsilon}\varkappa\tau\upsilon\pi\sigma$. Therefore in self-consciousness the known, consequently the will, must be the first and original thing; the knower, on the other hand, must be only the secondary thing, that which has been added, the mirror. They are related somewhat as the self-luminous is to the reflecting body; or as the vibrating strings are to the sounding-board, where the resulting note would then be consciousness. We can also consider the plant as such a symbol of consciousness. As we know, it has two poles, root and corona; the former reaching down into darkness, moisture and cold, and the latter up into brightness, dryness and warmth; then as the point of indifference of the two poles where they part from each other close to the ground, the collum or root-stock *(rhizoma, le collet)*. The root is what is essential, original, perennial, whose death entails the death of the corona; it is therefore primary. The corona, on the other hand, is the ostensible, that which has sprouted forth, that which passes away without the root dying; it is therefore the secondary. The root represents the will, the corona the intellect, and the point of indifference of the two, namely the collum, would be the *I*, which, as their common extreme point, belongs to both. This I is the *pro tempore* identical subject of knowing and willing, whose identity I call in my very first essay *(On the Principle of Sufficient Reason)* and in my first philosophical astonishment, the miracle $\varkappa\alpha\tau'$ $\acute{\epsilon}\xi\sigma\chi\acute{\eta}\nu$. It is the point of departure and of contact of the whole phenomenon, in other words, of the objectification of the will; it is true that it conditions the phenomenon, but the phenomenon also conditions it. The comparison here given can be carried even as far as the individual character and nature of men. Thus, just as usually a large corona springs only from a large root, so the greatest mental abilities are found only with a vehement and passionate will. A genius of phlegmatic character and feeble passions would be like succulent plants that have very small roots in spite of an imposing corona consisting of thick leaves; yet he will not be found. Vehemence of the will and passionate ardour of the character are a condition of enhanced intelligence, and this is shown physiologically through the brain's activity being conditioned by the movement communicated to it with every pulsation through the great arteries running up to the *basis cerebri*. Therefore an energetic pulse, and even, according to Bichat, a short neck are necessary for great activity of the brain. But the opposite of the above is of course found; that is, vehement desires, passionate, violent character, with weak intellect, in other words, with a small brain of inferior conformation in a thick skull. This is a phenomenon as common as it is repulsive; it might perhaps be compared to the beetroot.

2. But in order not merely to describe consciousness figuratively, but to know it thoroughly, we have first to find out what exists in every consciousness in the same manner, and what therefore will be, as the common and constant element, that which is essential. We shall then consider what distinguishes one consciousness from another, and this accordingly will be the accidental and secondary element.

Consciousness is known to us positively only as a property of animal nature; consequently we may not, indeed we cannot, think of it otherwise than as *animal consciousness,* so that this expression is in fact tautological. Therefore what is always to be found in *every* animal consciousness, even the most imperfect and feeblest, in fact what is always its foundation, is the immediate awareness of a *longing,* and of its alternate satisfaction and non-satisfaction in very different degrees. To a certain extent we know this *a priori.* For amazingly varied as the innumerable species of animals may be, and strange as some new form of them, never previously seen, may appear to us, we nevertheless assume beforehand with certainty its innermost nature as something well known, and indeed wholly familiar to us. Thus we know that the animal *wills,* indeed even *what* it wills, namely existence, well-being, life, and propagation. Since we here presuppose with perfect certainty an identity with ourselves, we have no hesitation in attributing to it unchanged all the affections of will known to us in ourselves; and we speak positively and plainly of its desire, aversion, fear, anger, hatred, love, joy, sorrow, longing, and so on. On the other hand, as soon as we come to speak of phenomena of mere knowledge, we run into uncertainty. We do not venture to say that the animal conceives, thinks, judges, or knows; we attribute to it with certainty only representations in general, since without these its *will* could not be stirred or agitated in the ways previously mentioned. But as regards the animals' definite way of knowing, and its precise limits in a given species, we have only indefinite concepts, and make conjectures. Therefore understanding between us and them is often difficult, and is brought about ingeniously only in consequence of experience and practice. Here, then, are to be found distinctions of consciousness. On the other hand, longing, craving, willing, or aversion, shunning, and not-willing, are peculiar to every consciousness; man has them in common with the polyp. Accordingly, this is the essential and the basis of every consciousness. The difference of its manifestations in the various species of animal beings depends on the different extension of their spheres of knowledge in which the motives of those manifestations are to be found. Directly from our own nature we understand all the actions and attitudes of animals that express stirrings and agitations of the will; and so to this extent we sympathize with them in many different ways. On the other hand, the gulf between us and them arises simply and solely from a difference of intellect. The gulf between a very intelligent animal and a man of very limited capacity is possibly not much greater than that between a blockhead and a genius. Therefore here also, the resemblance between them in another aspect, springing from the likeness of their inclinations and emotions and again assimilating both, sometimes stands out surprisingly, and excites astonishment. This consideration makes it clear that in all animal beings the *will* is the primary and substantial thing; the *intellect,* on the other hand, is something secondary and additional, in fact a mere tool in the service of the will, which is more or less complete and complicated according to the requirements of this service. Just as a species of animals appears equipped with hoofs, claws, hands, wings, horns, or teeth according to the aims of its will, so is it furnished with a more or less developed brain, whose function is the intelligence requisite for its continued existence. Thus the more complicated the organization becomes in the ascending series of animals, the more manifold do its needs become, and the more varied and specially determined the objects capable of satisfying them, consequently the more tortuous and lengthy the paths for arriving at these, which must now all be known and found. Therefore, to the same extent, the animal's representations must also be more versatile, accurate, definite, and connected, and its attention more eager, more continuous, and more easily roused; consequently its intellect must be more developed and complete. Accordingly we see the organ of intelligence, the cerebral system, together with the organs of sense, keep pace with an increase of needs and wants, and with the complication of the organism. We see the increase of the *representing* part of consciousness (as opposed to the *willing* part) bodily manifesting itself in the ever-increasing proportion of the brain in general to the rest of the nervous system, and of the cerebrum to the cerebellum. For (according to Flourens) the former is the workshop of representations, while the latter is the guide and regulator of movements. But the last step taken by nature in this respect is disproportionately great. For in man not only does the power of representation in *perception,* which hitherto has existed alone, reach the highest degree of perfection, but the *abstract* representation, thinking, i.e., *reason (Vernunft)* is added, and with it reflection. Through this important enhancement of the intellect, and hence of the secondary part of consciousness, it obtains a preponderance over the primary part in so far as it becomes from now on the predominantly active part. Thus, whereas in the case of the animal the immediate awareness of its satisfied or unsatisfied desire constitutes by far the principal part of its consciousness, and indeed the more so the lower the animal stands, so that the lowest animals are distinguished from plants only by the addition of a dull representation, with man the opposite is the case. Intense as his desires may be, more intense even than those of any animal and rising to the level of passions, his consciousness nevertheless remains continuously and predominantly concerned and engrossed with representations and ideas. Undoubtedly this is mainly what has given rise to that fundamental error of all philosophers, by virtue of which they make thinking the essential and primary element of the so-called soul, in other words, of man's inner or spiritual life, always putting it first, but regard willing as a mere product of thinking, and as something secondary, additional, and subsequent. But if willing resulted merely from knowing, how could the animals, even the lowest of them, manifest a will that is often so indomitable and vehement, in spite of such extremely limited knowledge? Accordingly, since that fundamental error of the philosophers makes, so to speak, the accident into the substance, it leads them on to wrong paths from which there is no longer a way out. Therefore that relative predominance of the *knowing* consciousness over the *desiring,* and consequently of the secondary part over the primary, which appears in man, can in certain abnormally favoured individuals go so far that, in moments of supreme enhancement, the secondary or knowing part of consciousness is entirely detached from the willing part, and passes by itself into free activity, in other words, into an activity not stimulated by the will, and therefore no longer serving it. Thus the knowing part of consciousness becomes purely objective and the clear mirror of the world, and from this the conceptions of *genius* arise, which are the subject of our third book.

3. If we descend through the series of grades of animals, we see the intellect becoming weaker and weaker and more and more imperfect; but we certainly do not observe a corresponding degradation of the will. On the contrary, the will everywhere retains its identical nature, and shows itself as a great attachment to life, care for the individual and for the species, egoism and lack of consideration for all others, together with the emotions springing therefrom. Even in the smallest insect the will is present complete and entire; it wills what it wills as decidedly and completely as does man. The difference lies merely in *what* it wills, that is to say, in the motives; but these are the business of the intellect. As that which is secondary and tied to bodily organs, the intellect naturally has innumerable degrees of perfection, and in general is essentially limited and imperfect. The *will,* on the other hand, as that which is original and the thing-in-itself, can never be imperfect, but every act of will is wholly what it can be. By virtue of the simplicity belonging to the will as the thing-in-itself, as the metaphysical in the phenomenon, its *essential nature* admits of no degrees, but is always entirely itself. Only its *stimulation or excitement* has degrees, from the feeblest inclination up to passion, and also its excitability, and thus its vehemence, from the phlegmatic to the choleric temperament. On the other hand, the *intellect* has not merely degrees of *excitement,* from sleepiness up to the mood and inspiration, but also degrees of its *real nature,* of the completeness thereof; accordingly, this rises gradually from the lowest animal which perceives only obscurely up to man, and in man again from the blockhead to the genius. The *will* alone is everywhere entirely itself, for its function is of the greatest simplicity; for this consists in willing and in not-willing, which operates with the greatest ease and without effort, and requires no practice. On the other hand, knowing has many different functions, and never takes place entirely without effort, which it requires for fixing the attention and making the object clear, and at a higher degree, also for thinking and deliberation; it is therefore capable of great improvement through practice and training. If the intellect holds out to the will something simple and perceptible, the will at once expresses its approval or disapproval. This is the case even when the intellect has laboriously pondered and ruminated, in order finally to produce from numerous data by means of difficult combinations the result that seems most in agreement with the interests of the will. Meanwhile, the will has been idly resting; after the result is reached, it enters, as the sultan does on the divan, merely to express again its monotonous approval or disapproval. It is true that this can turn out different in degree, but in essence it remains always the same.

This fundamentally different nature of the will and the intellect, the simplicity and originality essential in the former in contrast to the complicated and secondary character of the latter, become even clearer to us when we observe their strange interplay within us, and see in a particular case how the images and ideas arising in the intellect set the will in motion, and how entirely separated and different are the roles of the two. Now it is true that we can already observe this in the case of actual events that vividly excite the will, whereas primarily and in themselves they are merely objects of the intellect. But, to some extent, it is not so obvious here that this reality as such primarily exists only in the intellect; and again, the change generally does not occur as rapidly as is necessary, if the thing is to be easily seen at a glance, and thus really comprehensible. On the other hand, both these are the case if it is mere ideas and fantasies that we allow to act on the will. If, for example, we are alone, and think over our personal affairs, and then vividly picture to ourselves, say, the menace of an actually present danger, and the possibility of an unfortunate outcome, anxiety at once compresses the heart, and the blood ceases to flow. But if the intellect then passes to the possibility of the opposite outcome, and allows the imagination to picture the happiness long hoped-for as thereby attained, all the pulses at once quicken with joy, and the heart feels as light as a feather, until the intellect wakes up from its dream. But then let some occasion lead the memory to an insult or injury suffered long ago, and anger and resentment at once storm through the breast that a moment before was at peace. Then let the image of a long-lost love arise, called up by accident, with which is connected a whole romance with its magic scenes, and this anger will at once give place to profound longing and sadness. Finally, if there occur to us some former humiliating incident, we shrivel up, would like to be swallowed up, blush with shame, and often try to divert and distract ourselves forcibly from it by some loud exclamation, scaring away evil spirits as it were. We see that the intellect strikes up the tune, and the will must dance to it; in fact, the intellect causes it to play the part of a child whom its nurse at her pleasure puts into the most different moods by chatter and tales alternating between pleasant and melancholy things. This is due to the fact that the will in itself is without knowlege, but the understanding associated with it is without will. Therefore the will behaves like a body that is moved, the understanding like the causes that set it in motion, for it is the medium of motives. Yet with all this, the primacy of the will becomes clear again when this will, that becomes, as we have shown, the sport of the intellect as soon as it allows the intellect to control it, once makes its supremacy felt in the last resort. This it does by prohibiting the intellect from having certain representations, by absolutely preventing certain trains of thought from arising, because it knows, or in other words experiences from the self-same intellect, that they would arouse in it any one of the emotions previously described. It then curbs and restrains the intellect, and forces it to turn to other things. However difficult this often is, it is bound to succeed the moment the will is in earnest about it; for the resistance then comes not from the intellect, which always remains indifferent, but from the will itself; and the will has an inclination in one respect for a representation it abhors in another. Thus the representation is in itself interesting to the will, just because it excites it. At the same time, however, abstract knowledge tells the will that this representation will cause it a shock of painful and unworthy emotion to no purpose. The will then decides in accordance with this last knowledge, and forces the intellect to obey. This is called "being master of oneself"; here obviously the master is the will, the servant the intellect, for in the last instance the will is always in command, and therefore constitutes the real core, the being-in-itself, of man. In this respect Ἡγεμονικόν would be a fitting title for the *will;* yet again this title seems to apply to the *intellect,* in so far as that is the guide and leader, like the footman who walks in front of the stranger. In truth, however, the most striking figure for the relation of the two is that of the strong blind man carrying the sighted lame man on his shoulders.

The relation of the will to the intellect here described can further be recognized in the fact that the intellect is originally quite foreign to the decisions of the will. It furnishes the will with motives; but only subsequently, and thus wholly *a posteriori,* does it learn how these have acted, just as a man making a chemical experiment applies the reagents, and then waits for the result. In fact, the intellect remains so much excluded from the real resolutions and secret decisions of its own will that sometimes it can only get to know them, like those of a stranger, by spying out and taking unawares; and it must surprise the will in the act of expressing itself, in order merely to discover its real intentions. For example, I have devised a plan, but I still have some scruple regarding it; on the other hand, the feasibility of the plan, as regards its possibility, is completely uncertain, since it depends on external circumstances that are still undecided. Therefore at all events it is unnecessary for the present to come to a decision about it, and so for the time being I let the matter rest. Now I often do not know how firmly I am already attached in secret to this plan, and how much I desire that it be carried into effect, in spite of the scruple; in other words, my intellect does not know this. But only let a favourable report reach me as to its feasibility, and at once there arises within me a jubilant, irresistible gladness, diffused over my whole being and taking permanent possession of it, to my own astonishment. For only now does my intellect learn how firmly my will had already laid hold of the plan, and how entirely it was in agreement therewith, whereas the intellect had still regarded it as entirely problematical and hardly a match for that scruple. Or in another case, I have entered very eagerly into a mutual obligation that I believe to be very much in accordance with my wishes. As the matter progresses, the disadvantages and hardships make themselves felt, and I begin to suspect that I even repent of what I pursued so eagerly. However, I rid myself of this suspicion by assuring myself that, even if I were not bound, I should continue on the same course. But then the obligation is unexpectedly broken and dissolved by the other party, and I observe with astonishment that this happens to my great joy and relief. We often do not know what we desire or fear. For years we can have a desire without admitting it to ourselves or even letting it come to clear consciousness, because the intellect is not to know anything about it, since the good opinion we have of ourselves would inevitably suffer thereby. But if the wish is fulfilled, we get to know from our joy, not without a feeling of shame, that this is what we desired; for example, the death of a near relation whose heir we are. Sometimes we do not know what we really fear, because we lack the courage to bring it to clear consciousness. In fact, we are often entirely mistaken as to the real motive from which we do or omit to do something, till finally some accident discloses the secret to us, and we know that our real motive was not what we thought of it as being, but some other that we were unwilling to admit to ourselves, because it was by no means in keeping with our good opinion of ourselves. For example, as we imagine we omit to do something for purely moral reasons; yet we learn subsequently that we were deterred merely by fear, since we do it as soon as all danger is removed. In individual cases this may go so far that a man does not even guess the real motive of his action, in fact does not regard himself as capable of being influenced by such a motive; yet it is the real motive of his action. Incidentally, we have in all this a confirmation and illustration of the rule of La Rochefoucauld: *"L'amour-propre est plus habile que le plus habile homme du monde,"* in fact even a commentary on the Delphic γνῶθι σαυτόγ, and its difficulty. Now if, on the other hand, as all philosophers imagine, the intellect constituted our true inner nature, and the decisions of the will were a mere result of knowledge, then precisely *that* motive alone, from which we *imagined* we acted, would necessarily be decisive for our moral worth, on the analogy that the intention, not the result, is decisive in this respect. But then the distinction between imagined and actual motive would really be impossible. Therefore, all cases described here, and moreover the analogous cases which anyone who is attentive can observe in himself, enable us to see how the intellect is such a stranger to the will that occasionally it is even mystified thereby. For it is true that it furnishes the will with motives; but it does not penetrate into the secret workshop of the will's decisions. It is, of course, a confidant of the will, yet a confidant that does not get to know everything. A confirmation of this is also afforded by the fact that occasionally the intellect does not really trust the will; and at some time or other almost everyone will have an opportunity of observing this in himself. Thus, if we have formed some great and bold resolution—which, however, as such is only a promise given by the will to the intellect—there often remains within us a slight, unconfessed doubt whether we are quite in earnest about it, whether, in carrying it out, we shall not waver or flinch, but shall have firmness and determination enough to carry it through. It therefore requires the deed to convince us of the sincerity of the resolve.

All these facts are evidence of the complete difference between the will and the intellect, and demonstrate the former's primacy and the latter's subordinate position.

4. The *intellect* grows tired; the *will* is untiring. After continuous work with the head, we feel fatigue of the brain, just as we feel fatigue of the arm after continuous bodily work. All *knowing* is associated with effort and exertion; *willing,* on the contrary, is our very nature, whose manifestations occur without any weariness and entirely of their own accord. Therefore, if our *will* is strongly excited, as in all emotions such as anger, fear, desire, grief, and so on, and we are then called upon to *know,* perhaps with the intention of correcting the motives of those emotions, then the violence we must do to ourselves for this purpose is evidence of the transition from the original, natural activity proper to us to the activity that is derived, indirect, and forced. For the will alone is αὐτόματος and therefore ἀκάματος καὶ ἀγήρατος ἤματα πάντα *(lassitudinis et senii expers in sempiternum).* It alone is active, unbidden and of its own accord, and hence often too early and too much; and it knows no weariness. Infants, who show scarcely the first feeble trace of intelligence, are already full of self-will; through uncontrollable, aimless storming and screaming, they show the pressure of will with which they are full to overflowing, whereas their willing as yet has no object, in other words, they will without knowing what they will. The remarks of Cabanis are to the point here: *Toutes*

ces passions, qui se succèdent d'une manière si rapide, et se peignent avec tant de naïveté, sur le visage mobile des enfans. Tandis que les faibles muscles de leurs bras et de leurs jambes savent encore à peine former quelques mouvemens indécis, les muscles de la face expriment déjà par des mouvemens distincts presque toute la suite des affections générales propres à la nature humaine: et l'observateur attentif reconnait facilement dans ce tableau les traits caractéristiques de l'homme futur. (Rapports du physique et moral, Vol. I, p. 123.) The intellect, on the contrary, develops slowly, following on the completion of the brain and the maturity of the whole organism. These are the conditions of the intellect, just because it is only a somatic function. Because the brain has already attained its full size in the seventh year, children after that age become remarkably intelligent, inquisitive, and sensible. But then comes puberty; to a certain extent, it affords a support to the brain, or a sounding-board, and all at once raises the intellect by a large step, by an octave as it were, corresponding to the lowering of the voice by a like amount. But at the same time the animal desires and passions that now appear oppose the reasonableness that has hitherto prevailed, and this is progressive. Further evidence of the indefatigable nature of the will is afforded by the fault more or less peculiar to all people by nature, and overcome only by training—*precipitancy* or *rashness.* This consists in the will's hurrying prematurely to its business. This is the purely active and executive part that should appear only after the exploratory, deliberate, and thus the knowing part has thoroughly completed its business; but rarely does one actually wait for this time. Scarcely are a few data superficially comprehended and hastily gathered up by knowledge concerning the circumstances before us, or the event that has occurred, or the opinion of someone else that is conveyed to us, when from the depths of our nature the will, always ready and never tired, steps forth unbidden. It shows itself as terror, fear, hope, joy, desire, envy, grief, zeal, anger, or courage, and leads to hasty words or actions. These are often followed by repentance, after time has taught us that the hegemonikon, namely the intellect, has not been able to finish even half its business of comprehending the circumstances, reflecting on their connexion, and deciding what is advisable. This is because the will did not wait for it, but sprang forward long before its time with "Now it is my turn!" and at once took up an active part without the intellect's offering any resistance. But as a mere slave and bondman of the will, the intellect is not, like it αὐτόματος, or active from its own power and its own impulse. It is therefore easily pushed aside by the will, and brought to silence by a nod therefrom; whereas on its own part it is hardly able, even with the greatest effort, to bring the will even to a brief pause, in order to get a word in edgeways. This is why people are so rare, and are found almost exclusively among Spaniards, Turks, and possibly Englishmen, who, even in the most provocative circumstances, *keep their heads.* Imperturbably they continue to comprehend and investigate the state of affairs, and where others would already be beside themselves, ask a further question *con mucho sosiego.* This is something quite different from the composure and unconcern, based on indolence and apathy, of many Germans and Dutchmen. Iffland used to give an incomparable illustration of this admirable quality when taking the part of Hetman of the Cossacks in Benyowski. When the conspirators enticed him into their tent, they held a rifle at his head, intimating that it would be fired the moment he uttered a cry; Iffland blew into the muzzle of the rifle to test whether it was loaded. Of ten things that annoy us, nine could not do so if we thoroughly understood them from their causes, and so knew their necessity and true nature; but we should do this much oftener if we made them the object of reflection before making them the object of indignation and annoyance. For what bridle and bit are to an unmanageable horse, the intellect is to the will in man; it must be led by this bridle by means of instruction, exhortation, training, and so on; for in itself the will is as wild and impetuous an impulse as is the force appearing in the plunging waterfall; in fact, it is, as we know, ultimately identical therewith. In the height of anger, in intoxication, in despair, the will has taken the bit between its teeth; it has bolted, and follows its original nature. In *mania sine delirio,* it has completely lost bridle and bit, and then shows most clearly its original and essential nature, and that the intellect is as different from it as the bridle is from the horse. In this state it can also be compared to a clock that runs down without a stop after a certain screw is removed.

This consideration, therefore, also shows us the will as something original and thus metaphysical, but the intellect as something secondary and physical. For as such the intellect, like everything physical, is subject to *vis inertiae,* and is therefore active only when it is put in motion by something else, by the will; and this will rules it, guides it, incites it to further effort, in short imparts to it the activity that is not originally inherent in it. Therefore it willingly rests as soon as it is allowed to do so, and often declares itself to be *indolent* and disinclined to activity. Through continued effort it becomes tired to the point of complete dulness; it is exhausted just as the voltaic pile is through repeated shocks. Therefore all continuous mental work requires pauses and rest, otherwise stupidity and incapacity are the result. Of course these are at first only temporary; but if this rest is constantly denied to the intellect, it becomes excessively and perpetually strained. The consequence is that it becomes permanently dull, and in old age this dulness can pass into complete incapacity, childishness, imbecility, and madness. It is not to be ascribed to old age in and by itself, but to long-continued tyrannical overstraining of the intellect or the brain, when these disorders appear in the last years of life. From this can be explained the fact that Swift became mad, Kant childish, Sir Walter Scott, and also Wordsworth, Southey, and many of less eminence, dull and incapable. Goethe to the end remained clear, and mentally vigorous and active, because he, who was always a man of the world and a courtier, never pursued his mental occupations with self-compulsion. The same holds good of Wieland and the ninety-one-year-old Knebel, as well as Voltaire. But all this proves how very secondary and physical the intellect is, what a mere tool it is. For this reason it needs, for almost a third of its life, the entire suspension of its activity in sleep, in resting the brain. The intellect is the mere function of the brain, which therefore precedes it just as the stomach precedes digestion, or as bodies precede their impact, and together with which it flags and becomes exhausted in old age. The *will,* on the contrary, as thing-in-itself, is never indolent, is absolutely untiring. Its activity is its essence; it never ceases to will, and when, during deep sleep, it is forsaken by the intellect, and is therefore unable to act outwardly from motives, it is active as vital force, looks after the inner economy of the organism with the less interruption, and, as *vis naturae medicatrix,* again sets in order the irregularities that had found their way into it. For it is not, like the intellect, a function of the body, but *the body is its function;* therefore *ordine rerum* it is prior to that body, as it is the metaphysical substratum of that body, the in-itself of that body's phenomenal appearance. For the duration of life it communicates its indefatigability to the *heart,* that *primum mobile* of the organism, which has therefore become its symbol and synonym. Moreover it does not disappear in old age, but still goes on willing what it has willed. It becomes, in fact, firmer and more inflexible than it was in youth, more irreconcilable, implacable, self-willed, and intractable, because the intellect has become less responsive and susceptible. Therefore we can perhaps get the better of a person in old age only by taking advantage of the weakness of his intellect.

B. Art as Experience

John Dewey

W e cannot answer these questions any more than we can trace the development of art out of everyday experience, unless we have a clear and coherent idea of what is meant when we say "normal experience." Fortunately, the road to arriving at such an idea is open and well marked. The nature of experience is determined by the essential conditions of life. While man is other than bird and beast, he shares basic vital functions with them and has to make the same basal adjustments if he is to continue the process of living. Having the same vital needs, man derives the means by which he breathes, moves, looks and listens, the very brain with which he coördinates his senses and his movements, from his animal forbears. The organs with which he maintains himself in being are not of himself alone, but by the grace of struggles and achievements of a long line of animal ancestry.

Fortunately a theory of the place of the esthetic in experience does not have to lose itself in minute details when it starts with experience in its elemental form. Broad outlines suffice. The first great consideration is that life goes on in an environment; not merely *in* it but because of it, through interaction with it. No creature lives merely under its skin; its subcutaneous organs are means of connection with what lies beyond its bodily frame, and to which, in order to live, it must adjust itself, by accommodation and defense but also by conquest. At every moment, the living creature is exposed to dangers from its surroundings, and at every moment, it must draw upon something in its surroundings to satisfy its needs. The career and destiny of a living being are bound up with its interchanges with its environment, not externally but in the most intimate way.

The growl of a dog crouching over his food, his howl in time of loss and loneliness, the wagging of his tail at the return of his human friend are expressions of the implication of a living in a natural medium which includes man along with the animal he has domesticated. Every need, say hunger for fresh air or food, is a lack that denotes at least a temporary absence of adequate adjustment with surroundings. But it is also a demand, a reaching out into the environment to make good the lack and to restore adjustment by building at least a temporary equilibrium. Life itself consists of phases in which the organism falls out of step with the march of surrounding things and then recovers unison with it—either through effort or by some happy chance. And, in a growing life, the recovery is never mere return to a prior state, for it is enriched by the state of disparity and resistance through which it has successfully passed. If the gap between organism and environment is too wide, the creature dies. If its activity is not enhanced by the temporary alienation, it merely subsists. Life grows when a temporary falling out is a transition to a more extensive balance of the energies of the organism with those of the conditions under which it lives.

These biological commonplaces are something more than that; they reach to the roots of the esthetic in experience. The world is full of things that are indifferent and even hostile to life; the very processes by which life is maintained tend to throw it out of gear with its surroundings. Nevertheless, if life continues and if in continuing it expands, there is an overcoming of factors of opposition and conflict; there is a transformation of them into differentiated aspects of a higher powered and more significant life. The marvel of organic, of vital, adaptation through expansion (instead of by contraction and passive accommodation) actually takes place. Here in germ are balance and harmony attained through rhythm. Equilibrium comes about not mechanically and inertly but out of, and because of, tension.

There is in nature, even below the level of life, something more than mere flux and change. Form is arrived at whenever a stable, even though moving, equilibrium is reached. Changes interlock and sustain one another. Wherever there is this coherence there is endurance. Order is not imposed from without but is made out of the relations of harmonious interactions that energies bear to one another. Because it is active (not anything static because foreign to what goes on) order itself develops. It comes to include within its balanced movement a greater variety of changes.

Order cannot but be admirable in a world constantly threatened with disorder—in a world where living creatures can go on living only by taking advantage of whatever order exists about them, incorporating it into themselves. In a world like ours, every living creature that attains sensibility welcomes order with a response of harmonious feeling whenever it finds a congruous order about it.

For only when an organism shares in the ordered relations of its environment does it secure the stability essential to living. And when the participation comes after a phase of disruption and conflict, it bears within itself the germs of a consummation akin to the esthetic.

The rhythm of loss of integration with environment and recovery of union not only persists in man but becomes conscious with him; its conditions are material out of which he forms purposes. Emotion is the conscious sign of a break, actual or impending. The discord is the occasion that induces reflection. Desire for restoration of the union converts mere emotion into interest in objects as conditions of realization of harmony. With the realization, material of reflection is incorporated into objects as their meaning. Since the artist cares in a peculiar way for the phase of experience in which union is achieved, he does not shun moments of resistance and tension. He rather cultivates them, not for their own sake but because of their potentialities, bringing to living consciousness an experience that is unified and total. In contrast with the person whose purpose is esthetic, the scientific man is interested in problems, in situations wherein tension between the matter of observation and of thought is marked. Of course he cares for their resolution. But he does not rest in it; he passes on to another problem using an attained solution only as a stepping stone from which to set on foot further inquiries.

The difference between the esthetic and the intellectual is thus one of the place where emphasis falls in the constant rhythm that marks the interaction of the live creature with his surroundings. The ultimate matter of both emphases in experience is the same, as is also their general form. The odd notion that an artist does not think and a scientific inquirer does nothing else is the result of converting a difference of tempo and emphasis into a difference in kind. The thinker has his esthetic moment when his ideas cease to be mere ideas and become the corporate meanings of objects. The artist has his problems and thinks as he works. But his thought is more immediately embodied in the object. Because of the comparative remoteness of his end, the scientific worker operates with symbols, words and mathematical signs. The artist does his thinking in the very qualitative media he works in, and the terms lie so close to the object that he is producing that they merge directly into it.

The live animal does not have to project emotions into the objects experienced. Nature is kind and hateful, bland and morose, irritating and comforting, long before she is mathematically qualified or even a congeries of "secondary" qualities like colors and their shapes. Even such words as long and short, solid and hollow, still carry to all, but those who are intellectually specialized, a moral and emotional connotation. The dictionary will inform any one who consults it that the early use of words like sweet and bitter was not to denote qualities of sense as such but to discriminate things as favorable and hostile. How could it be otherwise? Direct experience comes from nature and man interacting with each other. In this interaction, human energy gathers, is released, dammed up, frustrated and victorious. There are rhythmic beats of want and fulfillment, pulses of doing and being withheld from doing.

All interactions that effect stability and order in the whirling flux of change are rhythms. There is ebb and flow, systole and diastole: ordered change. The latter moves within bounds. To overpass the limits that are set is destruction and death, out of which, however, new rhythms are built up. The proportionate interception of changes establishes an order that is spatially, not merely temporally patterned: like the waves of the sea, the ripples of sand where waves have flowed back and forth, the fleecy and the black-bottomed cloud. Contrast of lack and fullness, of struggle and achievement, of adjustment after consummated irregularity, form the drama in which action, feeling, and meaning are one. The outcome is balance and counterbalance. These are not static nor mechanical. They express power that is intense because measured through overcoming resistance. Environing objects avail and counteravail.

There are two sorts of possible worlds in which esthetic experience would not occur. In a world of mere flux, change would not be cumulative; it would not move toward a close. Stability and rest would have no being. Equally is it true, however, that a world that is finished, ended, would have no traits of suspense and crisis, and would offer no opportunity for resolution. Where everything is already complete, there is no fulfillment. We envisage with pleasure Nirvana and a uniform heavenly bliss only because they are projected upon the background of our present world of stress and conflict. Because the actual world, that in which we live, is a combination of movement and culmination, of breaks and re-unions, the experience of a living creature is capable of esthetic quality. The live being recurrently loses and reëstablishes equilibrium with his surroundings. The moment of passage from disturbance into harmony is that of intensest life. In a finished world, sleep and waking could not be distinguished. In one wholly perturbed, conditions could not even be struggled with. In a world made after the pattern of ours, moments of fulfillment punctuate experience with rhythmically enjoyed intervals.

Inner harmony is attained only when, by some means, terms are made with the environment. When it occurs on any other than an "objective" basis, it is illusory—in extreme cases to the point of insanity. Fortunately for variety in experience, terms are made in many ways—ways ultimately decided by selective interest. Pleasures may come about through chance contact and stimulation; such pleasures are not to be despised in a world full of pain. But happiness and delight are a different sort of thing. They come to be through a fulfillment that reaches to the depths of our being—one that is an adjustment of our whole being with the conditions of existence. In the process of living, attainment of a period of equilibrium is at the same time the initiation of a new relation to the environment, one that brings with it potency of new adjustments to be made through struggle. The time of consummation is also one of beginning anew. Any attempt to perpetuate beyond its term the enjoyment attending the time of fulfillment and harmony constitutes withdrawal from the world. Hence it marks the lowering and loss of vitality. But, through the phases of perturbation and conflict, there abides the deep-seated memory of an underlying harmony, the sense of which haunts life like the sense of being founded on a rock.

Most mortals are conscious that a split often occurs between their present living and their past and future. Then the past hangs upon them as a burden; it invades the present with a sense of regret, of opportunities not used, and of consequences we wish undone. It rests upon the present as an oppression, instead of being a storehouse of resources by which to move confidently forward. But the live creature adopts its past; it can make friends with even its stupidities, using them as warnings that increase present wariness. Instead of trying to live upon whatever may have been achieved in the past, it uses past successes to inform the present. Every living experience owes its richness to what Santayana well calls "hushed reverberations."

To the being fully alive, the future is not ominous but a promise; it surrounds the present as a halo. It consists of possibilities that are felt as a possession of what is now and here. In life that is truly life, everything overlaps and merges. But all too often we exist in apprehensions of what the future may bring, and are divided within ourselves. Even when not overanxious, we do not enjoy the present because we subordinate it to that which is absent. Because of the frequency of this abandonment of the present to the past and future, the happy periods of an experience that is now complete because it absorbs into itself memories of the past and anticipations of the future, come to constitute an esthetic ideal. Only when the past ceases to trouble and anticipations of the future are not perturbing is a being wholly united with his environment and therefore fully alive. Art celebrates with peculiar intensity the moments in which the past reënforces the present and in which the future is a quickening of what now is.

To grasp the sources of esthetic experience it is, therefore, necessary to have recourse to animal life below the human scale. The activities of the fox, the dog, and the thrush may at least stand as reminders and symbols of that unity of experience which we so fractionize when work is labor, and thought withdraws us from the world. The live animal is fully present, all there, in all of its actions: in its wary glances, its sharp sniffings, its abrupt cocking of ears. All senses are equally on the *qui vive.* As you watch, you see motion merging into sense and sense into motion—constituting that animal grace so hard for man to rival. What the live creature retains from the past and what it expects from the future operate as directions in the present. The dog is never pedantic nor academic; for these things arise only when the past is severed in consciousness from the present and is set up as a model to copy or a storehouse upon which to draw. The past absorbed into the present carries on; it presses forward.

There is much in the life of the savage that is sodden. But, when the savage is most alive, he is most observant of the world about him and most taut with energy. As he watches what stirs about him, he, too, is stirred. His observation is both action in preparation and foresight of the future. He is as active through his whole being when he looks and listens as when he stalks his quarry or stealthily retreats from a foe. His senses are sentinels of immediate thought and outposts of action, and not, as they so often are with us, mere pathways along which material is gathered to be stored away for a delayed and remote possibility.

C. Being and Time

Martin Heidegger

In our preparatory discussions (Section 9) we have brought out some characteristics of Being which will provide us with a steady light for our further investigation, but which will at the same time become structurally concrete as that investigation continues. Dasein is an entity which, in its very Being, comports itself understandingly towards that Being. In saying this, we are calling attention to the formal concept of existence. Dasein exists. Furthermore, Dasein is an entity which in each case I myself am. Mineness belongs to any existent Dasein, and belongs to it as the condition which makes authenticity and inauthenticity possible. In each case Dasein exists in one or the other of these two modes, or else it is modally undifferentiated.

But these are both ways in which Dasein's Being takes on a definite character, and they must be seen and understood *a priori* as grounded upon that state of Being which we have called *"Being-in-the-world"*. An interpretation of this constitutive state is needed if we are to set up our analytic of Dasein correctly.

The compound expression 'Being-in-the-world' indicates in the very way we have coined it, that it stands for a *unitary* phenomenon. This primary datum must be seen as a whole. But while Being-in-the-world cannot be broken up into contents which may be pieced together, this does not prevent it from having several constitutive items in its structure. Indeed the phenomenal datum which our expression indicates is one which may, in fact, be looked at in three ways. If we study it, keeping the whole phenomenon firmly in mind beforehand, the following items may be brought out for emphasis:

First, the *'in-the-world'*. With regard to this there arises the task of inquiring into the ontological structure of the 'world' and defining the idea of *worldhood* as such. (See the third chapter of this Division.)

Second, that *entity* which in every case has Being-in-the-world as the way in which it is. Here we are seeking that which one inquires into when one asks the question 'Who?' By a phenomenological demonstration we shall determine who is in the mode of Dasein's average everydayness. (See the fourth chapter of this Division.)

Third, *Being-in [In-sein]* as such. We must set forth the ontological Constitution of inhood [Inheit] itself. (See the fifth chapter of this

Division.) Emphasis upon any one of these constitutive items signifies that the others are emphasized along with it; this means that in any such case the whole phenomenon gets seen. Of course Being-in-the-world is a state of Dasein which is necessary *a priori,* but it is far from sufficient for completely determining Dasein's Being. Before making these three phenomena the themes for special analyses, we shall attempt by way of orientation to characterize the third of these factors.

What is meant by *"Being-in"?* Our proximal reaction is to round out this expression to "Being-in 'in the world' ", and we are inclined to understand this Being-in as 'Being in something' ["Sein in . . . "]. This latter term designates the kind of Being which an entity has when it is 'in' another one, as the water is 'in' the glass, or the garment is 'in' the cupboard. By this 'in' we mean the relationship of Being which two entities extended 'in' space have to each other with regard to their location in that space. Both water and glass, garment and cupboard, are 'in' space and 'at' a location, and both in the same way. This relationship of Being can be expanded: for instance, the bench is in the lecture-room, the lecture-room is in the university, the university is in the city, and so on, until we can say that the bench is 'in world-space'. All entities whose Being 'in' one another can thus be described have the same kind of Being—that of Being-present-at-hand—as Things occurring 'within' the world. Being-present-at-hand 'in' something which is likewise present-at-hand, and Being-present-at-hand-along-with [Mitvorhandensein] in the sense of a definite location-relationship with something else which has the same kind of Being, are ontological characteristics which we call *"categorial":* they are of such a sort as to belong to entities whose kind of Being is not of the character of Dasein.

Being-in, on the other hand, is a state of Dasein's Being; it is an existentiale. So one cannot think of it as the Being-present-at-hand of some corporeal Thing (such as a human body) 'in' an entity which is present-at-hand. Nor does the term "Being-in" mean a spatial 'in-one-another-ness' of things present-at-hand, any more than the word 'in' primordially signifies a spatial relationship of this kind. 'In' is derived from *"innan"*—"to reside", *"habitare"*, "to dwell" [sich auf halten]. *'An'* signifies "I am accustomed", "I am familiar with", "I look after something". It has the signification of *"colo"* in the senses of *"habito"* and *"diligo".* The entity to which Being-in in this signification belongs is one which we have characterized as that entity which in each case I myself am [bin]. The expression *'bin'* is connected with *'bei',* and so *'ich bin'* ['I am'] means in its turn "I reside" or "dwell alongside" the world, as that which is familiar to me in such and such a way. "Being" [Sein], as the infinitive of *'ich bin'* (that is to say, when it is understood as an *existentiale*), signifies "to reside alongside . . . ", "to be familiar with . . . ". *"Being-in" is thus the formal existential expression for the Being of Dasein, which has Being-in-the-world as its essential state.*

'Being alongside' the world in the sense of being absorbed in the world (a sense which calls for still closer interpretation) is an *existentiale* founded upon Being-in. In these analyses the issue is one of *seeing* a primordial structure of Dasein's Being—a structure in accordance with whose phenomenal content the concepts of Being must be Articulated; because of this, and because this structure is in principle one which cannot be grasped by the traditional ontological categories, this 'Being-alongside' must be examined still more closely. We shall again choose the method of contrasting it with a relationship of Being which is essentially different ontologically—*viz.* categorial—but which we express by the same linguistic means. Fundamental ontological distinctions are easily obliterated; and if they are to be envisaged phenomenally in this way, this must be done *explicitly,* even at the risk of discussing the 'obvious'. The status of the ontological analytic shows, however, that we have been far from interpreting these obvious matters with an adequate 'grasp', still less with regard for the meaning of their Being; and we are even farther from possessing a stable coinage for the appropriate structural concepts.

As an *existentiale,* 'Being alongside' the world never means anything like the Being-present-at-hand-together of Things that occur. There is no such thing as the 'side-by-side-ness' of an entity called 'Dasein' with another entity called 'world'. Of course when two things are present-at-hand together alongside one another, we are accustomed to express this occasionally by something like 'The table stands "by" ['bei'] the door' or 'The chair "touches" ['berührt'] the wall'. Taken strictly, 'touching' is never what we are talking about in such cases, not because accurate reexamination will always eventually establish that there is a space between the chair and the wall, but because in principle the chair can never touch the wall, even if the space between them should be equal to zero. If the chair could touch the wall, this would presuppose that the wall is the sort of thing 'for' which a chair would be *encounterable.* An entity present-at-hand within the world can be touched by another entity only if by its very nature the latter entity has Being-in as its own kind of Being—only if, with its Being-there [Dasein], something like the world is already revealed to it, so that from out of that world another entity can manifest itself in touching, and thus become accessible in its Being-present-at-hand. When two entities are present-at-hand within the world, and furthermore are *worldless* in themselves, they can never 'touch' each other, nor can either of them 'be' 'alongside' the other. The clause 'furthermore are worldless' must not be left out; for even entities which are not worldless—Dasein itself, for example—are present-at-hand 'in' the world, or, more exactly *can* with some right and within certain limits be *taken* as merely present-at-hand. To do this, one must completely disregard or just not see the existential state of Being-in. But the fact that 'Dasein' can be taken as something which is present-at-hand and just present-at-hand, is not to be confused with a certain way of 'presence-at-hand' which is Dasein's *own*. This latter kind of presence-at-hand becomes accessible not by disregarding Dasein's specific structures but only by understanding them in advance. Dasein understands its ownmost Being in the sense of a certain 'factual Being-present-at-hand'. And yet the 'factuality' of the fact [Tatsache] of one's own Dasein is at bottom quite different ontologically from the factual occurrence of some kind of mineral, for example. Whenever Dasein is, it is as a Fact; and the factuality of such a Fact is what we shall call Dasein's *"facticity"*. This is a definite way of Being [Seinsbestimmtheit], and it has a complicated structure which cannot even be grasped *as a problem* until Dasein's basic existential states have been worked out. The concept of "facticity" implies that an entity 'within-the-world' has Being-in-the-world in such a way that it can understand itself as bound up in its 'destiny' with the Being of those entities which it encounters within its own world.

In the first instance it is enough to see the ontological difference between Being-in as an *existentiale* and the category of the 'insideness' which things present-at-hand can have with regard to one another. By thus delimiting Being-in, we are not denying every kind of 'spatiality' to Dasein. On the contrary, Dasein itself has a 'Being-in-space' of its own; but this in turn is possible only *on the basis of Being-in-the-world in general.* Hence Being-in is not to be explained ontologically by some ontical characterization, as if one were to say, for instance, that Being-in in a world is a spiritual property, and that man's 'spatiality' is a result of his bodily nature (which, at the same time, always gets 'founded' upon corporeality). Here again we are faced with the Being-present-at-hand-together of some such spiritual Thing along with a corporeal Thing, while the Being of the entity thus compounded remains more obscure than ever. Not until we understand Being-in-the-world as an essential structure of Dasein can we have any insight into Dasein's *existential spatiality.* Such an insight will keep us from failing to see this structure or from previously cancelling it out—a procedure motivated not ontologically but rather 'metaphysically' by the naïve supposition that man is, in the first instance, a spiritual Thing which subsequently gets misplaced 'into' a space.

Dasein's facticity is such that its Being-in-the-world has always dispersed [zerstreut] itself or even split itself up into definite ways of Being-in. The multiplicity of these is indicated by the following examples: having to do with something, producing something, attending to something and looking after it, making use of something, giving something up and letting it go, undertaking, accomplishing, evincing, interrogating, considering, discussing, determining. . . . All these ways of Being-in have *concern* as their kind of Being—a kind of Being which we have yet to characterize in detail. Leaving undone, neglecting, renouncing, taking a rest—these too are ways of concern; but these are all *deficient* modes, in which the possibilities of concern are kept to a 'bare minimum'. The term 'concern' has, in the first instance, its colloquial [vorwissenschaftliche] signification, and can mean to carry out something, to get it done [erledigen], to 'straighten it out'. It can also mean to 'provide oneself with something'. We use the expression with still another characteristic turn of phrase when we say "I am concerned for the success of the undertaking." Here 'concern' means something like apprehensiveness. In contrast to these colloquial ontical significations, the expression 'concern' will be used in this investigation as an ontological term for an *existentiale,* and will designate the Being of a possible way of Being-in-the-world. This term has been chosen not because Dasein happens to be proximally and to a large extent 'practical' and economic, but because the Being of Dasein itself is to be made visible as *care.* This expression too is to be taken as an ontological structural concept. (See Chapter 6 of this Division.) It has nothing to do with 'tribulation', 'melancholy', or the 'cares of life', though ontically one can come across these in every Dasein. These—like their opposites, 'gaiety' and 'freedom from care'—are ontically possible only because Dasein, when understood *ontologically,* is care. Because Being-in-the-world belongs essentially to Dasein, its Being towards the world [Sein zur Welt] is essentially concern.

From what we have been saying, it follows that Being-in is not a 'property' which Dasein sometimes has and sometimes does not have, and *without* which it could *be* just as well as it could with it. It is not the case that man 'is' and then has, by way of an extra, a relationship-of-Being towards the 'world'—a world with which he provides himself occasionally. Dasein is never 'proximally' an entity which is, so to speak, free from Being-in, but which sometimes has the inclination to take up a 'relationship' towards the world. Taking up relationships towards the world is possible only *because* Dasein, as Being-in-the-world, is as it is. This state of Being does not arise just because some other entity is present-at-hand outside of Dasein and meets up with it.

Such an entity can 'meet up with' Dasein only in so far as it can, of its own accord, show itself with a *world.*

Nowadays there is much talk about 'man's having an environment [Umwelt]'; but this says nothing ontologically as long as this 'having' is left indefinite. In its very possibility this 'having' is founded upon the existential state of Being-in. Because Dasein is essentially an entity with Being-in, it can explicitly discover those entities which it encounters environmentally, it can know them, it can avail itself of them, it can *have* the 'world'. To talk about 'having an environment' is ontically trivial, but ontologically it presents a problem. To solve it requires nothing else than defining the Being of Dasein, and doing so in a way which is ontologically adequate. Although this state of Being is one of which use was made in biology, especially since K. von Baer, one must not conclude that its philosophical use implies 'biologism'. For the environment is a structure which even biology as a positive science can never find and can never define, but must presuppose and constantly employ. Yet, even as an *a priori* condition for the objects which biology takes for its theme, this structure itself can be explained philosophically only if it has been conceived beforehand as a structure of Dasein. Only in terms of an orientation towards the ontological structure thus conceived can 'life' as a state of Being be defined *a priori,* and this must be done in a private manner. Ontically as well as ontologically, the priority belongs to Being-in-the world as concern. In the analytic of Dasein this structure undergoes a basic Interpretation.

But have we not confined ourselves to negative assertions in all our attempts to determine the nature of this state of Being? Though this Being-in is supposedly so fundamental, we always keep hearing about what it is *not.* Yes indeed. But there is nothing accidental about our characterizing it predominantly in so negative a manner. In doing so we have rather made known what is peculiar to this phenomenon, and our characterization is therefore positive in a genuine sense—a sense appropriate to the phenomenon itself. When Being-in-the-world is exhibited phenomenologically, disguises and concealments are rejected *because* this phenomenon itself always gets 'seen' in a certain way in every Dasein. And it thus gets 'seen' *because* it makes up a basic state of Dasein, and in every case is already disclosed for Dasein's understanding of Being, and disclosed along with that Being itself. But for the most part this phenomenon has been explained in a way which is basically wrong, or interpreted in an ontologically inadequate manner. On the other hand, this 'seeing in a certain way and yet for the most part wrongly explaining' is itself based upon nothing else than this very state of Dasein's Being, which is such that Dasein itself—and this means also its Being-in-the world—gets its ontological understanding of itself in the first instance from those entities which it itself is *not* but which it encounters 'within' its world, and from the Being which they possess.

Both in Dasein and for it, this state of Being is always in some way familiar [bekannt]. Now if it is also to become known [erkannt], the *knowing* which such a task explicitly implies takes *itself* (as a knowing of the world [Welterkennen]) as the chief exemplification of the 'soul's' relationship to the world. Knowing the world *(νοεῖν)*—or rather addressing oneself to the 'world' and discussing it *(λόγος)*—thus functions as the primary mode of Being-in-the-world, even though Being-in-the-world does not as such get conceived. But because this structure of Being remains ontologically inaccessible, yet is experienced ontically as a 'relationship' between one entity (the world) and another (the soul), and because one proximally understands Being by taking entities as entities within-the-world for one's ontological foothold, one tries to conceive the relationship between world and soul as grounded in these two entities themselves and in the meaning of their Being—namely, to conceive it as Being-present-at-hand. And even though Being-in-the-world is something of which one has pre-phenomenological experience and acquaintance [erfahren und gekannt], it becomes *invisible* if one interprets it in a way which is ontologically inappropriate. This state of Dasein's Being is now one with which one is just barely acquainted (and indeed as something obvious), with the stamp of an inappropriate interpretation. So in this way it becomes the 'evident' point of departure for problems of epistemology or the 'metaphysics of knowledge'. For what is more obvious than that a 'subject' is related to an 'Object' and *vice versa?* This 'subject-Object-relationship' must be presupposed. But while this presupposition is unimpeachable in its facticity, this makes it indeed a baleful one, if its ontological necessity and especially its ontological meaning are to be left in the dark.

Thus the phenomenon of Being-in has for the most part been represented exclusively by a single exemplar—knowing the world. This has not only been the case in epistemology; for even practical behaviour has been understood as behaviour which is '*non*-theoretical' and 'atheoretical'. Because knowing has been given this priority, our understanding of its ownmost kind of Being gets led astray, and accordingly Being-in-the-world must be exhibited even more precisely with regard to knowing the world, and must itself be made visible as an existential 'modality' of Being-in.

D. The Future of Man

Pierre Teilhard de Chardin

THE PLACE OF MAN IN THE FOREFRONT OF LIFE

In what I have said thus far I have been looking at Life in general, in its entirety. We come now to the particular case which interests us most—the problem of Man.

The existence of an ascendant movement in the Universe has been revealed to us by the study of palaeontology. Where is Man to be situated in this line of progress?

The answer is clear. If, as I maintain, the movement of the cosmos towards the highest degree of consciousness is not an optical illusion, but represents the essence of biological evolution, then, in the curve traced by Life, Man is unquestionably situated at the topmost point; and it is he, by his emergence and existence, who finally proves the reality and defines the direction of the trajectory—'the dot on the i'. . . .

Indeed, within the field accessible to our experience, does not the birth of Thought stand out as a critical point through which all the striving of previous ages passes and is consummated—the critical point traversed by consciousness, when, by force of concentration, it ends by reflecting upon itself?

Prior to Galileo science thought of Man as the mathematical and moral centre of a World composed of spheres turning statically upon themselves. But in terms of our modern neo-anthropocentricity, Man, both diminished and enlarged, becomes the *head* (terrestrial) of a Universe that is in the process of psychic transformation—Man, the last-formed, most complex and most conscious of 'molecules'. From which it follows that, borne on the tide of millions of years of psychogenesis, we have the right to consider ourselves the fruit of a progression—the children of progress.

The world did at least progress to the point where the first-born of our race appeared. Here we have a fixed and solid point on which to base our philosophy of life.

Let us now take a further step.

We may agree that zoological evolution culminated in Man. But having reached this peak did it come to a stop? Life continued to move until Thought entered the world, this we may admit. But has it advanced since then? Can it make any further progress?

THE MOVEMENT OF MANKIND UPON ITSELF

Ancient though prehistory may make it seem to our eyes, Mankind is still very young. We can trace its existence for not much more than a hundred thousand years, a period so short that it has left no mark on the majority of the animal forms that preceded us on the earth and which still surround us. It may seem impossible, and it is certainly a very delicate matter, to measure any movement of Life in so slender a fragment of the past. Nevertheless, owing to the exceptionally rapid development which is a characteristic of the human wave, a direct assessment of the advance of our own group in terms of a consciousness is possible to the practised eye, even within this limited tract of time.

a It seems in the first place that, anatomically, a gradual evolution of the brain can be discerned during the earliest phases of our phylogenesis. Pithecanthropus and Sinanthropus possessed intelligence, but there are solid grounds for supposing that they were not cerebrally as well developed as ourselves.

b We may accept that the human brain reached the limit of its development at the stage which anthropologists call *Homo sapiens;* or at least, if it has continued to develop since then, that the change cannot be detected by our present methods of observation. But although, since the Age of the Reindeer (that is to say, within a period of twenty or thirty thousand years) no progress is perceptible in either the physical or the mental faculties of Individual Man, the fact of organo-psychic development seems to be clearly manifest in Collective Man: and this, whatever we may think of it, represents as true an advance as the acquisition of an added convolution by the brain.

Let me here repeat the two fundamental equations or equivalents which we have established:

Progress = growth of consciousness.
Growth of Consciousness = effect of organisation.

Taken together these mean that, in order to discover or verify the existence of biological progress within a given system, we have only to observe, for the period of time and the field we are considering, how far the state of organisation varies within that system.

This being posited we may compare the world of the cave-dweller with the world of today. Setting all theory aside there can be no question but that, within this period of 30,000 years, Mankind has advanced almost unbelievably in its state of concentration.

Economic concentration, manifest in the unification of the earth's energies.

Intellectual concentration, manifest in the unification of our knowledge in a coherent system (science).

Social concentration, manifest in the unification of the human mass as a thinking whole.

To those who have not studied its implications, this slow and irresistible flow of our history in the direction of more and more unified groupings has no particular meaning; they relegate it to the trivial category of surface and incidental phenomena, no more. But to the enlightened eye this human development, succeeding all the twists and turns of pre-human consciousness, assumes a dazzling significance. *For the two curves are a prolongation one of the other.* Tremendous events such as those through which we are now passing are seen to take shape, and with a brilliant clarity. This tremendous war which so afflicts us, this remoulding, this universal longing for a new order, what are they but the shock, the tremor and the crisis, beyond which we may glimpse a more synthetic organisation of the human world? And this new order, the thought of which is in all our minds, what form can it take other than a higher degree of self-awareness on the part of a Mankind become at once more complex and more centred upon itself?

No, truly: Life in emerging into Thought did not come to a stop. Not only has it moved and progressed from the protozoa to Man, but since the coming of Man it has continued to advance along its most essential path. We can feel it at this moment quivering beneath our feet! The ship that bears us is still making headway.

And it is here that the ultimate and decisive question arises, finally the only question that interests us. Thus far Life, and Man himself, has progressed. So be it. But what of the future? We are still moving, but can we continue much longer to advance?

Have we not reached a dead-end? Can we talk seriously of a future for Mankind?

THE FUTURE OF MANKIND

I make no claim to be a prophet. Moreover I know, as a scientist, how dangerous it is to extend a curve beyond the facts, that is to say, to extrapolate. Nevertheless I believe that, basing the argument upon our general knowledge of the world's history over a period of 300 million years, we can advance the following two propositions without losing ourselves in a fog of speculation:

a Firstly, Mankind still shows itself to possess a *reserve,* a formidable potential of concentration, i.e. of progress. We have only to think of the immensity of the forces, ideas and human beings that have still to be born or discovered or applied or synthesized. ... 'Energetically' as well as biologically the human group is still young, still fresh. If we are to judge by what history teaches us about other living groups, it still has, organically speaking, some millions of years in which to live and develop.

b Everything leads us to believe that it really does dispose of this vast reservoir of time, which is necessary for the normal achievement of its evolution. The earth is far from having completed its sidereal evolution. We may envisage all kinds of mischance (disaster or disease) which might in theory put an end to our evolutionary progress: but the fact remains that for 300 million years Life has paradoxically flourished in the Improbable. Does not this suggest that its advance may be sustained by *some sort of complicity on the part of the 'blind' forces of the Universe*—that is to say, that it is inexorable?

The more we ponder these matters the more must we realise that, scientifically speaking, the real difficulty presented by Man is not the problem of whether he is a centre of constant progress: it is far more the question of how long this progress can continue, at the speed at which it is going, without Life blowing up upon itself or causing the earth on which it was born to explode. Our modern world was created in less than 10,000 years, and in the past 200 years it has changed more than in all the preceding millennia. Have we ever thought of what our planet may be like, psychologically, in a million years' time? It is finally the Utopians, not the 'realists', who make scientific sense. They at least, though their flights of fancy may cause us to smile, have a feeling for the true dimensions of the phenomenon of Man.

THE ADVANCE

Having clarified our ideas, let us see what action they require of us. If progress is to continue, it will not do so of its own accord. *Evolution, by the very mechanism of its syntheses, charges itself with an every-growing measure of freedom.*

If indeed an almost limitless field of action lies open to us in the future, what shall our moral dispositions be, as we contemplate this march ahead?

I can think of two, which may be summarised in six words: *a great hope held in common.*

a First, the hope. This must spring to life spontaneously in every generous spirit faced by the task that awaits us; and it is also the essential *impulse,* without which nothing can be done. A passionate longing to grow, to be, is what we need. There can be no place for the poor in spirit, the sceptics, the pessimists, the sad of heart, the weary and the immobilists. Life is ceaseless discovery. Life is movement.

b A hope held in common. Here again the history of Life is decisive. Not all directions are good for our advance: one alone leads upward, that which through increasing organisation leads to greater synthesis and unity. Here we part company with the whole-hearted individualists, the egoists who seek to grow by excluding or diminishing their fellows, individually, nationally or racially. Life moves towards unification. Our hope can only be realised if it finds its expression in greater cohesion and greater human solidarity.

This double point is finally established by the verdict of the Past.

THE CROSSROADS

But here there is a grave uncertainty to be resolved. The future, I have said, depends on the courage and resourcefulness which men display in overcoming the forces of isolationism, even of repulsion, which seem to drive them apart rather than draw them together. How is the drawing together to be accomplished? How shall we so contrive matters that the human mass merges in a single whole, instead of ceaselessly scattering in dust?

A priori, there seem to be two methods, two possible roads.

a The first is a process of tightening-up in response to external pressures. We are in any case inescapably subject to this through the negative action of terrestrial causes. The human mass, because on the confined surface of this planet it is in a state of continuous additive growth, in numbers and inter-connections, must automatically become more and more tightly concentrated upon itself. To this formidable process of natural compression there may well be added the artificial constraint imposed by a stronger human group upon a weaker; we have only to look about us at the present time to see how this idea is seeking, indeed rushing towards, its realisation.

b But there is another way. This is that, *prompted by some favouring influence,* the elements of Mankind should succeed in making effective a profound force of mutual attraction, deeper and more powerful than the surface-repulsion which causes them to diverge. Forced upon one another by the dimensions and mechanics of the earth, men will purposefully bring to life a common soul in this vast body.

Unification by external or by internal force? Compulsion or Unanimity?

I spoke earlier of the present war. Does it not precisely express the tension and interior dislocation of Mankind shaken to its roots as it stands at the crossroads, faced by the need to decide upon its future?

THE CHOICE

Gloriously situated by life at this critical point in the evolution of Mankind, what ought we to do? We hold Earth's future in our hands. What shall we decide?

In my view the road to be followed is clearly revealed by the teaching of all the past.

We can progress only by uniting: this, as we have seen, is the law of Life. But unification through coercion leads only to a superficial pseudo-unity. It may establish a mechanism, but it does not achieve any fundamental synthesis; and in consequence it engenders no growth of consciousness. It materialises, in short, instead of spiritualising. Only unification through unanimity is biologically valid. This alone can work the miracle of causing heightened personality to emerge from the forces of collectivity. It alone represents a genuine extension of the psychogenesis that gave us birth.

Therefore it is inwardly that we must come together, and in entire freedom.

But this brings us to the last question of all. To create this unanimity we need the bond, as I said, the cement of a favouring influence. Where shall we look for it; how shall we conceive of this principle of togetherness, this soul of the Earth?

Is it to be in the development of a common *vision,* that is to say, the establishment of a universally accepted body of knowledge, in which all intelligences will join in knowing the same facts interpreted in the same way?

Or will it rather be in common *action,* in the determination of an Objective universally recognised as being so desirable that all activity will naturally converge towards it under the impulse of a common fear and a common ambition?

These two kinds of unanimity are undoubtedly real, and will, I believe, have their place in our future progress. But they need to be complemented by something else if they are not to remain precarious, insufficient and incomplete. A common body of knowledge brings together nothing but the geometrical point of intelligences. A common aspiration, no matter how ardent, can only touch individuals indirectly and in an impersonal way that is depersonalising in itself.

It is not a *tête-à-tête* or a *corps-à-corps* that we need; it is a heart-to-heart.

This being so, the more I consider the fundamental question of the future of the earth, the more it appears to me that the generative principle of its unification is finally to be sought, not in the sole contemplation of a single Truth or in the sole desire for a single Thing, but in the common attraction exercised by a single *Being.* For on the one hand, if the synthesis of the Spirit is to be brought about in its entirety (and this is the only possible definition of progress) it can only be done, in the last resort, through the meeting, *centre to centre,* of human units, such as can only be realised in a universal, mutual love. And on the other hand there is but one possible way in which human elements, innumerably diverse by nature, can love one another: it is by knowing themselves all to be centred upon a single 'supercentre' common to all, to which they can only attain, each at the extreme of himself, through their unity.

'Love one another, recognising in the heart of each of you the same God who is being born.' Those words, first spoken two thousand years ago, now begin to reveal themselves as the essential structural law of what we call progress and evolution. They enter the scientific field of cosmic energy and its necessary laws.

VII

THE INTERPERSONAL SELF

A. The Symposium

Plato

Eryximachus then spoke as follows: 'Pausanias, after an admirable beginning, has not brought his argument to an adequate conclusion; I think therefore that it is incumbent on me to try to put the finishing touches to it. He was quite right, in my opinion, in the distinction which he drew between the two kinds of love, but my professional experience as a doctor has shown me that love does not operate only in men's souls and has not only beautiful boys as its object, but that it has many other objects and other spheres of action, the bodies of all animals, for example, and plants which grow in the earth, and practically all existing things; in fact Love is a great and wonderful god whose influence extends everywhere, and embraces the worlds of gods and men alike.

'I will begin with medicine, to show my respect for the craft. Our physical constitution involves a double love; a healthy body is admittedly different from a diseased body and unlike it. Now the objects of the desire and love felt by unlike things are themselves unlike; so the love which exists in a healthy body is different from the love which exists in a diseased body. The fact is that in dealing with men's bodies we find an analogy with what Pausanias said a moment ago; just as honour and dishonour consist in yielding to the desires of virtuous and vicious men respectively, so it is the duty of a good practitioner to gratify the sound and healthy parts of the body and to thwart the unsound and diseased, and this is the business of what we call medicine, which is, in a word, the knowledge of the principles of love at work in the body in regard to repletion and evacuation. The most skilful doctor is the doctor who can distinguish between noble and base loves in this sphere, and the man who can cause a body to change the latter for the former, and can implant love in a body which lacks but needs it, and remove it where it already exists, will be a good practitioner. He must be able to bring elements in the body which are most hostile to one another into mutual affection and love; such hostile elements are the opposites hot and cold, wet and dry, and the like; it was by knowing how to create love and harmony between these that our forefather Asclepius, as our poets here say and as I believe, founded our craft.

'Medicine then, I repeat, is entirely under the control of this god; and so are the arts of physical culture and of farming. That the same is true of music is plain to anyone who gives the smallest attention to the subject, and this is presumably what Heraclitus means to say, though he is not very happy in his choice of words, when he speaks of a unity which agrees with itself by being at variance, as in the stringing of a bow or a lyre. It is, of course, quite illogical to speak of a concord being in discord, or of its consisting of factors which are still in discord at the time when they compose it, but probably what he meant to say was that the art of music produces a harmony out of factors which are first in discord but subsequently in concord, namely treble and bass notes. There can be no accord of treble and bass as long as they are in discord, for concord is consonance, and consonance is a kind of agreement, and it is impossible for there to be agreement between discordant elements as long as they are in discord; but it is possible to harmonize what is in discord and disagreement, just as rhythm results from the combination of fast and slow, factors which are originally discordant but consequently in agreement. Music, by implanting mutual love and sympathy, causes agreement between these elements, just as medicine does in its different sphere, and music in its turn may be called a knowledge of the principles of love in the realm of harmony and rhythm. In the actual constitution of a harmony there is no difficulty in perceiving the principle of love at work, and the question of the double nature of love does not so far arise; but when one has to deal with the effect upon human beings of rhythm and harmony, either in their creation by the process known as composition, or in the right use of melodies and verse-forms in what is called education, difficulties occur which demand a skilful artist. We come back to our old notion that it is the love felt by virtuous men which should be gratified and preserved, with the object of making those more virtuous who are as yet less so. This is the noble, the heavenly love, which is associated with the heavenly muse, Urania. But there is also a vulgar or common love, associated with Polyhymnia, and anyone who employs this must exercise great caution in his choice of people upon whom to employ it, so as to cull the pleasure which it affords without implanting any taint of debauchery. Similarly in my profession it is a matter of no little skill to make the right use of men's appetite for rich food, so that they may enjoy the pleasure it brings without incurring disease. Both kinds of love then must be the object of our vigilant care, in music and in medicine and in all other matters, both human and divine, for both are to be found in them all.

'Moreover, the seasons of the year are so ordained as to exhibit the operation of both kinds of love. When the elements of which I spoke before, hot and cold and dry and wet, are bound together in love which is orderly, and combined harmoniously in due proportions, man and the other animals and plants thrive and are healthy and take no harm. But when inordinate love gets the upper hand in the matter of the seasons, it causes widespread destruction and injury; from this, epidemics and many other various ailments are apt to spring; frost, hail, and blight are the result of the mutual disorderly aggression of these elements under the influence of love. The effects of that influence upon the courses of the stars and the seasons of the year are the object of the department of knowledge which is called astronomy.

'Again, all sacrifices and acts which fall within the province of divination (and these comprise the whole subject of the mutual relations of gods and men) are entirely directed to the preservation or the cure of love. Sin of all kinds is the result of gratifying and honouring and exalting in one's every action the vicious instead of the virtuous love, whether the persons affected by such behaviour be one's parents, either living or dead, or the gods. In these matters it is the function of divination to oversee the two kinds of love, and to effect a cure where it is needed; divination is the craft which establishes good-will between gods and men, because it understands the principles of love which, in human life, issue in virtuous and god-fearing behaviour.

'So then love in general exercises a multifarious and great, or, to speak more accurately, an omnipotent sway, but it is the love whose object is good and whose fulfilment is attended by sobriety and virtue, whether in heaven or earth, that possesses the greater power, and is the author of all our happiness, and makes it possible for us to live in harmony and concord with our fellow-creatures and with the gods, our masters. It may be that in my panegyric of love I have omitted several points, but, if so, it has been unwittingly. If I *have* left anything out, it is for you, Aristophanes, to fill the gaps, unless you plan to take some other line in praising the god. Now is your time to speak, since your hiccup has stopped.'

So it came to Aristophanes' turn, who began, according to Aristodemus, as follows:

'Yes, it stopped, but not till I applied the sneezing treatment. I can't help wondering whether it is the virtuous love in my body which desires such noises and tickling sensations as a sneeze. At any rate, the hiccup stopped at once as soon as I applied your method.'

'My dear Aristophanes,' said Eryximachus, 'take care what you're about. If you preface what you have to say by making us laugh, you will force me to be on the watch for jokes in your speech, which might otherwise run its course in peace.'

'Quite right, Eryximachus,' replied Aristophanes, laughing. 'I take back what I said. As for what I am going to say, don't watch me too strictly, for my fear is, not that it may raise a smile—that would be all to the good and quite in accordance with the nature of my muse—but that it may be downright absurd.'

'Ah, you think that you can have your joke and escape the consequences, Aristophanes. But take care, and remember in making your speech that you will be called to account, and then perhaps, if I see fit, I may let you off.'

'Well, Eryximachus,' began Aristophanes, 'it is quite true that I intend to take a different line from you and Pausanias. Men seem to me to be utterly insensible of the power of Love; otherwise he would have had the largest temples and altars and the largest sacrifices. As it is, he has none of these things, though he deserves them most of all. For of all the gods he is the most friendly to man, and his helper and physician in those diseases whose cure constitutes the greatest happiness of the human race. I shall therefore try to initiate you into the secret of his power, and you in turn shall teach others.

'First of all, you must learn the constitution of man and the modifications which it has undergone, for originally it was different from what it is now. In the first place there were three sexes, not, as with us, two, male and female; the third partook of the nature of both the others and has vanished, though its name survives. The hermaphrodite was a distinct sex in form as well as in name, with the characteristics of both male and female, but now the name alone remains, and that solely as a term of abuse. Secondly, each human being was a whole, with its back and flanks rounded to form a circle; it had four hands and an equal number of legs, and two identically similar faces upon a circular neck, with one head common to both the faces, which were turned in opposite directions. It had four ears and two organs of generation and everything else to correspond. These people could walk upright like us in either direction, backwards or forwards, but when they wanted to run quickly they used all their eight limbs, and turned rapidly over and over in a circle, like tumblers who perform a cartwheel and return to an upright position. The reason for the existence of three sexes and for their being of such a nature is that originally the male sprang from the sun and the female from the earth, while the sex which was both male and female came from the moon, which partakes of the nature of both sun and earth. Their spherical shape and their hoop-like method of progression were both due to the fact that they were like their parents. Their strength and vigour made them very formidable, and their pride was overweening; they attacked the gods, and Homer's story of Ephialtes and Otus attempting to climb up to heaven and set upon the gods is related also to these beings.

'So Zeus and the other gods debated what was to be done with them. For a long time they were at a loss, unable to bring themselves either to kill them by lightning, as they had the giants, and extinguish the race—thus depriving themselves for ever of the honours and sacrifices due from humanity—or to let them go on in their insolence. At last, after much painful thought, Zeus had an idea. "I think," he said, "that I have found a way by which we can allow the human race to continue to exist and also put an end to their wickedness by making them weaker. I will cut each of them in two; in this way they will be weaker, and at the same time more profitable to us by being more numerous. They shall walk upright upon two legs. If there is any sign of wantonness in them after that, and they will not keep quiet, I will bisect them again, and they shall hop on one leg." With these words he cut the members of the human race in half, just like fruit which is to be dried and preserved, or like eggs which are cut with a hair. As he bisected each, he bade Apollo turn round the face and the half-neck attached to it towards the cut side, so that the victim, having the evidence of bisection before his eyes, might behave better in future. He also bade him heal the wounds. So Apollo turned round the faces, and gathering together the skin, like a purse with drawstrings, on to what is now called the belly, he tied it tightly in the middle of the belly round a single aperture which men call the navel. He smoothed out the other wrinkles, which were numerous, and moulded the chest with a tool like those which cobblers use to smooth wrinkles in the leather on their last. But he left a few on the belly itself round the navel, to remind man of the state from which he had fallen.

'Man's original body having been thus cut in two, each half yearned for the half from which it had been severed. When they met they threw their arms round one another and embraced, in their longing to grow together again, and they perished of hunger and general neglect of their concerns, because they would not do anything apart. When one member of a pair died and the other was left, the latter sought after and embraced another partner, which might be the half either of a female whole (what is now called a woman) or a male. So they went on perishing till Zeus took pity on them, and hit upon a second plan. He moved their reproductive organs to the front: hitherto they had been placed on the outer side of their bodies, and the processes of begetting and birth had been carried on not by the physical

union of the sexes, but by emission on to the ground, as is the case
with grasshoppers. By moving their genitals to the front, as they are
now, Zeus made it possible for reproduction to take place by the intercourse of the male with the female. His object in making this change
was twofold; if male coupled with female, children might be begotten
and the race thus continued, but if male coupled with male, at any rate
the desire for intercourse would be satisfied, and men set free from it
to turn to other activities and to attend to the rest of the business of
life. It is from this distant epoch, then, that we may date the innate
love which human beings feel for one another, the love which restores
us to our ancient state by attempting to weld two beings into one and
to heal the wounds which humanity suffered.

'Each of us then is the mere broken tally of a man, the result of a
bisection which has reduced us to a condition like that of flat fish, and
each of us is perpetually in search of his corresponding tally. Those
men who are halves of a being of the common sex, which was called,
as I told you, hermaphrodite, are lovers of women, and most adulter-
ers come from this class, as also do women who are mad about men
and sexually promiscuous. Women who are halves of a female whole
direct their affections towards women and pay little attention to men;
Lesbians belong to this category. But those who are halves of a male
whole pursue males, and being slices, so to speak, of the male, love
men throughout their boyhood, and take pleasure in physical contact
with men. Such boys and lads are the best of their generation, because
they are the most manly. Some people say that they are shameless, but
they are wrong. It is not shamelessness which inspires their behaviour,
but high spirit and manliness and virility, which lead them to welcome
the society of their own kind. A striking proof of this is that such boys
alone, when they reach maturity, engage in public life. When they grow
to be men, they become lovers of boys, and it requires the compulsion
of convention to overcome their natural disinclination to marriage
and procreation; they are quite content to live with one another
unwed. In a word, such persons are devoted to lovers in boyhood and
themselves lovers of boys in manhood, because they always cleave to
what is akin to themselves.

'Whenever the lover of boys—or any other person for that matter—has the good fortune to encounter his own actual half, affection
and kinship and love combined inspire in him an emotion which is
quite overwhelming, and such a pair practically refuse ever to be separated even for a moment. It is people like these who form lifelong
partnerships, although they would find it difficult to say what they
hope to gain from one another's society. No one can suppose that it is

mere physical enjoyment which causes the one to take such intense delight in the company of the other. It is clear that the soul of each has some other longing which it cannot express, but can only surmise and obscurely hint at. Suppose Hephaestus with his tools were to visit them as they lie together, and stand over them and ask: "What is it, mortals, that you hope to gain from one another?" Suppose too that when they could not answer he repeated his question in these terms: "Is the object of your desire to be always together as much as possible, and never to be separated from one another day or night? If that is what you want, I am ready to melt and weld you together, so that, instead of two, you shall be one flesh; as long as you live you shall live a common life, and when you die, you shall suffer a common death, and be still one, not two, even in the next world. Would such a fate as this content you, and satisfy your longings?" We know what their answer would be; no one would refuse the offer; it would be plain that this is what everybody wants, and everybody would regard it as the precise expression of the desire which he had long felt but had been unable to formulate, that he should melt into his beloved, and that henceforth they should be one being instead of two. The reason is that this was our primitive condition when we were wholes, and love is simply the name for the desire and pursuit of the whole. Originally, as I say, we were whole beings, before our wickedness caused us to be split by Zeus, as the Arcadians have been split apart by the Spartans. We have reason to fear that if we do not behave ourselves in the sight of heaven, we may be split in two again, like dice which are bisected for tallies, and go about like the people represented in profile on tombstones, sawn in two vertically down the line of our noses. That is why we ought to exhort everyone to conduct himself reverently towards the gods; we shall thus escape a worse fate, and even win the blessings which Love has in his power to bestow, if we take him for our guide and captain. Let no man set himself in opposition to Love—which is the same thing as incurring the hatred of the gods—for if we are his friends and make our peace with him, we shall succeed, as few at present succeed, in finding the person to love who in the strictest sense belongs to us. I know that Eryximachus is anxious to make fun of my speech, but he is not to suppose that in saying this I am pointing at Pausanias and Agathon. They may, no doubt, belong to this class, for they are both unquestionably halves of male wholes, but I am speaking of men and women in general when I say that the way to happiness for our race lies in fulfilling the behests of Love, and in each finding for himself the mate who properly belongs to him; in a word, in returning to our original condition. If that condition was the best, it follows that it is best for us to come as near to it as our present circumstances allow; and the way to do that is to find a sympathetic and congenial object for our affections.

'If we are to praise the god who confers this benefit upon us, it is to Love that our praises should be addressed. It is Love who is the author of our well-being in this present life, by leading us towards what is akin to us, and it is Love who gives us a sure hope that, if we conduct ourselves well in the sight of heaven, he will hereafter make us blessed and happy by restoring us to our former state and healing our wounds.

'There is my speech about Love, Eryximachus, and you will see that it is of quite a different type from yours. Remember my request, and don't make fun of it, but let us hear what each of the others has to say. I should have said "each of the other two", for only Agathon and Socrates are left.'

B. Friendship

Aristotle

After what we have said, a discussion of friendship would naturally follow, since it is a virtue or implies virtue, and is besides most necessary with a view to living. For without friends no one would choose to live, though he had all other goods; even rich men and those in possession of office and of dominating power are thought to need friends most of all; for what is the use of such prosperity without the opportunity of beneficence, which is exercised chiefly and in its most laudable form towards friends? Or how can prosperity be guarded and preserved without friends? The greater it is, the more exposed is it to risk. And in poverty and in other misfortunes men think friends are the only refuge. It helps the young, too, to keep from error; it aids older people by ministering to their needs and supplementing the activities that are failing from weakness; those in the prime of life it stimulates to noble actions— 'two going together'—for with friends men are more able both to think and to act. Again, parent seems by nature to feel it for offspring and offspring for parent, not only among men but among birds and among most animals; it is felt mutually by members of the same race, and especially by men, whence we praise lovers of their fellowmen. We may see even in our travels how near and dear every man is to every other. Friendship seems too to hold states together, and lawgivers to care more for it than for justice; for unanimity seems to be something like friendship, and this they aim at most of all, and expel faction as their worst enemy; and when men are friends they have no need of justice, while when they are just they need friendship as well, and the truest form of justice is thought to be a friendly quality.

But it is not only necessary but also noble; for we praise those who love their friends, and it is thought to be a fine thing to have many friends; and again we think it is the same people that are good men and are friends.

Not a few things about friendship are matters of debate. Some define it as a kind of likeness and say like people are friends, whence come the sayings 'like to like', 'birds of a feather flock together', and so on; others on the contrary say 'two of a trade never agree'. On this very question they inquire for deeper and more physical causes, Euripides saying that 'parched earth loves the rain, and stately heaven when

295

filled with rain loves to fall to earth', and Heraclitus that 'it is what opposes that helps' and 'from different tones comes the fairest tune' and 'all things are produced through strife'; while Empedocles, as well as others, expresses the opposite view that like aims at like. The physical problems we may leave alone (for they do not belong to the present inquiry); let us examine those which are human and involve character and feeling, e.g. whether friendship can arise between any two people or people cannot be friends if they are wicked, and whether there is one species of friendship or more than one. Those who think there is only one because it admits of degrees have relied on an inadequate indication; for even things different in species admit of degree. We have discussed this matter previously.

The kinds of friendship may perhaps be cleared up if we first come to know the object of love. For not everything seems to be loved but only the lovable, and this is good, pleasant, or useful; but it would seem to be that by which some good or pleasure is produced that is useful, so that it is the good and the useful that are lovable as ends. Do men love, then, *the* good, or what is good for *them*? These sometimes clash. So too with regard to the pleasant. Now it is thought that each loves what is good for himself, and that the good is without qualification lovable, and what is good for each man is lovable for him; but each man loves not what is good for him but what seems good. This however will make no difference; we shall just have to say that this is 'that which seems lovable'. Now there are three grounds on which people love; of the love of lifeless objects we do not use the word 'friendship'; for it is not mutual love, nor is there a wishing of good to the other (for it would surely be ridiculous to wish wine well; if one wishes anything for it, it is that it may keep, so that one may have it oneself); but to a friend we say we ought to wish what is good for his sake. But to those who thus wish good we ascribe only goodwill, if the wish is not reciprocated; goodwill when it *is* reciprocal being friendship. Or must we add 'when it is recognized'? For many people have goodwill to those whom they have not seen but judge to be good or useful; and one of these might return this feeling. These people seem to bear goodwill to each other; but how could one call them friends when they do not know their mutual feelings? To be friends, then, they must be mutually recognized as bearing goodwill and wishing well to each other for one of the aforesaid reasons.

Now these reasons differ from each other in kind; so, therefore, do the corresponding forms of love and friendship. There are therefore three kinds of friendship, equal in number to the things that are lovable; for with respect to each there is a mutual and recognized love, and those who love each other wish well to each other in that respect in which they love one another. Now those who love each other for their utility do not love each other for themselves but in virtue of some good which they get from each other. So too with those who love for the sake of pleasure; it is not for their character that men love ready-witted people, but because they find them pleasant. Therefore those who love for the sake of utility love for the sake of what is good for *themselves,* and those who love for the sake of pleasure do so for the sake of what is pleasant to *themselves,* and not in so far as the other is the person loved but in so far as he is useful or pleasant. And thus these friendships are only incidental; for it is not as being the man he is that the loved person is loved, but as providing some good or pleasure. Such friendships, then, are easily dissolved, if the parties do not remain like themselves; for if the one party is no longer pleasant or useful the other ceases to love him.

Now the useful is not permanent but is always changing. Thus when the motive of the friendship is done away, the friendship is dissolved, inasmuch as it existed only for the ends in question. This kind of friendship seems to exist chiefly between old people (for at that age people pursue not the pleasant but the useful), and, of those who are in their prime or young, between those who pursue utility. And such people do not live much with each other either; for sometimes they do not even find each other pleasant; therefore they do not need such companionship unless they are useful to each other; for they are pleasant to each other only in so far as they rouse in each other hopes of something good to come. Among such friendships people also class the friendship of host and guest. On the other hand the friendship of young people seems to aim at pleasure; for they live under the guidance of emotion, and pursue above all what is pleasant to themselves and what is immediately before them; but with increasing age their pleasures become different. This is why they quickly become friends and quickly cease to be so; their friendship changes with the object that is found pleasant, and such pleasure alters quickly.

Young people are amorous too; for the greater part of the friendship of love depends on emotion and aims at pleasure; this is why they fall in love and quickly fall out of love, changing often within a single day. But these people do wish to spend their days and lives together; for it is thus that they attain the purpose of their friendship.

Perfect friendship is the friendship of men who are good, and alike in virtue; for these wish well alike to each other *qua* good, and they are good in themselves. Now those who wish well to their friends for their sake are most truly friends; for they do this by reason of their own nature and not incidentally; therefore their friendship lasts as long as they are good—and goodness is an enduring thing. And each is good without qualification and to his friend, for the good are both good without qualification and useful to each other. So too they are pleasant; for the good are pleasant both without qualification and to each other, since to each his own activities and others like them are pleasurable, and the actions of the good are the same or like. And such a friendship is as might be expected permanent, since there meet in it all the qualities that friends should have. For all friendship is for the sake of good or of pleasure—good or pleasure either in the abstract or such as will be enjoyed by him who has the friendly feeling—and is based on a certain resemblance; and to a friendship of good men all the qualities we have named belong in virtue of the nature of the friends themselves; for in the case of this kind of friendship the other qualities also are alike in both friends, and that which is good without qualification is also without qualification pleasant, and these are the most lovable qualities. Love and friendship therefore are found most and in their best form between such men.

But it is natural that such friendships should be infrequent; for such men are rare. Further, such friendship requires time and familiarity; as the proverb says, men cannot know each other till they have 'eaten salt together'; nor can they admit each other to friendship or be friends till each has been found lovable and been trusted by each. Those who quickly show the marks of friendship to each other wish to be friends; but are not friends unless they both are lovable and know the fact; for a wish for friendship may arise quickly, but friendship does not.

C. Mind, Self and Society

George Herbert Mead

W e come now to the position of the self-conscious self or mind in the community.
Such a self finds its expression in self-assertion, or in the devotion of
itself to the cause of the community. The self appears as a new type of
individual in the social whole. There is a new social whole because
of the appearance of the type of individual mind I have described, and
because of the self with its own assertion of itself or its own identification with the community. The self is the important phase in the
development because it is in the possibility of the importation of this
social attitude into the responses of the whole community that such a
society could arise. The change that takes place through this importation of the conversation of gestures into the conduct of the individual
is one that takes place in the experience of all of the component
individuals.

These, of course, are not the only changes that take place in the
community. In speech definite changes take place that nobody is aware
of at all. It requires the investigation of scientists to discover that such
processes have taken place. This is also true of other phases of human
organization. They change, we say, unconsciously, as is illustrated in
such a study of the myth as Wundt has carried out in his *Völkerpsy-
chologie*. The myth carries an account of the way in which organization has taken place while largely without any conscious direction—
and that sort of change is going on all the time. Take a person's attitude
toward a new fashion. It may at first be one of objection. After a while
he gets to the point of thinking of himself in this changed fashion,
noticing the clothes in the window and seeing himself in them. The
change has taken place in him without his being aware of it. There is,
then, a process by means of which the individual in interaction with
others inevitably becomes like others in doing the same thing, without
that process appearing in what we term consciousness. We become
conscious of the process when we do definitely take the attitude of the
others, and this situation must be distinguished from the previous one.
Perhaps one says that he does not care to dress in a certain fashion,
but prefers to be different; then he is taking the attitude of others
toward himself into his own conduct. When an ant from another nest
is introduced into the nest of other forms, these turn on it and tear it

301

to pieces. The attitude in the human community may be that of the individual himself, refusing to submit himself because he does take that common attitude. The ant case is an entirely external affair, but in the human individual it is a matter of taking the attitudes of the others and adjusting one's self or fighting it out. It is this recognition of the individual as a self in the process of using his self-consciousness which gives him the attitude of self-assertion or the attitude of devotion to the community. He has become, then, a definite self. In such a case of self-assertion there is an entirely different situation from that of the member of the pack who perhaps dominates it, and may turn savagely on different members of it. There an individual is just acting instinctively, we say, in a certain situation. In the human society we have an individual who not only takes his own attitude but takes the attitude in a certain sense of his subjects; in so far as he is dominating he knows what to expect. When that occurs in the experience of the individual a different response results with different emotional accompaniments, from that in the case of the leader of the pack. In the latter case there is simple anger or hostility, and in the other case there is the experience of the self asserting itself consciously over against other selves, with the sense of power, of domination. In general, when the community reaction has been imported into the individual there is a new value in experience and a new order of response.

We have discussed the self from the point of view of the "I" and the "me," the "me" representing that group of attitudes which stands for others in the community, especially that organized group of responses which we have detailed in discussing the game on the one hand and social institutions on the other. In these situations there is a certain organized group of attitudes which answer to any social act on the part of the individual organism. In any co-operative process, such as the family, the individual calls out a response from the other members of the group. Now, to the extent that those responses can be called out in the individual so that he can answer to them, we have both those contents which go to make up the self, the "other" and the "I." The distinction expresses itself in our experience in what we call the recognition of others and the recognition of ourselves in the others. We cannot realize ourselves except in so far as we can recognize the other in his relationship to us. It is as he takes the attitude of the other that the individual is able to realize himself as a self.

We are referring, of course, to a social situation as distinct from such bare organic responses as reflexes of the organism, some of which we have already discussed, as in the case where a person adjusts himself unconsciously to those about him. In such an experience there is no self-consciousness. One attains self-consciousness only as he takes, or finds himself stimulated to take, the attitude of the other. Then he is in a position of reacting in himself to that attitude of the other. Suppose we find ourselves in an economic situation. It is when we take the attitude of the other in making an offer to us that we can express ourselves in accepting or declining such an offer. That is a different response of the self from a distinctly automatic offering that can take place without self-consciousness. A small boy thrusts an advertising bill into our hand and we take it without any definite consciousness of him or of ourselves. Our thought may be elsewhere but the process still goes on. The same thing is true, of course, in the care of infants. Young children experience that which comes to them, they adjust themselves to it in an immediate fashion, without there being present in their experience a self.

When a self does appear it always involves an experience of another; there could not be an experience of a self simply by itself. The plant or the lower animal reacts to its environment, but there is no experience of a self. When a self does appear in experience it appears over against the other, and we have been delineating the condition under which this other does appear in the experience of the human animal, namely in the presence of that sort of stimulation in the co-operative activity which arouses in the individual himself the same response it arouses in the other. When the response of the other becomes an essential part in the experience or conduct of the individual; when taking the attitude of the other becomes an essential part in his behavior—then the individual appears in his own experience as a self; and until this happens he does not appear as a self.

Rational society, of course, is not limited to any specific set of individuals. Any person who is rational can become a part of it. The attitude of the community toward our own response is imported into ourselves in terms of the meaning of what we are doing. This occurs in its widest extent in universal discourse, in the reply which the rational world makes to our remark. The meaning is as universal as the community; it is necessarily involved in the rational character of that community; it is the response that the world made up out of rational beings inevitably makes to our own statement. We both get the object and ourselves into experience in terms of such a process; the other appears in our own experience in so far as we do take such an organized and generalized attitude.

If one meets a person on the street whom he fails to recognize, one's reaction toward him is that toward any other who is a member of the same community. He is the other, the organized, generalized other, if you like. One takes his attitude over against one's self. If he turns in one direction one is to go in another direction. One has his response as an attitude within himself. It is having that attitude within himself that makes it possible for one to be a self. That involves something beyond the mere turning to the right, as we say, instinctively, without self-consciousness. To have self-consciousness one must have the attitude of the other in one's own organism as controlling the thing that he is going to do. What appears in the immediate experience of one's self in taking that attitude is what we term the "me." It is that self which is able to maintain itself in the community, that is recognized in the community in so far as it recognizes the others. Such is the phase of the self which I have referred to as that of the "me."

Over against the "me" is the "I." The individual not only has rights, but he has duties; he is not only a citizen, a member of the community, but he is one who reacts to this community and in his reaction to it, as we have seen in the conversation of gestures, changes it. The "I" is the response of the individual to the attitude of the community as this appears in his own experience. His response to that organized attitude in turn changes it. As we have pointed out, this is a change which is not present in his own experience until after it takes place. The "I" appears in our experience in memory. It is only after we have acted that we know what we have done; it is only after we have spoken that we know what we have said. The adjustment to that organized world which is present in our own nature is one that represents the "me" and is constantly there. But if the response to it is a response which is of the nature of the conversation of gestures, if it creates a situation which is in some sense novel, if one puts up his side of the case, asserts himself over against others and insists that they take a different attitude toward himself, then there is something important occurring that is not previously present in experience.

The general conditions under which one is going to act may be present in one's experience, but he is as ignorant of just how he is going to respond as is the scientist of the particular hypothesis he will evolve out of the consideration of a problem. Such and such things are happening that are contrary to the theory that has been held. How are they to be explained? Take the discovery that a gram of radium would keep a pot of water boiling, and seemingly lead to no expenditure of energy. Here something is happening that runs contrary to the theory of physics up to the conception of radium activity. The scientist who has these facts before him has to pick out some explanation. He suggests that the radium atom is breaking down, and is consequently setting free energy. On the previous theory an atom was a permanent affair out of which one could not get energy. But now if it is assumed that the atom itself is a system involving an interrelationship of energies, then the breaking down of such a system sets free what is relatively an enormous amount of energy. The point I am making is that the idea of the scientist comes to him, it is not as yet there in his own mind. His mind, rather, is the process of the appearance of that idea. A person asserting his rights on a certain occasion has rehearsed the situation in his own mind; he has reacted toward the community and when the situation arises he arouses himself and says something already in his mind. But when he said it to himself in the first place he did not know what he was going to say. He then said something that was novel to himself, just as the scientist's hypothesis is a novelty when it flashes upon him.

Such a novel reply to the social situation involved in the organized set of attitudes constitutes the "I" as over against the "me." The "me" is a conventional, habitual individual. It is always there. It has to have those habits, those responses which everybody has; otherwise the individual could not be a member of the community. But an individual is constantly reacting to such an organized community in the way of expressing himself, not necessarily asserting himself in the offensive sense but expressing himself, being himself in such a co-operative process as belongs to any community. The attitudes involved are gathered from the group, but the individual in whom they are organized has the opportunity of giving them an expression which perhaps has never taken place before.

This brings out the general question as to whether anything novel can appear. Practically, of course, the novel is constantly happening and the recognition of this gets its expression in more general terms in the concept of emergence. Emergence involves a reorganization, but the reorganization brings in something that was not there before. The first time oxygen and hydrogen come together, water appears. Now water is a combination of hydrogen and oxygen, but water was not there before in the separate elements. The conception of emergence is a concept which recent philosophy has made much of. If you look at the world simply from the point of view of a mathematical equation in which there is absolute equality of the different sides, then, of course, there is no novelty. The world is simply a satisfaction of that equation. Put in any values for X and Y and the same equation holds. The equations do hold, it is true, but in their holding something else in fact arises that was not there before. For instance, there is a group of individuals that have to work together. In a society there must be a set of common organized habits of response found in all, but the way in which individuals act under specific circumstances gives rise to all of the individual differences which characterize the different persons. The fact that they have to act in a certain common fashion does not deprive them of originality. The common language is there, but a different use of it is made in every new contact between persons; the element of novelty in the reconstruction takes place through the reaction of the individuals to the group to which they belong. That reconstruction is no more given in advance than is the particular hypothesis which the scientist brings forward given in the statement of the problem. Now, it is that reaction of the individual to the organized "me," the "me" that is in a certain sense simply a member of the community, which represents the "I" in the experience of the self.

The relative values of the "me" and the "I" depend very much on the situation. If one is maintaining his property in the community, it is of primary importance that he is a member of that community, for it is his taking of the attitude of the others that guarantees to him the recognition of his own rights. To be a "me" under those circumstances is the important thing. It gives him his position, gives him the dignity of being a member in the community, it is the source of his emotional response to the values that belong to him as a member of the community. It is the basis for his entering into the experience of others.

At times it is the response of the ego or "I" to a situation, the way in which one expresses himself, that brings to one a feeling of prime importance. One now asserts himself against a certain situation, and the emphasis is on the response. The demand is freedom from conventions, from given laws. Of course, such a situation is only possible where the individual appeals, so to speak, from a narrow and restricted community to a larger one, that is, larger in the logical sense of having rights which are not so restricted. One appeals from fixed conventions which no longer have any meaning to a community in which the rights shall be publicly recognized, and one appeals to others on the assumption that there is a group of organized others that answer to one's own appeal—even if the appeal be made to posterity. In that case there is the attitude of the "I" as over against the "me."

Both aspects of the "I" and "me" are essential to the self in its full expression. One must take the attitude of the others in a group in order to belong to a community; he has to employ that outer social world taken within himself in order to carry on thought. It is through his relationship to others in that community, because of the rational social processes that obtain in that community, that he has being as a citizen. On the other hand, the individual is constantly reacting to the social attitudes, and changing in this co-operative process the very community to which he belongs. Those changes may be humble and trivial ones. One may not have anything to say, although he takes a long time to say it. And yet a certain amount of adjustment and readjustment takes place. We speak of a person as a conventional individual; his ideas are exactly the same as those of his neighbors; he is hardly more than a "me" under the circumstances; his adjustments are only the slight adjustments that take place, as we say, unconsciously. Over against that there is the person who has a definite personality, who replies to the organized attitude in a way which makes a significant difference. With such a person it is the "I" that is the more important phase of the experience. Those two constantly appearing phases are the important phases in the self.

D. The Knowledge of Man

Martin Buber

THE SOCIAL AND THE INTERHUMAN

It is usual to ascribe what takes place between men to the social realm, thereby blurring a basically important line of division between two essentially different areas of human life. I myself, when I began nearly fifty years ago to find my own bearings in the knowledge of society, making use of the then unknown concept of the interhuman, made the same error. From that time it became increasingly clear to me that we have to do here with a separate category of our existence, even a separate dimension, to use a mathematical term, and one with which we are so familiar that its peculiarity has hitherto almost escaped us. Yet insight into its peculiarity is extremely important not only for our thinking, but also for our living.

We may speak of social phenomena wherever the life of a number of men, lived with one another, bound up together, brings in its train shared experiences and reactions. But to be thus bound up together means only that each individual existence is enclosed and contained in a group existence. It does not mean that between one member and another of the group there exists any kind of personal relation. They do feel that they belong together in a way that is, so to speak, fundamentally different from every possible belonging together with someone outside the group. And there do arise, especially in the life of smaller groups, contacts which frequently favour the birth of individual relations, but, on the other hand, frequently make it more difficult. In no case, however, does membership in a group necessarily involve an existential relation between one member and another. It is true that there have been groups in history which included highly intensive and intimate relations between two of their members—as, for instance, in the homosexual relations among the Japanese Samurai or among Doric warriors—and these were countenanced for the sake of the stricter cohesion of the group. But in general it must be said that the leading elements in groups, especially in the later course of human history, have rather been inclined to suppress the personal relation in favour of the purely collective element. Where this latter element

311

reigns alone or is predominant, men feel themselves to be carried by the collectivity, which lifts them out of loneliness and fear of the world and lostness. When this happens—and for modern man it is an essential happening—the life between person and person seems to retreat more and more before the advance of the collective. The collective aims at holding in check the inclination to personal life. It is as though those who are bound together in groups should in the main be concerned only with the work of the group and should turn to the personal partners, who are tolerated by the group, only in secondary meetings.

The difference between the two realms became very palpable to me on one occasion when I had joined the procession through a large town of a movement to which I did not belong. I did it out of sympathy for the tragic development which I sensed was at hand in the destiny of a friend who was one of the leaders of the movement. While the procession was forming, I conversed with him and with another, a goodhearted 'wild man', who also had the mark of death upon him. At that moment I still felt that the two men really were there, over against me, each of them a man near to me, near even in what was most remote from me; so different from me that my soul continually suffered from this difference, yet by virtue of this very difference confronting me with authentic being. Then the formations started off, and after a short time I was lifted out of all confrontation, drawn into the procession, falling in with its aimless step; and it was obviously the very same for the two with whom I had just exchanged human words. After a while we passed a café where I had been sitting the previous day with a musician whom I knew only slightly. The very moment we passed it the door opened, the musician stood on the threshold, saw me, apparently saw me alone, and waved to me. Straightway it seemed to me as though I were taken out of the procession and of the presence of my marching friends, and set there, confronting the musician. I forgot that I was walking along with the same step; I felt that I was standing over there by the man who had called out to me, and without a word, with a smile of understanding, was answering him. When consciousness of the facts returned to me, the procession, with my companions and myself at its head, had left the café behind.

The realm of the interhuman goes far beyond that of sympathy. Such simple happenings can be part of it as, for instance, when two strangers exchange glances in a crowded streetcar, at once to sink back again into the convenient state of wishing to know nothing about each other. But also every casual encounter between opponents belongs to this realm, when it affects the opponent's attitude—that is, when something, however imperceptible, happens between the two, no matter whether it is marked at the time by any feeling or not. The only thing that matters is that for each of the two men the other happens as the particular other, that each becomes aware of the other and is thus related to him in such a way that he does not regard and use him as his object, but as his partner in a living event, even if it is no more than a boxing match. It is well known that some existentialists assert that the basic factor between men is that one is an object for the other. But so far as this is actually the case, the special reality of the interhuman, the fact of the contact, has been largely eliminated. It cannot indeed be entirely eliminated. As a crude example, take two men who are observing one another. The essential thing is not that the one makes the other his object, but the fact that he is not fully able to do so and the reason for his failure. We have in common with all existing beings that we can be made objects of observation. But it is my privilege as man that by the hidden activity of my being I can establish an impassable barrier to objectification. Only in partnership can my being be perceived as an existing whole.

The sociologist may object to any separation of the social and the interhuman on the ground that society is actually built upon human relations, and the theory of these relations is therefore to be regarded as the very foundation of sociology. But here an ambiguity in the concept 'relation' becomes evident. We speak, for instance, of a comradely relation between two men in their work, and do not merely mean what happens between them as comrades, but also a lasting disposition which is actualized in those happenings and which even includes purely psychological events such as the recollection of the absent comrade. But by the sphere of the interhuman I mean solely actual happenings between men, whether wholly mutual or tending to grow into mutual relations. For the participation of both partners is in principle indispensable. The sphere of the interhuman is one in which a person is confronted by the other. We call its unfolding the dialogical.

In accordance with this, it is basically erroneous to try to understand the interhuman phenomena as psychological. When two men converse together, the psychological is certainly an important part of the situation, as each listens and each prepares to speak. Yet this is only the hidden accompaniment to the conversation itself, the phonetic event fraught with meaning, whose meaning is to be found neither in one of the two partners nor in both together, but only in their dialogue itself, in this 'between' which they live together.

BEING AND SEEMING

The essential problem of the sphere of the interhuman is the duality of being and seeming.

Although it is a familiar fact that men are often troubled about the impression they make on others, this has been much more discussed in moral philosophy than in anthropology. Yet this is one of the most important subjects for anthropological study.

We may distinguish between two different types of human existence. The one proceeds from what one really is, the other from what one wishes to seem. In general, the two are found mixed together. There have probably been few men who were entirely independent of the impression they made on others, while there has scarcely existed one who was exclusively determined by the impression made by him. We must be content to distinguish between men in whose essential attitude the one or the other predominates.

This distinction is most powerfully at work, as its nature indicates, in the interhuman realm—that is, in men's personal dealings with one another.

Take as the simplest and yet quite clear example the situation in which two persons look at one another—the first belonging to the first type, the second to the second. The one who lives from his being looks at the other just as one looks at someone with whom he has personal dealings. His look is 'spontaneous', 'without reserve'; of course he is not uninfluenced by the desire to make himself understood by the other, but he is uninfluenced by any thought of the idea of himself which he can or should awaken in the person whom he is looking at. His opposite is different. Since he is concerned with the image which his appearance, and especially his look or glance, produces in the other, he 'makes' this look. With the help of the capacity, in greater or lesser degree peculiar to man, to make a definite element of his being appear in his look, he produces a look which is meant to have, and often enough does have, the effect of a spontaneous utterance—not only the utterance of a psychical event supposed to be taking place at that very moment, but also, as it were, the reflection of a personal life of such-and-such a kind.

This must, however, be carefully distinguished from another area of seeming whose ontological legitimacy cannot be doubted. I mean the realm of 'genuine seeming', where a lad, for instance, imitates his heroic model and while he is doing so is seized by the actuality of heroism, or a man plays the part of a destiny and conjures up authentic destiny. In this situation there is nothing false; the imitation is genuine imitation and the part played is genuine; the mask, too, is a mask and no deceit. But where the semblance originates from the lie and is permeated by it, the interhuman is threatened in its very existence. It is not that someone utters a lie, falsifies some account. The lie I mean does not take place in relation to particular facts, but in relation to existence itself, and it attacks interhuman existence as such. There are times when a man, to satisfy some stale conceit, forfeits the great chance of a true happening between I and Thou.

Let us now imagine two men, whose life is dominated by appearance, sitting and talking together. Call them Peter and Paul. Let us list the different configurations which are involved. First, there is Peter as he wishes to appear to Paul, and Paul as he wishes to appear to Peter. Then there is Peter as he really appears to Paul, that is, Paul's image of Peter, which in general does not in the least coincide with what Peter wishes Paul to see; and similarly there is the reverse situation. Further, there is Peter as he appears to himself, and Paul as he appears to himself. Lastly, there are the bodily Peter and the bodily Paul. Two living beings and six ghostly appearances, which mingle in many ways in the conversation between the two. Where is there room for any genuine interhuman life?

Whatever the meaning of the word 'truth' may be in other realms, in the interhuman realm it means that men communicate themselves to one another as what they are. It does not depend on one saying to the other everything that occurs to him, but only on his letting no seeming creep in between himself and the other. It does not depend on one letting himself go before another, but on his granting to the man to whom he communicates himself a share in his being. This is a question of the authenticity of the interhuman, and where this is not to be found, neither is the human element itself authentic.

Therefore, as we begin to recognize the crisis of man as the crisis of what is between man and man, we must free the concept of uprightness from the thin moralistic tones which cling to it, and let it take its tone from the concept of bodily uprightness. If a presupposition of human life in primeval times is given in man's walking upright, the fulfilment of human life can only come through the soul's walking upright, through the great uprightness which is not tempted by any seeming because it has conquered all semblance.

But, one may ask, what if a man by his nature makes his life subservient to the images which he produces in others? Can he, in such a case, still become a man living from his being, can he escape from his nature?

The widespread tendency to live from the recurrent impression one makes instead of from the steadiness of one's being is not a 'nature'. It originates, in fact, on the other side of interhuman life itself, in men's dependence upon one another. It is no light thing to be confirmed in one's being by others, and seeming deceptively offers itself as a help in this. To yield to seeming is man's essential cowardice, to resist it is his essential courage. But this is not an inexorable state of affairs which is as it is and must so remain. One can struggle to come to oneself—that is, to come to confidence in being. One struggles, now more successfully, now less, but never in vain, even when one thinks he is defeated. One must at times pay dearly for life lived from the being; but it is never too dear. Yet is there not bad being, do weeds not grow everywhere? I have never known a young person who seemed to me irretrievably bad. Later indeed it becomes more and more difficult to penetrate the increasingly tough layer which has settled down on a man's being. Thus there arises the false perspective of the seemingly fixed 'nature' which cannot be overcome. It is false; the foreground is deceitful; man as man can be redeemed.

Again we see Peter and Paul before us surrounded by the ghosts of the semblances. A ghost can be exorcized. Let us imagine that these two find it more and more repellent to be represented by ghosts. In each of them the will is stirred and strengthened to be confirmed in their being as what they really are and nothing else. We see the forces of real life at work as they drive out the ghosts, till the semblance vanishes and the depths of personal life call to one another.

PERSONAL MAKING PRESENT

By far the greater part of what is today called conversation among men would be more properly and precisely described as speechifying. In general, people do not really speak to one another, but each, although turned to the other, really speaks to a fictitious court of appeal whose life consists of nothing but listening to him. Chekhov has given poetic expression to this state of affairs in *The Cherry Orchard,* where the only use the members of a family make of their being together is to talk past one another. But it is Sartre who has raised to a principle of existence what in Chekhov still appears as the deficiency of a person who is shut up in himself. Sartre regards the walls between the partners in a conversation as simply impassable. For him it is inevitable human destiny that a man has directly to do only with himself and his own affairs. The inner existence of the other is his own concern, not mine; there is no direct relation with the other, nor can there be. This is perhaps the clearest expression of the wretched fatalism of modern man, which regards degeneration as the unchangeable nature of *Homo sapiens* and the misfortune of having run into a blind alley as his primal fate, and which brands every thought of a breakthrough as reactionary romanticism. He who really knows how far our generation has lost the way of true freedom, of free giving between I and Thou, must himself, by virtue of the demand implicit in every great knowledge of this kind, practise directness—even if he were the only man on earth who did it—and not depart from it until scoffers are struck with fear, and hear in his voice the voice of their own suppressed longing.

The chief presupposition for the rise of genuine dialogue is that each should regard his partner as the very one he is. I become aware of him, aware that he is different, essentially different from myself, in the definite, unique way which is peculiar to him, and I accept whom I thus see, so that in full earnestness I can direct what I say to him as the person he is. Perhaps from time to time I must offer strict opposition to his view about the subject of our conversation. But I accept this person, the personal bearer of a conviction, in his definite being out of which his conviction has grown—even though I must try to show, bit by bit, the wrongness of this very conviction. I affirm the person I struggle with: I struggle with him as his partner, I confirm him as creature and as creation, I confirm him who is opposed to me as him who is over against me. It is true that it now depends on the other whether genuine dialogue, mutuality in speech arises between us. But if I thus give to the other who confronts me his legitimate standing as a man with whom I am ready to enter into dialogue, then I may trust him and suppose him to be also ready to deal with me as his partner.

But what does it mean to be 'aware' of a man in the exact sense in which I use the word? To be aware of a thing or a being means, in quite general terms, to experience it as a whole and yet at the same time without reduction or abstraction, in all its concreteness. But a man, although he exists as a living being among living beings and even as a thing among things, is nevertheless something categorically different from all things and all beings. A man cannot really be grasped except on the basis of the gift of the spirit which belongs to man alone among all things, the spirit as sharing decisively in the personal life of the living man, that is, the spirit which determines the person. To be aware of a man, therefore, means in particular to perceive his wholeness as a person determined by the spirit; it means to perceive the dynamic centre which stamps his every utterance, action, and attitude with the recognizable sign of uniqueness. Such an awareness is impossible, however, if and so long as the other is the separated object of my contemplation or even observation, for this wholeness and its centre do not let themselves be known to contemplation or observation. It is only possible when I step into an elemental relation with the other, that is, when he becomes present to me. Hence I designate awareness in this special sense as 'personal making present'.

The perception of one's fellow man as a whole, as a unity, and as unique—even if his wholeness, unity, and uniqueness are only partly developed, as is usually the case—is opposed in our time by almost everything that is commonly understood as specifically modern. In our time there predominates an analytical, reductive, and deriving look between man and man. This look is analytical, or rather pseudo analytical, since it treats the whole being as put together and therefore able to be taken apart—not only the so-called unconscious which is accessible to relative objectification, but also the psychic stream itself, which can never, in fact, be grasped as an object. This look is a reductive one because it tries to contract the manifold person, who is nourished by the microcosmic richness of the possible, to some schematically surveyable and recurrent structures. And this look is a deriving one because it supposes it can grasp what a man has become, or even is becoming, in genetic formulae, and it thinks that even the dynamic central principle of the individual in this becoming can be represented by a general concept. An effort is being made today radically to destroy the mystery between man and man. The personal life, the ever near mystery, once the source of the stillest enthusiasms, is levelled down.

What I have just said is not an attack on the analytical method of the human sciences, a method which is indispensable wherever it furthers knowledge of a phenomenon without impairing the essentially different knowledge of its uniqueness that transcends the valid circle of the method. The science of man that makes use of the analytical method must accordingly always keep in view the boundary of such a contemplation, which stretches like a horizon around it. This duty makes the transposition of the method into life dubious; for it is excessively difficult to see where the boundary is in life.

If we want to do today's work and prepare tomorrow's with clear sight, then we must develop in ourselves and in the next generation a gift which lives in man's inwardness as a Cinderella, one day to be a princess. Some call it intuition, but that is not a wholly unambiguous concept. I prefer the name 'imagining the real', for in its essential being this gift is not a looking at the other, but a bold swinging—demanding the most intensive stirring of one's being—into the life of the other.

This is the nature of all genuine imagining, only that here the realm of my action is not the all-possible, but the particular real person who confronts me, whom I can attempt to make present to myself just in this way, and not otherwise, in his wholeness, unity, and uniqueness, and with his dynamic centre which realizes all these things ever anew.

Let it be said again that all this can only take place in a living partnership, that is, when I stand in a common situation with the other and expose myself vitally to his share in the situation as really his share. It is true that my basic attitude can remain unanswered, and the dialogue can die in seed. But if mutuality stirs, then the interhuman blossoms into genuine dialogue.

I have referred to two things which impede the growth of life between men: the invasion of seeming, and the inadequacy of perception. We are now faced with a third, plainer than the others, and in this critical hour more powerful and more dangerous than ever.

There are two basic ways of affecting men in their views and their attitude to life. In the first a man tries to impose himself, his opinion and his attitude, on the other in such a way that the latter feels the psychical result of the action to be his own insight, which has only been freed by the influence. In the second basic way of affecting others, a man wishes to find and to further in the soul of the other the disposition toward what he has recognized in himself as the right. Because it is the right, it must also be alive in the microcosm of the other, as one possibility. The other need only be opened out in this potentiality of his; moreover, this opening out takes place not essentially by teaching, but by meeting, by existential communication between someone that is in actual being and someone that is in a process of becoming. The first way has been most powerfully developed in the realm of propaganda, the second in that of education.

The propagandist I have in mind, who imposes himself, is not in the least concerned with the person whom he desires to influence, as a person; various individual qualities are of importance only in so far as he can exploit them to win the other and must get to know them for this purpose. In his indifference to everything personal the propagandist goes a substantial distance beyond the party for which he works. For the party, persons in their difference are of significance because each can be used according to his special qualities in a particular function. It is true that the personal is considered only in respect of the specific use to which it can be put, but within these limits it is recognized in practice. To propaganda as such, on the other hand, individual qualities are rather looked on as a burden, for propaganda is concerned simply with *more*—more members, more adherents, an increasing extent of support. Political methods, where they rule in an extreme form, as here, simply mean winning power over the other by depersonalizing him. This kind of propaganda enters upon different relations with force; it supplements it or replaces it, according to the need or the prospects, but it is in the last analysis nothing but sublimated violence, which has become imperceptible as such. It places men's souls under a pressure which allows the illusion of autonomy. Political methods at their height mean the effective abolition of the human factor.

The educator whom I have in mind lives in a world of individuals, a certain number of whom are always at any one time committed to his care. He sees each of these individuals as in a position to become a unique, single person, and thus the bearer of a special task of existence which can be fulfilled through him and through him alone. He sees every personal life as engaged in such a process of actualization, and he knows from his own experience that the forces making for actualization are all the time involved in a microcosmic struggle with counterforces. He has come to see himself as a helper of the actualizing forces. He knows these forces; they have shaped and they still shape him. Now he puts this person shaped by them at their disposal for a new struggle and a new work. He cannot wish to impose himself, for he believes in the effect of the actualizing forces, that is, he believes that in every man what is right is established in a single and uniquely personal way. No other way may be imposed on a man, but another way, that of the educator, may and must unfold what is right, as in this case it struggles for achievement, and help it to develop.

The propagandist, who imposes himself, does not really believe even in his own cause, for he does not trust it to attain its effect of its own power without his special methods, whose symbols are the loudspeaker and the television advertisement. The educator who unfolds what is there believes in the primal power which has scattered itself, and still scatters itself, in all human beings in order that it may grow up in each man in the special form of that man. He is confident that this growth needs at each moment only that help which is given in meeting, and that he is called to supply that help.

I have illustrated the character of the two basic attitudes and their relation to one another by means of two extremely antithetical examples. But wherever men have dealings with one another, one or the other attitude is to be found in more or less degree.

These two principles of imposing oneself on someone and helping someone to unfold should not be confused with concepts such as arrogance and humility. A man can be arrogant without wishing to impose himself on others, and it is not enough to be humble in order to help another unfold. Arrogance and humility are dispositions of the soul, psychological facts with a moral accent, while imposition and helping to unfold are events between men, anthropological facts which point to an ontology, the ontology of the interhuman.

In the moral realm Kant expressed the essential principle that one's fellow man must never be thought of and treated merely as a means, but always at the same time as an independent end. The principle is expressed as an 'ought' which is sustained by the idea of human dignity. My point of view, which is near to Kant's in its essential features, has another source and goal. It is concerned with the presuppositions of the interhuman. Man exists anthropologically not in his isolation, but in the completeness of the relation between man and man; what humanity is can be properly grasped only in vital reciprocity. For the proper existence of the interhuman it is necessary, as I have shown, that the semblance not intervene to spoil the relation of personal being to personal being. It is further necessary, as I have also shown, that each one means and makes present the other in his personal being. That neither should wish to impose himself on the other is the third basic presupposition of the interhuman. These presuppositions do not include the demand that one should influence the other in his unfolding; this is, however, an element that is suited to lead to a higher stage of the interhuman.

That there resides in every man the possibility of attaining authentic human existence in the special way peculiar to him can be grasped in the Aristotelian image of entelechy, innate self-realization; but one must note that it is an entelechy of the work of creation. It would be mistaken to speak here of individuation alone. Individuation is only the indispensable personal stamp of all realization of human existence. The self as such is not ultimately the essential, but the meaning of human existence given in creation again and again fulfils itself as self. The help that men give each other in becoming a self leads the life between men to its height. The dynamic glory of the being of man is first bodily present in the relation between two men each of whom in meaning the other also means the highest to which this person is called, and serves the self-realization of this human life as one true to creation without wishing to impose on the other anything of his own realization.

GENUINE DIALOGUE

We must now summarize and clarify the marks of genuine dialogue.

In genuine dialogue the turning to the partner takes place in all truth, that is, it is a turning of the being. Every speaker 'means' the partner or partners to whom he turns as this personal existence. To 'mean' someone in this connection is at the same time to exercise that degree of making present which is possible to the speaker at that moment. The experiencing senses and the imagining of the real which completes the findings of the senses work together to make the other present as a whole and as a unique being, as the person that he is. But the speaker does not merely perceive the one who is present to him in this way; he receives him as his partner, and that means that he confirms this other being, so far as it is for him to confirm. The true turning of his person to the other includes this confirmation, this acceptance. Of course, such a confirmation does not mean approval; but no matter in what I am against the other, by accepting him as my partner in genuine dialogue I have affirmed him as a person.

Further, if genuine dialogue is to arise, everyone who takes part in it must bring himself into it. And that also means that he must be willing on each occasion to say what is really in his mind about the subject of the conversation. And that means further that on each occasion he makes the contribution of his spirit without reduction and without shifting his ground. Even men of great integrity are under the illusion that they are not bound to say everything 'they have to say'. But in the great faithfulness which is the climate of genuine dialogue, what I have to say at any one time already has in me the character of something that wishes to be uttered, and I must not keep it back, keep it in myself. It bears for me the unmistakable sign which indicates that it belongs to the common life of the word. Where the dialogical word genuinely exists, it must be given its right by keeping nothing back. To keep nothing back is the exact opposite of unreserved speech. Everything depends on the legitimacy of 'what I have to say'. And of course I must also be intent to raise into an inner word and then into a spoken word what I have to say at this moment but do not yet possess as speech. To speak is both nature and work, something that grows and something that is made, and where it appears dialogically, in the climate of great faithfulness, it has to fulfill ever anew the unity of the two.

Associated with this is that overcoming of semblance to which I have referred. In the atmosphere of genuine dialogue, he who is ruled by the thought of his own effect as the speaker of what he has to speak, has a destructive effect. If instead of what has to be said, I try to bring attention to my *I*, I have irrevocably miscarried what I had to say; it enters the dialogue as a failure, and the dialogue is a failure. Because genuine dialogue is an ontological sphere which is constituted by the authenticity of being, every invasion of semblance must damage it.

But where the dialogue is fulfilled in its being, between partners who have turned to one another in truth, who express themselves without reserve and are free of the desire for semblance, there is brought into being a memorable common fruitfulness which is to be found nowhere else. At such times, at each such time, the word arises in a substantial way between men who have been seized in their depths and opened out by the dynamic of an elemental togetherness. The interhuman opens out what otherwise remains unopened.

This phenomenon is indeed well known in dialogue between two persons; but I have also sometimes experienced it in a dialogue in which several have taken part.

About Easter of 1914 there met a group consisting of representatives of several European nations for a three-day discussion that was intended to be preliminary to further talks. We wanted to discuss together how the catastrophe, which we all believed was imminent, could be avoided. Without our having agreed beforehand on any sort of modalities for our talk, all the presuppositions of genuine dialogue were fulfilled. From the first hour immediacy reigned between all of us, some of whom had just got to know one another; everyone spoke with an unheard-of unreserve, and clearly not a single one of the participants was in bondage to semblance. In respect of its purpose the meeting must be described as a failure (though even now in my heart it is still not a certainty that it had to be a failure); the irony of the situation was that we arranged the final discussion for the middle of August, and in the course of events the group was soon broken up. Nevertheless, in the time that followed, not one of the participants doubted that he shared in a triumph of the interhuman.

One more point must be noted. Of course it is not necessary for all who are joined in a genuine dialogue actually to speak; those who keep silent can on occasion be especially important. But each must be determined not to withdraw when the course of the conversation makes it proper for him to say what he has to say. No one, of course, can know in advance what it is that he has to say; genuine dialogue cannot be arranged beforehand. It has indeed its basic order in itself from the beginning, but nothing can be determined, the course is of the spirit, and some discover what they have to say only when they catch the call of the spirit.

But it is also a matter of course that all the participants, without exception, must be of such nature that they are capable of satisfying the presuppositions of genuine dialogue and are ready to do so. The genuineness of the dialogue is called in question as soon as even a small number of those present are felt by themselves and by the others as not being expected to take any active part. Such a state of affairs can lead to very serious problems.

I had a friend whom I account one of the most considerable men of our age. He was a master of conversation, and he loved it: his genuineness as a speaker was evident. But once it happened that he was sitting with two friends and with the three wives, and a conversation arose in which by its nature the women were clearly not joining, although their presence in fact had a great influence. The conversation among the men soon developed into a duel between two of them (I was the third). The other 'duelist', also a friend of mine, was of a noble nature; he too was a man of true conversation, but given more to objective fairness than to the play of the intellect, and a stranger to any controversy. The friend whom I have called a master of conversation did not speak with his usual composure and strength, but he scintillated, he fought, he triumphed. The dialogue was destroyed.

VIII

THE RELIGIOUS SELF

A. The Dynamics of Faith

Paul Tillich

The last consideration is decisive for the relation of faith to the problems of man's life as a personality. If faith is the state of being ultimately concerned, all preliminary concerns are subject to it. The ultimate concern gives depth, direction and unity to all other concerns and, with them, to the whole personality. A personal life which has these qualities is integrated, and the power of a personality's integration is his faith. It must be repeated at this point that such an assertion would be absurd if faith were what it is in its distorted meaning, the belief in things without evidence. Yet the assertion is not absurd, but evident, if faith is ultimate concern.

Ultimate concern is related to all sides of reality and to all sides of the human personality. The ultimate is one object beside others, and the ground of all others. As the ultimate is the ground of everything that is, so ultimate concern is the integrating center of the personal life. Being without it is being without a center. Such a state, however, can only be approached but never fully reached, because a human being deprived completely of a center would cease to be a human being. For this reason one cannot admit that there is any man without an ultimate concern or without faith.

The center unites all elements of man's personal life, the bodily, the unconscious, the conscious, the spiritual ones. In the act of faith every nerve of man's body, every striving of man's soul, every function of man's spirit participates. But body, soul, spirit, are not three parts of man. They are dimensions of man's being, always within each other; for man is a unity and not composed of parts. Faith, therefore, is not a matter of the mind in isolation, or of the soul in contrast to mind and body, or of the body (in the sense of animal faith), but is the centered movement of the whole personality toward something of ultimate meaning and significance.

Ultimate concern is passionate concern; it is a matter of infinite passion. Passion is not real without a bodily basis, even if it is the most spiritual passion. In every act of genuine faith the body participates, because genuine faith is a passionate act. The way in which it participates is manifold. The body can participate both in vital ecstasy and in asceticism leading to spiritual ecstasy. But whether in vital fulfillment or vital restriction, the body participates in the life of faith. The same is true of the unconscious strivings, the so-called instincts of man's psyche. They determine the choice of symbols and types of faith. Therefore, every community of faith tries to shape the unconscious strivings of its members, especially of the new generations. If the faith of somebody expresses itself in symbols which are adequate to his unconscious strivings, these strivings cease to be chaotic. They do not need repression, because they have received "sublimation" and are united with the conscious activities of the person. Faith also directs man's conscious life by giving it a central object of "con-centration." The disrupting trends of man's consciousness are one of the great problems of all personal life. If a uniting center is absent, the infinite variety of the encountered world, as well as of the inner movements of the human mind, is able to produce or complete disintegration of the personality. There can be no other uniting center than the ultimate concern of the mind. There are various ways in which faith unites man's mental life and gives it a dominating center. It can be the way of discipline which regulates the daily life; it can be the way of meditation and contemplation; it can be the way of concentration on the ordinary work, or on a special aim or on another human being. In each case, faith is presupposed; none of it could be done without faith. Man's spiritual function, artistic creation, scientific knowledge, ethical formation and political organization are consciously or unconsciously expressions of an ultimate concern which gives passion and creative *eros* to them, making them inexhaustible in depth and united in aim.

We have shown how faith determines and unites all elements of the personal life, how and why it is its integrating power. In doing so we have painted a picture of what faith can do. But we have not brought into this picture the forces of disintegration and disease which prevent faith from creating a fully integrated personal life, even in those who represent the power of faith most conspicuously, the saints, the great mystics, the prophetic personalities. Man is integrated only fragmentarily and has elements of disintegration or disease in all dimensions of his being.

One can also say that the integrating power of faith has healing power. This statement, however, needs comment in view of linguistic and actual distortions of the relation of faith and healing. Linguistically (and materially) one must distinguish the integrating power of faith from what has been called "faith healing." Faith healing, as the term is actually used, is the attempt to heal others or oneself by mental concentration on the healing power in others or in oneself. There is such healing power in nature and man, and it can be strengthened by mental acts. In a nondepreciating sense one could speak of the use of magic power; and certainly there is healing magic in human relationships as well as in the relation to oneself. It is a daily experience and sometimes one that is astonishing in its intensity and success. But one should not use the word "faith" for it, and one should not confuse it with the integrating power of an ultimate concern.

The integrating power of faith in a concrete situation is dependent on the subjective and objective factors. The subjective factor is the degree to which a person is open for the power of faith, and how strong and passionate is his ultimate concern. Such openness is what religion calls "grace." It is given and cannot be produced intentionally. The objective factor is the degree to which a faith has conquered its idolatrous elements and is directed toward the really ultimate. Idolatrous faith has a definite dynamic: it can be extremely passionate and exercise a preliminary integrating power. It can heal and unite the personality, including its soul and body. The gods of polytheism have shown healing power, not only in a magic way but also in terms of genuine reintegration. The objects of modern secular idolatry, such as nation and success, have shown healing power, not only by the magic fascination of a leader, a slogan or a promise but also by the fulfillment of otherwise unfulfilled strivings for a meaningful life. But the basis of the integration is too narrow. Idolatrous faith breaks down sooner or later and the disease is worse than before. The one limited element which has been elevated to ultimacy is attacked by other limited elements. The mind is split, even if each of these elements represents a high value. The fulfillment of the unconscious drives does not last; they are repressed or explode chaotically. The concentration of the mind vanishes because the object of concentration has lost its convincing character. Spiritual creativity shows an increasingly shallow and empty character, because no infinite meaning gives depth to it. The passion of faith is transformed into the suffering of unconquered doubt and despair, and in many cases into an escape to neurosis and psychosis. Idolatrous faith has more disintegrating power than indifference, just because it is faith and produces a transitory integration. This is the extreme danger of misguided, idolatrous faith, and the reason why the prophetic Spirit is above all the Spirit which fights against the idolatrous distortion of faith.

The healing power of faith raises the question of its relation to other agencies of healing. We have already referred to an element of magic influence from mind to mind without referring to the medical art, its scientific presuppositions and its technical methods. There is an overlapping of all agencies of healing and none of them should claim exclusive validity. Nevertheless, it is possible conceptually to limit each of them to a special function. Perhaps one can say that the healing power of faith is related to the whole personality, independent of any special disease of body or mind, and effective positively or negatively in every moment of one's life. It precedes, accompanies and follows all other activities of healing. But it does not suffice alone in the development of the personality. In finitude and estrangement man is not a whole, but is disrupted into different elements. Each of these elements can disintegrate independently of the other elements. Parts of the body can become sick, without producing mental disease; and the mind can become sick without visible bodily failures. In some forms of mental sickness, especially neurosis, and in almost all forms of bodily disease the spiritual life can remain completely healthy and even gain in strength. Therefore, medical art must be used wherever such separated elements of the whole of the personality are disintegrating for external or internal reasons. This is true of mental as well as of bodily medicine. And there is no conflict between them and the healing power of the state of ultimate concern. It is also clear that medical activities, including mental healing, cannot produce a reintegration of the personality as a whole. Only faith can do this. The tension between the two agencies of health would disappear if both sides knew their special functions and their special limits. Then they would not be worried about the third agency, the healing by magic concentration on the powers of healing. They would accept its help while revealing at the same time its great limitations.

There are as many types of integrated personalities as there are types of faith. There is also the type of integration which unites many characteristics of the different types of personal integration. It was this kind of personality which was created by early Christianity, and missed again and again in the history of the Church. Its character cannot be described from the point of view of faith alone; it leads to the questions of faith and love, and of faith and action.

B. The Essence of Religion in General

Ludwig Feuerbach

W hat we have so far maintained concerning the general relationship between man and his object, and between man and sensuous objects, is particularly true of man's relationship to the religious object.

In view of its relation to the objects of the senses, the consciousness of the object can be distinguished from self-consciousness; but, in the case of the religious object, consciousness and self-consciousness directly coincide. A sensuous object exists apart from man, but the religious object exists within him—it is itself an inner, intimate object, indeed, the closest object, and hence an object which forsakes him as little as his self-consciousness or conscience. "God," says Augustine, for example, "is nearer, more closely related to us and therefore more easily known by us than sensuous and physical things." Strictly speaking, the object of the senses is in itself indifferent, having no relevance to our disposition and judgment. But the object of religion is a distinguished object—the most excellent, the first, the highest being. It essentially presupposes a critical judgment—the discrimination between the divine and the non-divine, between that which is worthy of adoration and that which is not. It is in this context, therefore, that the following statement is unconditionally true: The object of man is nothing else than his objective being itself. As man thinks, as is his understanding of things, so is his God; so much worth as a man has, so much and no more has his God. The consciousness of God is the self-consciousness of man; the knowledge of God is the self-knowledge of man. Man's notion of himself is his notion of God, just as his notion of God is his notion of himself—the two are identical. What is God to man, that is man's own spirit, man's own soul; what is man's spirit, soul, and heart—that is his God. God is the manifestation of man's inner nature, his expressed self; religion is the solemn unveiling of man's hidden treasures, the avowal of his innermost thoughts, the open confession of the secrets of his love.

But if religion, i.e., the consciousness of God, is characterized as the self-consciousness of man, this does not mean that the religious man is directly aware that his consciousness of God is his self-consciousness, for it is precisely the absence of such an awareness that is responsible for the peculiar nature of religion. Hence, in order to eliminate this misunderstanding, it would be better to say that religion is the first, but indirect, self-consciousness of man. That is why religion precedes philosophy everywhere, in the history of mankind as well as in the history of the individual. Man transposes his essential being outside himself before he finds it within himself. His own being becomes the object of his thought first as another being. Religion is the essential being of man in his infancy; but the child sees his essential being, namely, man outside himself, as a child; a man is object to himself as another man. Hence, the historical development occurring within religions takes the following course: What an earlier religion regarded as objective, is now recognized as subjective; i.e., what was regarded and worshiped as God, is now recognized as something human. From the standpoint of a later religion, the earlier religion turns out to be idolatry: Man is seen to have worshiped his own essence. Man has objectified himself, but he has not yet recognized the object as his own essential being—a step taken by later religion. Every progress in religion means, therefore, a deepening of man's knowledge of himself. But every religion, while designating older religions as idolatrous, looks upon itself as exempted from their fate. It does so necessarily, for otherwise it would no longer be religion; it sees only in other religions what is the fault—if a fault it can be called—of religion as such. Because its object, its content, is a different one, because it has superseded the content of earlier religions, it presumes to be exalted above the necessary and eternal laws that constitute the essence of religion; it gives itself to the illusion that its object, its content, is superhuman. However, the hidden nature of religion, which remains opaque to religion itself, is transparent to the thinker who makes it the object of his thought. And our task consists precisely in showing that the antithesis of the divine and human is illusory; that is, that it is nothing other than the antithesis between the essential being of man and his individual being, and that consequently the object and the content of the Christian religion are altogether human.

Religion, at least the Christian religion, is the expression of how man relates to himself, or more correctly, to his essential being; but he relates to his essential being as to another being. The Divine Being is nothing other than the being of man himself, or rather, the being of man abstracted from the limits of the individual man or the real, corporeal man, and objectified, i.e., contemplated and worshiped as another being, as a being distinguished from his own. All determinations of the Divine Being are, therefore, determinations of the being of man.

In relation to the predicates—attributes or determinations—of God, this is admitted without hesitation, but by no means admitted in relation to the subject of these predicates, in relation to the being in which they are grounded. The negation of the subject is taken to mean the negation of religion, atheism, but not the negation of the predicates. That which has no determinations, also has no effect upon me; that which has no effect upon me, also does not exist for me. To eliminate all determinations of a being is the same as to eliminate that being itself. A being without determinations is a being that cannot be an object of thought; it is a nonentity. Where man removes all determinations from God, God is reduced to a negative being, to a being that is not a being. To a truly religious man, however, God is not a being without determinations, because he is a definite, real being to him. Hence, the view that God is without determinations, that he cannot be known, is a product of the modern era, of modern unbelief.

Just as reason can be, and is, determined as finite only where man regards sensual enjoyment, religious feeling, aesthetic contemplation, or moral sentiment as the absolute, the true, so the view as to the unknowability or indeterminateness of God can be fixed as a dogma only where this object commands no interest for cognition, where reality alone claims the interest of man or where the real alone has for him the significance of being an essential, absolute, divine object, but where at the same time this purely worldly tendency is contradicted by a still-existing remnant of old religiosity. By positing God as unknowable, man excuses himself to what is still left of his religious conscience for his oblivion of God, his surrender to the world. He negates God in practice—his mind and his senses have been absorbed by the world—but he does not negate him in theory. He does not attack his existence; he leaves it intact. But this existence neither affects nor incommodes him, for it is only a negative existence, an existence without existence; it is an existence that contradicts itself—a being that, in view of its effects, is indistinguishable from non-being. The negation of determinate, positive predicates of the Divine Being is nothing else than the negation of religion, but one which still has an appearance of religion, so that it is not recognized as a negation—it is nothing but a subtle, sly atheism. The alleged religious horror of limiting God by determinate predicates is only the irreligious wish to forget all about God, to banish him from the mind. He who is afraid to be finite is afraid to exist. All real existence, that is, all existence that really is existence, is qualitative, determinate existence. He who seriously, truly believes in the existence of God is not disturbed even by grossly sensuous qualities attributed to God. He who regards the fact of his existence as an insult, he who recoils from that which is gross, may just as well give up existing. A God to whom his determinateness is an insult lacks the courage and strength to exist. Determinateness is the fire, the oxygen, the salt of existence. An existence in general, an existence without qualities, is an insipid and preposterous existence. But there is nothing more, and nothing less, in God than what religion puts in him. Only when man loses his taste for religion, that is, when religion itself becomes insipid, does God become an insipid existence.

Moreover, there is yet a milder way of denying the divine predicates than the direct one just described. One admits that the predicates of the Divine Being are finite and, more particularly, human determinations, but one rejects the idea of rejecting them. One even defends them on the ground that they are necessary for man; that being man, he cannot conceive God in any way other than human. One argues that although these determinations have no meaning in relation to God, the fact is that God, if he is to exist for man, can appear to man in no other way than he does, namely, as a being with human attributes. However, this distinction between what God is in himself and what he is for man destroys the peace of religion as well as being an unfeasible and unfounded distinction. It is not at all possible for me to know whether God as he is in and for himself is something different from what he is for me. The manner in which he exists for me is also the totality of his existence for me. The determinations in terms of which he exists for me contain also the "in-itself-ness" of his being, his essential nature itself; he exists for me in a way in which he can exist for me alone. The religious man is completely satisfied with how he sees God in relation to himself—and he knows nothing of any other relation—for God is to him what he can be to man at all. In the distinction made above, man transgresses the boundaries of himself, his being and its absolute measure, but this transcending is only an illusion. For I can make the distinction between the object as it is in itself and the object as it is for me only where an object can really appear different from what it actually appears to me. I cannot make such a distinction where the object appears to me as it does according to my absolute measure; that is, as it must appear to me. It is true that my conception can be subjective; that is, one which is not bound by the essential constitution of my species. However, if my conception corresponds to the measure of my species, the distinction between what something is in itself and what it is for me ceases; for in that case this conception is itself an absolute one. The measure of the species is the absolute measure, law, and criterion of man. Yet religion has the conviction that its conceptions and determinations of God are such as every man ought to have if he is to have true conceptions, that these are conceptions necessitated by human nature, that they are indeed objective, conforming to the nature of God. To every religion, the gods of other religions are only conceptions of God; but its own conception of God is itself its God—God as it conceives him to be, God genuinely and truly so, God as he is in himself. Religion is satisfied only with a complete and total God—it will not have merely an appearance of God, it can be satisfied with nothing less than God himself, God in person. Religion abandons itself if it abandons God in his essential being; it is no longer true if it renounces its possession of the true God. Skepticism is the archenemy of religion. But the distinction between object and concept, between God as he is in himself and as he is for me, is a skeptical, that is, irreligious distinction.

That which is subsumed by man under the concept of "being-in-itself," that which he regards as the most supreme being or as the being of which he can conceive none higher, that is the Divine Being. How can he therefore still ask, what this being is in itself? If God were an object to the bird, he would be an object to it only as a winged being— the bird knows nothing higher, nothing more blissful than the state of being winged. How ludicrous would it be if this bird commented: "God appears to me as a bird, but I do not know what he is in himself." The highest being to the bird is the "bird-being." Take from it its conception of "bird-being," and you take from it its conception of the highest being. How, therefore, could the bird ask whether God in himself were winged? To ask whether God is in himself what he is for me, is to ask whether God is God; it is to raise oneself above God and to rebel against him.

Given, therefore, the situation in which man is seized by the awareness that religious predicates are mere anthropomorphisms, his faith has also come under the sway of doubt and unbelief. And if this awareness does not lead him to the formal negation of the predicates and thence to the negation of the being in which they are grounded, it is only due to an inconsistency for which his faint-heartedness and irresolute intellect are responsbile. If you doubt the objective truth of the predicates, you must also doubt the objective truth of the subject to which they belong. If your predicates are anthropomorphisms, their subject, too, is an anthropomorphism. If love, goodness, and personality are human determinations, the being which constitutes their source and, according to you, their presupposition is also an anthropomorphism; so is the existence of God; so is the belief that there is a God—in short, all presuppositions that are purely human. What tells you that the belief in a God at all is not an indication of the limitedness of man's mode of conception? Higher beings—and you assume that such beings exist—are perhaps so blissful in themselves, so at unity with themselves that they are not exposed to a tension between themselves and a higher being. To know God and not to be God, to know blissfulness and not to enjoy it, is to be in conflict with oneself, is to be delivered up to unhappiness.

C. The Divine Milieu

Pierre Teilhard de Chardin

Nemo sibi vivit, aut sibi moritur ... Sive vivimus, sive morimur, Christi sumus.

No man lives or dies to himself. But whether through our life or through our death we belong to Christ.

T he first two parts of this Essay are simply an analysis and verification of the above words of St. Paul. We have considered, in turn, the sphere of activity, development and life, and the sphere of passivity, diminishment and death in our lives. All around us, to right and left, in front and behind, above and below, we have only had to go a little beyond the frontier of sensible appearances in order to see the divine welling up and showing through. But it is not only close to us, in front of us, that the divine Presence has revealed itself. It has sprung up so universally, and we find ourselves so surrounded and transfixed by it, that there is no room left to fall down and adore it, even within ourselves.

By means of all created things, without exception, the divine assails us, penetrates us and moulds us. We imagined it as distant and inaccessible, whereas in fact we live steeped in its burning layers. *In eo vivimus.* As Jacob said, awakening from his dream, the world, this palpable world, to which we brought the boredom and callousness reserved for profane places, is in truth a holy place, and we did not know it. *Venite, adoremus.*

Let us withdraw to the higher and more spiritual ether which bathes us in living light. And let us take joy in making an inventory of its attributes and recognising their nature, before examining in a general way the means by which we can open ourselves ever more to its penetration.

The essential marvel of the divine milieu is the ease with which it assembles and harmonises within itself qualities which appear to us to be contradictory.

As vast as the world and much more formidable than the most immense energies of the universe, it nevertheless possesses in a supreme degree the concentration and the specific qualities which are the charm and warmth of human persons.

Vast and innumerable as the dazzling surge of creatures that are sustained and sur-animated by its ocean, it nevertheless retains the

343

concrete transcendence that allows it to bring back the elements of the world, without the least confusion, within its triumphant and personal unity.

Incomparably near and tangible—for it presses in upon us through all the forces of the universe—it nevertheless eludes our grasp so constantly that we can never seize it here below except by raising ourselves, uplifted on its waves, to the extreme limit of our efforts: present in, and drawing at the inaccessible depth of, each creature, it withdraws always further, bearing us along with it towards the common centre of all consummation.

Through it, the touch of matter is a purification, and chastity flowers as the sublimation of love.

In it, development culminates in renunciation; attachment to things separates us from everything disintegrating in them. Death becomes a resurrection.

Now, if we try to discover the source of so many astonishingly coupled perfections, we shall find they all spring from the same 'fontal' property which we can express thus: God reveals Himself everywhere, beneath our groping efforts, *as a universal milieu,* only because he is *the ultimate point* upon which all realities converge. Each element of the world, whatever it may be, only subsists, *hic et nunc,* in the manner of a cone whose generatrices meet in God who draws them together— (meeting at the term of their individual perfection and at the term of the general perfection of the world which contains them). It follows that all created things, every one of them, cannot be looked at, in their nature and action, without the same reality being found in their innermost being—like sunlight in the fragments of a broken mirror—one beneath its multiplicity, unattainable beneath its proximity, and spiritual beneath its materiality. No object can influence us by its essence without our being touched by the radiance of the focus of the universe. Our minds are incapable of grasping a reality, our hearts and hands of seizing the essentially desirable in it, without our being compelled *by the very structure of things* to go back to the first source of its perfections. This focus, this source, are thus everywhere. It is *precisely because* he is so infinitely profound and punctiform that God is infinitely near, and dispersed everywhere. It is *precisely because* He is the centre that He fills the whole sphere. The omnipresence of the divine is simply the effect of its extreme spirituality and is the exact contrary of the fallacious ubiquity which matter seems to derive from its extreme dissociation and dispersal. In the light of this discovery, we can resume our march through the inexhaustible wonders which the divine milieu has in store for us.

However vast the divine milieu may be, it is in reality a *centre*. It therefore has the properties of a centre, and above all the absolute and final power to unite (and consequently to complete) all beings within its breast. In the divine milieu all the elements of the universe *touch each other* by that which is most inward and ultimate in them. There they concentrate, little by little, all that is purest and most attractive in them without loss and without danger of subsequent corruption. There they shed, in their meeting, the mutual exteriority and the incoherences which form the basic pain of human relationships. Let those seek refuge there who are saddened by the separations, the parsimonies and the prodigalities of the world. In the external spheres of the world, man is always torn by the separations which set distance between bodies, which set the impossibility of mutual understanding between souls, which set death between lives. Moreover at every minute he must lament that he cannot pursue and embrace everything within the compass of a few years. Finally, and not without reason, he is incessantly distressed by the crazy indifference or the heart-breaking muteness of a natural milieu in which the greater part of individual endeavour seems wasted or lost, where the blow and the cry seem stifled on the spot, without awakening any echo.

All that is only surface desolation.

But let us leave the surface, and, without leaving the world, plunge into God. There, and from there, in Him and through Him, we shall hold all things and have command of all things. There we shall one day rediscover the essence and brilliance of all the flowers and lights which we were forced to abandon so as to be faithful to life. The things we despaired of reaching and influencing are all there, all reunited by the most vulnerable, receptive and enriching point in their substance. In this place the least of our desires and efforts is harvested and tended and can at any moment cause the marrow of the universe to vibrate.

Let us establish ourselves in the divine milieu. There we shall find ourselves where the soul is most deep and where matter is most dense. There we shall discover, with the confluence of all beauties, the ultravital, the ultra-sensitive, the ultra-active point of the universe. And, at the same time, we shall feel the *plenitude* of our powers of action and adoration effortlessly ordered within our deepest selves.

But the fact that all the external springs of the world should be co-ordinated and harmonised at that privileged point is not the only marvel. By a complementary marvel, the man who abandons himself to the divine milieu feels his inward powers clearly directed and vastly expanded by it with a sureness which enables him to avoid, like child's play, the reefs on which mystical ardour has so often foundered.

In the first place, the sojourner in the divine milieu is not a pantheist. At first sight, perhaps, the depths of the divine which St. Paul reveals to us may seem to resemble the fascinating domains unfolded before our eyes by monistic philosophies or religions. In fact they are very different, far more reassuring to our minds, far more comforting to our hearts. Pantheism seduces us by its vistas of perfect universal union. But ultimately, if it were true, it would give us only fusion and unconsciousness; for, at the end of the evolution it claims to reveal, the elements of the world vanish in the God they create or by which they are absorbed. Our God, on the contrary, pushes to its furthest possible limit the differentiation among the creatures He concentrates within Himself. At the peak of their adherence to Him, the elect also discover in Him the consummation of their individual fulfilment. Christianity alone therefore saves, with the rights of thought, the essential aspiration of all mysticism: *to be united* (that is, to become the other) *while remaining oneself.* More attractive than any world-Gods, whose eternal seduction it embraces, transcends, and purifies—*in omnibus omnia Deus (En pasi panta Theos)*—our divine milieu is at the antipodes of false pantheism. The Christian can plunge himself into it whole-heartedly without the risk of finding himself one day a monist.

Nor is there any reason to fear that in abandoning himself to those deep waters, he will lose his foothold in revelation and in life, and become either unrealistic in the object of his cult or else chimerical in the substance of his work. The Christian lost within the divine layers will not find his mind subject to the forbidden distortions that go to make the 'modernist' or the 'illuminati.'

To the Christian's sensitised vision, it is true, the Creator and, more specifically, the Redeemer (as we shall see) have steeped themselves in all things and penetrated all things to such a degree that, as Blessed Angela of Foligno said, 'the world is full of God.' But this aggrandisement is only valuable in his eyes in so far as the light, in which everything seems to him bathed, radiates from *an historical centre* and is transmitted along *a traditional and solidly defined axis.* The immense enchantment of the divine milieu owes all its value in the long run to the human-divine contact which was revealed at the Epiphany of Jesus. If you suppress the historical reality of Christ, the divine omnipresence which intoxicates us becomes, like all the other dreams of metaphysics, uncertain, vague, conventional—lacking the decisive experimental verification by which to impose itself on our minds, and without the moral directives to assimilate our lives into it. Thenceforward, however dazzling the expansions which we shall try in a moment to discern in the resurrected Christ, their beauty and their stuff of reality will always remain inseparable from the tangible and verifiable truth of the Gospel event. The mystical Christ, the universal Christ of St. Paul, has neither meaning nor value in our eyes except as an expansion of the Christ who was born of Mary and who died on the Cross. The former essentially draws His fundamental quality of undeniability and concreteness from the latter. However far we may be drawn into the divine spaces opened up to us by Christian mysticism, we never depart from the Jesus of the Gospels. On the contrary, we feel a growing need to enfold ourselves ever more firmly within His human truth. We are not, therefore, modernist in the condemned sense of the word. Nor shall we end up among the visionaries and the 'illuminati.'

The real error of the visionaries is to *confuse* the different *planes* of the world, and consequently to mix up their activities. In the view of the visionary, the divine presence illuminates not only the heart of things, but tends to invade their surface and hence to do away with their exacting but salutary reality. The gradual maturing of immediate causes, the complex network of material determinisms, the infinite susceptibilities of the universal order, no longer count. Through this veil without seam and these delicate threads, divine action is imagined as appearing naked and without order. And then the falsely miraculous comes to disconcert and obstruct the human effort.

As we have already abundantly shown, the effect produced upon human activity, by the true transformation of the world in Jesus Christ, is utterly different. At the heart of the divine milieu, as the Church reveals it, things are transfigured, but from within. They bathe inwardly in light, but, in this incandescence, they retain—this is not strong enough, they exalt—all that is most specific in their attributes. *We can only lose ourselves in God by prolonging the most individual characteristics of beings far beyond themselves:* that is the fundamental rule by which we can always distinguish the true mystic from his counterfeits. The heart of God is boundless, *multae mansiones.* And yet in all that immensity there is only one possible place for each one of us at any given moment, the one we are led to by unflagging fidelity to the natural and supernatural duties of life. At this point, which we can reach at the right moment only if we exert the maximum effort on every plane, God will reveal Himself in all His plenitude. Except at this point, the divine milieu, although it may still enfold us, exists only incompletely, or not at all, *for us.* Thus its great waters do not call us to defeat but to perpetual struggle to breast their floods. Their energy awaits, and provokes, our energy. Just as on certain days the sea lights up only as the ship's prow or the swimmer cleaves its surface, so the world is lit up with God only when reacting to our impetus. When God desires ultimately to subject and unite the Christian to Him, either by ecstasy or by death, it is as though He bears him away stiffened by love and by obedience in the full extent of his effort.

It might thenceforward look as though the believer in the divine milieu were falling back into the errors of a pagan naturalism in reaction against the excesses of quietism and illuminism. With his faith in the heavenly value of human endeavour, by his expectation of a new awakening of the faculties of adoration dormant in the world, by his respect for the spiritual powers still latent in matter, the Christian may often bear a striking resemblance to the worshippers of the earth.

But here again, as in the case of pantheism, the resemblance is only external and *such as is so often found in opposite things.*

The pagan loves the earth in order to enjoy it and confine himself within it; the Christian in order to make it purer and draw from it the strength to escape from it.

The pagan seeks to espouse sensible things so as to extract delight from them; *he adheres to the world.* The Christian multiplies his contacts with the world only so as to harness, or submit to, the energies which he will take back, or which will take him, to Heaven. *He pre-adheres to God.*

The pagan holds that man divinises himself by closing in upon himself; the final act of human evolution comes when the individual, or the totality, constitutes itself within itself. The Christian sees his divinisation only in the assimilation by an 'Other' of his achievement: the culmination of life, in his eyes, is death in union.

To the pagan, universal reality exists only in so far as it is projected on to the plane of the tangible: it is immediate and multiple. The Christian makes use of exactly the same elements: but he prolongs them along their common axis, which links them to God: and, by the same token, the universe is thus unified for him, although it is only attainable at the final centre of its consummation.

To sum up, one may say that, in relation to all the main historical forms assumed by the human religious spirit, Christian mysticism extracts *all* that is sweetest and strongest circulating in all the human mysticisms, though without absorbing their evil or suspect elements. It shows an astonishing equilibrium between the active and the passive, between possession of the world and its renunciation, between a taste for things and an indifference to them. But there is really no reason why we should be astonished by this shifting harmony, for is it not the natural and spontaneous reaction of the soul to the stimulus of a milieu which is exactly, by nature and grace, the one in which that soul is made to live and develop itself? Just as, at the centre of the divine milieu, all the sounds of created being are fused, without being confused, in a single note which dominates and sustains them (that seraphic note, no doubt, which bewitched St. Francis), so all the powers of the soul begin to resound in response to its call; and these multiple tones, in their turn, compose themselves into a single, ineffably simple vibration in which all the spiritual nuances—of love and of the intellect, of zeal and of tranquillity, of fullness and of ecstasy, of passion and of indifference, of assimilation and of surrender, of rest and of motion—are born and pass and shine forth, according to the times and the circumstances, like the countless possibilities of an inward attitude, inexpressible and unique.

And if any words could translate that permanent and lucid intoxication better than others, perhaps they would be 'passionate indifference.'

To have access to the divine milieu is to have found the One Thing needful: *Him who burns* by setting fire to everything that we would love badly or not enough; *Him who calms* by eclipsing with His blaze everything that we would love too much; *Him who consoles* by gathering up everything that has been snatched from our love or has never been given to it. To reach those priceless layers is to experience, with equal truth, that one has need of everything, and that one has need of nothing. Everything is needed because the world will never be large enough to provide our taste for action with the means of grasping God, or our thirst for undergoing with the possibility of being invaded by Him. And yet nothing is needed; for as the only reality which can satisfy us lies beyond the transparencies in which it is mirrored, everything that fades away and dies between us and it will only serve to give reality back to us with greater purity. Everything means both everything and nothing to me; everything is God to me and everything is dust to me: that is what man can say with equal truth, in accord with how the divine ray falls.

'Which is the greater blessing,' someone once asked, 'to have the sublime unity of God to centre and save the universe? or to have the concrete immensity of the universe by which to undergo and touch God?'

We shall not seek to escape this joyful uncertainty. But now that we are familiar with the attributes of the divine milieu, we shall turn our attention to the thing itself which appeared to us in the depth of each being, like a radiant countenance, like a fascinating abyss. We can now say 'Lord, who art Thou?'

D. The Body and the Members

Josiah Royce

Henceforth, in these lectures, I shall restrict the application of the term "community" to those social groups which conform to the definition stated at the close of our last lecture. Not every social group which behaves so that, to an observer, it seems to be a single unit, meets all the conditions of our definition. Our new use of the term "community" will therefore be more precise and restricted than was our earlier employment of the word. But our definition will clear the way for further generalizations. It will enable us to express our reasons for much that, in our study of the Christian doctrine of life, had to be stated dogmatically, and illustrated rather than intimately examined.

We have repeatedly spoken of two levels of human life, the level of the individual and the level of the community. We have now in our hands the means for giving a more precise sense to this expression, and for furnishing a further verification of what we asserted about these two levels of life. We have also repeatedly emphasized the ethical and religious significance of loyalty; but our definition will help us to throw clearer light upon the sources of this worth. And by thus sharpening the outlines of our picture of what a real community is, we shall be made ready to consider whether the concept of the community possesses a more than human significance. Let us recall our new definition to mind, and then apply it to our main problems.

I

Our definition presupposes that there exist many individual selves. Suppose these selves to vary in their present experiences and purposes as widely as you will. Imagine them to be sundered from one another by such chasms of mutual mystery and independence as, in our natural social life, often seem hopelessly to divide and secrete the inner world of each of us from the direct knowledge and estimate of his fellows. But let those selves be able to look beyond their present chaos of fleeting ideas and of warring desires, far away into the past whence they came, and into the future whither their hopes lead them. As they thus look, let each one of them ideally enlarge his own individual life, extending himself into the past and future, so as to say of some far-off event, belonging, perhaps, to other generations of men, "I view that event as a part of my own life." "That former happening or achievement so predetermined the sense and the destiny which are now mine, that I am moved to regard it as belonging to my own past." Or again: "For that coming event I wait and hope as an event of my own future."

And further, let the various ideal extensions, forwards and backwards, include at least one common event, so that each of these selves regards that event as a part of his own life.

Then, *with reference to the ideal common past and future in question, I say that these selves constitute a community.* This is henceforth to be our definition of a community. The present variety of the selves who are the members of the spiritual body so defined, is not hereby either annulled or slighted. The motives which determine each of them thus ideally to extend his own life, may vary from self to self in the most manifold fashion.

Our definition will enable us, despite all these varieties of the members, to understand in what sense any such community as we have defined exists, and is one.

Into this form, which, when thus summarily described, seems so abstract and empty, life can and does pour the rich contents and ideals which make the communities of our human world so full of dramatic variety and significance.

II

The *first* condition upon which the existence of a community, in our sense of the word, depends, is the power of an individual self to extend his life, in ideal fashion, so as to regard it as including past and future events which lie far away in time, and which he does not now personally remember. That this power exists, and that man has a self which is thus ideally extensible in time without any definable limit, we all know.

This power itself rests upon the principle that, however a man may come by his idea of himself, the self is no mere datum, but is in its essence a life which is interpreted, and which interprets itself, and which, apart from some sort of ideal interpretation, is a mere flight of ideas, or a meaningless flow of feelings, or a vision that sees nothing, or else a barren abstract conception. How deep the process of interpretation goes in determining the real nature of the self, we shall only later be able to estimate.

There is no doubt that what we usually call our personal memory does indeed give us assurances regarding our own past, so far as memory extends and is trustworthy. But our trust in our memories is itself an interpretation of their data. All of us regard as belonging, even to our recent past life, much that we cannot just now remember. And the future self shrinks and expands with our hopes and our energies. No one can merely, from without, set for us the limits of the life of the self, and say to us: "Thus far and no farther."

In my ideal extensions of the life of the self, I am indeed subject to some sort of control,—to what control we need not here attempt to formulate. I must be able to give myself some sort of reason, personal, or social, or moral, or religious, or metaphysical, for taking on or throwing off the burden, the joy, the grief, the guilt, the hope, the glory of past and of future deeds and experiences; but I must also myself personally share in this task of determining how much of the past and the future shall ideally enter into my life, and shall contribute to the value of that life.

And if I choose to say, "There is a sense in which *all* the tragedy and the attainment of an endless past and future of deeds and of fortunes enter into my own life," I say only what saints and sages of the most various creeds and experiences have found their several reasons for saying. The fact and the importance of such ideal extensions of the self must therefore be recognized. Here is the first basis for every clear idea of what constitutes a community.

The ideal extensions of the self may also include, as is well known, not only past and future events and deeds, but also physical things, whether now existent or not, and many other sorts of objects which are neither events nor deeds. The knight or the samurai regarded his sword as a part of himself. One's treasures and one's home, one's tools, and the things that one's hands have made, frequently come to be interpreted as part of the self. And any object in heaven or earth may be thus ideally appropriated by a given self. The ideal self of the Stoic or of the Mystic may, in various fashions, identify its will, or its very essence, with the whole universe. The Hindoo seer seeks to realize the words: "I am Brahm;" "That art thou."

In case such ideal extensions of the self are consciously bound up with deeds, or with other events, such as belong to the past or future life which the self regards as its own, our definition of the community warrants us in saying that many selves form one community when all are ideally extended so as to include the same object. But unless the ideal extensions of the self thus consciously involve past and future deeds and events that have to do with the objects in question, we shall not use these extensions to help us to define communities.

For our purposes, the community is a being that attempts to accomplish something in time and through the deeds of its members. These deeds belong to the life which each member regards as, in ideal, his own. It is in this way that both the real and the ideal Church are intended by the members to be communities in our sense. An analogous truth holds for such other communities as we shall need to consider. The concept of the community is thus, for our purposes, a practical conception. It involves the idea of deeds done, and ends sought or attained. Hence I shall define it in terms of members who themselves not only live in time, but conceive their own ideally extended personalities in terms of a time-process. In so far as these personalities possess a life that is for each of them his own, while it is, in some of its events, common to them all, they form a community.

Nothing important is lost, for our conception of the community, by this formal restriction, whereby common objects belong to a community only when these objects are bound up with the deeds of the community. For, when the warrior regards his sword as a part of himself, he does so because his sword is the instrument of his will, and because what he does with his sword belongs to his literal or ideal life. Even the mystic accomplishes his identification of the self and the world only through acts of renunciation or of inward triumph. And these acts are the goal of his life. Until he attains to them, they form part of his ideal future self. Whenever he fully accomplishes these crowning acts of identification, the separate self no longer exists. When knights or mystics form a community, in our sense, they therefore do so because they conceive of deeds done, in common, with their swords, or of mystical attainments that all of them win together.

Thus then, while no authoritative limit can be placed upon the ideal extensions of the self in time, those extensions of the self which need be considered for the purposes of our theory of the community are indeed extensions in time, past or future; or at all events involve such extensions in time.

Memory and hope constantly incite us to the extensions of the self which play so large a part in our daily life. Social motives of endlessly diverse sort move us to consider "far and forgot" as if to us it were near, when we view ourselves in the vaster perspectives of time. It is, in fact, the ideally extended self, and not, in general, the momentary self, whose life is worth living, whose sense outlasts our fleeting days, and whose destiny may be worthy of the interest of beings who are above the level of human individuals. The present self, the fleeting individual of to-day, is a mere gesticulation of a self. The genuine person lives in the far-off past and future as well as in the present. It is, then, the ideally extended self that is worthy to belong to a significant community.

III

The *second* condition upon which the existence of a community depends is the fact that there are in the social world a number of distinct selves capable of social communication, and, in general, engaged in communication.

The distinctness of the selves we have illustrated at length in our previous discussion. We need not here dwell upon the matter further, except to say, expressly, that a community does *not* become one, in the sense of my definition, by virtue of any reduction or melting of these various selves into a single merely present self, or into a mass of passing experience. That mystical phenomena may indeed form part of the life of a community, just as they may also form part of the life of an individual human being, I fully recognize.

About such mystical or quasi-mystical phenomena, occurring in their own community, the Corinthians consulted Paul. And Paul, whose implied theory of the community is one which my own definition closely follows, assured them in his reply that mystical phenomena are not essential to the existence of the community; and that it is on the whole better for the life of such a community as he was addressing, if the individual member, instead of losing himself "in a mystery," kept his own individuality, in order to contribute his own edifying gift to the common life. Wherein this common life consists we have yet further to see in what follows.

The *third* of the conditions for the existence of the community which my definition emphasizes consists in the fact that the ideally extended past and future selves of the members include at least some events which are, for all these selves, identical. This third condition is the one which furnishes both the most exact, the most widely variable, and the most important of the motives which warrant us in calling a community a real unit. The Pauline metaphor of the body and the members finds, in this third condition, its most significant basis,—a basis capable of exact description.

E. On The Ontological Mystery

Gabriel Marcel

We have now come to the centre of what I have called the ontological mystery, and the simplest illustrations will be the best. To hope against all hope that a person whom I love will recover from a disease which is said to be incurable is to say: It is impossible that I should be alone in willing this cure; it is impossible that reality in its inward depth should be hostile or so much as indifferent to what I assert is in itself a good. It is quite useless to tell me of discouraging *cases* or *examples:* beyond all experience, all probability, all statistics, I assert that a given order shall be re-established, that reality *is* on my side in willing it to be so. I do not wish: I assert; such is the prophetic tone of true hope.

No doubt I shall be told: "In the immense majority of cases this is an illusion." But it is of the essence of hope to exclude the consideration of cases; moreover, it can be shown that there exists an ascending dialectic of hope, whereby hope rises to a plane which transcends the level of all possible empirical disproof—the plane of salvation as opposed to that of success in whatever form.

It remains true, nevertheless, that the correlation of hope and despair subsists until the end; they seem to me inseparable. I mean that while the structure of the world we live in permits—and may even seem to counsel—absolute despair, yet it is only such a world that can give rise to an unconquerable hope. If only for this reason, we cannot be sufficiently thankful to the great pessimists in the history of thought; they have carried through an inward experience which needed to be made and of which the radical possibility no apologetics should disguise; they have prepared our minds to understand that despair can be what it was for Nietzsche (though on an infra-ontological level and in a domain fraught with mortal dangers) the springboard to the loftiest affirmation.

At the same time, it remains certain that, for as much as hope is a mystery, its mystery can be ignored or converted into a problem. Hope is then regarded as a desire which wraps itself up in illusory judgments to distort an objective reality which it is interested in disguising from itself. What happens in this case is what we have already observed in connection with encounter and with love; it is because mystery can—and, in a sense, logically must—be degraded into a

361

problem that an interpretation such as that of Spinoza, with all the confusion it implies, had to be put forward sooner or later. It is important and must be stressed that this attitude has nothing against it so long as our standpoint is on the hither-side of the realm of the ontological. Just as long as my attitude towards reality is that of someone who is not involved in it, but who judges it his duty to draw up its minutes as exactly as possible (and this is by definition the attitude of the scientist), I am justified in maintaining in regard to it a sort of principle of mistrust, which in theory is unlimited in its application; such is the legitimate standpoint of the workman in the laboratory, who must in no way prejudge the result of his analysis, and who can all the better envisage *the worst,* because at this level the very notion of worst is empty of meaning. But an investigation of this sort, which is just like that of an accountant going through the books, takes place on the hither-side of the order of mystery, an order in which the problem encroaches upon its own data.

It would indeed be a profound illusion to believe that I can still maintain this same attitude when I undertake an inquiry, say, into the value of life; it would be a paralogism to suppose that I can pursue such an inquiry as though my own life were not at issue.

Hence, between hope—the reality of hope in the heart of the one whom it inhabits—and the judgment brought to bear upon it by a mind chained to objectivity there exists the same barrier as that which separates a pure mystery from a pure problem.

This brings us to a nodal point of our subject, where certain intimate connections can be traced.

The world of the problematical is the world of fear and desire, which are inseparable; at the same time, it is that world of the functional—or of what can be functionalised—which was defined at the beginning of this essay; finally, it is the kingdom of technics of whatever sort. Every technique serves, or can be made to serve, some desire or some fear; conversely, every desire as every fear tends to invent its appropriate technique. From this standpoint, despair consists in the recognition of the ultimate inefficacy of all technics, joined to the inability or the refusal to change over to a new ground—a ground where all technics are seen to be incompatible with the fundamental nature of being, which itself escapes our grasp (in so far as our grasp is limited to the world of objects and to this alone). It is for this reason that we seem nowadays to have entered upon the very era of despair; we have not ceased to believe in technics, that is to envisage reality as a complex of problems; yet at the same time the failure of technics *as a whole* is as discernible to us as its *partial* triumphs. To the question:

what can man achieve? we continue to reply: He can achieve as much as his technics; yet we are obliged to admit that these technics are unable *to save man himself,* and even that they are apt to conclude the most sinister alliance with the enemy he bears within him.

I have said that man is *at the mercy of his technics.* This must be understood to mean that he is increasingly incapable of controlling his technics, or rather of *controlling his own control.* This control of his own control, which is nothing else than the expression on the plane of active life of what I have called thought at one remove, cannot find its centre or its support anywhere except in recollection.

It will be objected that even those whose faith in technics is strongest are bound to admit that there exist enormous realms which are outside man's control. But what matters is the spirit in which this admission is made. We have to recognise that we have no control over meteorological conditions, but the question is: do we consider it desirable and just that we should have such control? The more the sense of the ontological tends to disappear, the more unlimited become the claims of the mind which has lost it to a kind of cosmic governance, because it is less and less capable of examining its own credentials to the exercise of such dominion.

It must be added that the more the disproportion grows between the claims of the technical intelligence on the one hand, and the persisting fragility and precariousness of what remains its material substratum on the other, the more acute becomes the constant danger of despair which threatens this intelligence. From this standpoint there is truly an intimate dialectical correlation between the optimism of technical progress and the philosophy of despair which seems inevitably to emerge from it—it is needless to insist on the examples offered by the world of to-day.

It will perhaps be said: This optimism of technical progress is animated by great hope. How is hope in this sense to be reconciled with the ontological interpretation of hope?

I believe it must be answered that, *speaking metaphysically, the only genuine hope is hope in what does not depend on ourselves,* hope springing from humility and not from pride. This brings us to the consideration of another aspect of the mystery—a mystery which, in the last analysis, is one and unique—on which I am endeavouring to throw some light.

The metaphysical problem of pride—*hubris*—which was perceived by the Greeks and which has been one of the essential themes of Christian theology, seems to me to have been almost completely ignored by modern philosophers other than theologians. It has become a domain reserved for the moralist. Yet from my own standpoint it is an essential—if not the vital—question. It is sufficient to recall Spinoza's definition of *superbia* in his *Ethics* (III, def. XXVIII) to see how far he was from grasping the problem: "Pride is an exaggeratedly good opinion of ourselves which arises from self-love." In reality, this is a definition of vanity. As for pride, it consists in drawing one's strength solely from oneself. The proud man is cut off from a certain form of communion with his fellow men, which pride, acting as a principle of destruction, tends to break down. Indeed, this destructiveness can be equally well directed against the self; pride is in no way incompatible with self-hate; this is what Spinoza does not seem to have perceived.

An important objection may be raised at the point we have now reached.

It will perhaps be said: Is not that which you are justifying ontologically in reality a kind of moral quietism which is satisfied by passive acceptance, resignation and inert hope? But what, then, becomes of man as man, as active being? Are we to condemn action itself inasmuch as it implies a self-confidence which is akin to pride? Can it be that action itself is a kind of degradation?

This objection implies a series of misunderstandings.

To begin with, the idea of inert hope seems to me a contradiction in terms. Hope is not a kind of listless waiting; it underpins action or it runs before it, but it becomes degraded and lost once the action is spent. Hope seems to me, as it were, the prolongation into the unknown of an activity which is central—that is to say, rooted in being. Hence it has affinities, not with desire, but with the will. The will implies the same refusal to calculate possibilities, or at any rate it suspends this calculation. Could not hope therefore be defined as the will when it is made to bear on what does not depend on itself?

The experimental proof of this connection is that it is the most active saints who carry hope to its highest degree; this would be inconceivable if hope were simply an inactive state of the soul. The mistake so often made here comes from a stoical representation of the will as a stiffening of the soul, whereas it is on the contrary relaxation and creation.

The term "creation," which occurs here for the first time, is, nevertheless, decisive. Where there is creation there can be no degradation, and to the extent that technics are creative, or imply creativity, they are not degrading in any way. Degradation begins at the point where creativeness falls into self-imitation and self-hypnotism, stiffening and falling back on itself. This may, indeed, bring out the origin of the confusion which I denounced in the context of recollection.

Great is the temptation to confuse two distinct movements of the soul, whose opposition is blurred by the use of spacial metaphors. The stiffening, the contraction, the falling back on the self which are inseparable from pride, and which are indeed its symbol, must not be confused with the humble withdrawal which befits recollection and whereby I renew my contact with the ontological basis of my being.

There is every reason to think that such withdrawal in recollection is a presupposition of aesthetic creativity itself. Artistic creation, like scientific research, excludes the act of self-centring and self-hypnotism which is, ontologically speaking, pure negation.

It may perhaps seem that my thesis comes so near to that of Bergson as to coincide with it, but I do not think that this is the case. The terms almost invariably used by Bergson suggest that for him the essential character of creativity lay in its inventiveness, in its spontaneous innovation. But I wonder if by limiting our attention to this aspect of creation we do not lose sight of its ultimate significance, which is its deep-rootedness in being. It is at this point that I would bring in the notion of *creative fidelity;* it is a notion which is the more difficult to grasp and, above all, to define conceptually, because of its underlying and unfathomable paradox, and because it is at the very centre of the realm of the metaproblematical.

It is important to note that the idea of fidelity seems difficult to maintain in the context of Bergsonian metaphysics, because it will tend to be interpreted as a routine, as an observance in the pejorative sense of the word, as an arbitrary safeguard *against* the power of renewal which is the spirit itself.

I am inclined to think that there is something in this neglect of the values of fidelity which deeply vitiates the notion of static religion as it is put forward in *Les Deux Sources de la Morale et de la Religion.* It may perhaps be useful to devote some thought to creative fidelity in order to elucidate this point.

Faithfulness is, in reality, the exact opposite of inert conformism. It is the active recognition of something permanent, not formally, after the manner of a law, but ontologically; in this sense, it refers invariably to a presence, or to something which can be maintained within us and before us as a presence, but which, *ipso facto,* can be just as well ignored, forgotten and obliterated; and this reminds us of that menace of betrayal which, to my mind, overshadows our whole world.

It may perhaps be objected that we commonly speak of fidelity to a principle. But it remains to be seen if this is not an arbitrary transposition of the notion of fidelity. A principle, in so far as it is a mere abstract affirmation, can make no demands upon me because it owes the whole of its reality to the act whereby I sanction it or proclaim it. Fidelity to a principle as a principle is idolatry in the etymological sense of the word; it might be a sacred duty for me to deny a principle from which life has withdrawn and which I know that I no longer accept, for by continuing to conform my actions to it, it is myself—myself as presence—that I betray.

So little is fidelity akin to the inertia of conformism that it implies an active and continuous struggle against the forces of interior dissipation, as also against the sclerosis of habit. I may be told: This is nevertheless no more than a sort of active conservation which is the opposite of creation. We must, I think, go much further into the nature of fidelity and of presence before we can reply to this point.

If presence were merely an *idea* in us whose characteristic was that it was nothing more than itself, then indeed the most we could hope would be to maintain this idea in us or before us, as one keeps a photograph on a mantelpiece or in a cupboard. But it is of the nature of presence as presence to be uncircumscribed; and this takes us once again beyond the frontier of the problematical. Presence is mystery in the exact measure in which it is presence. Now fidelity is the active perpetuation of presence, the renewal of its benefits—of its virtue which consists in a mysterious incitement to create. Here again we may be helped by the consideration of aesthetic creativeness; for if artistic creation is conceivable, it can only be on condition that the world is present to the artist in a certain way—present to his heart and to his mind, present to his very being.

Thus if creative fideltiy is conceivable, it is because fidelity is ontological in its principle, because it prolongs presence which itself corresponds to a certain kind of hold which being has upon us; because it multiplies and deepens the effect of this presence almost unfathomably in our lives. This seems to me to have almost inexhaustible consequences, if only for the relationships between the living and the dead.

I must insist once again: A presence to which we are faithful is not at all the same thing as the carefully preserved effigy of an object which has vanished; an effigy is, when all is said and done, nothing but a likeness; metaphysically it is *less* than the object, it is a diminution of the object. Whereas presence, on the contrary, is *more* than the object, it exceeds the object on every side. We are here at the opening of a vista at whose term death will appear as the *test of presence.* This is an essential point and we must consider it carefully.

It will no doubt be said: What a strange way of defining death! Death *is* a phenomenon definable in biological terms; it *is not* a test.

It must be answered: It is what it signifies and, moreover, what it signifies to a being who rises to the highest spiritual level to which it is possible for us to attain. It is evident that if I read in the newspaper of the death of Mr. So-and-so, who is for me nothing but a name, this event *is* for me nothing more than the subject of an announcement. But it is quite another thing in the case of a being who has been granted to me as a presence. In this case, everything depends on me, on my inward attitude of maintaining this presence which could be debased into an effigy.

It will be objected: This is nothing more than a description in recondite and unnecessarily metaphysical terms of a common psychological fact. It is evident that it depends upon us in a certain measure to enable the dead to survive in our memory, but this existence is no more than subjective.

I believe that the truth is altogether different and infinitely more mysterious. In saying, "It depends upon us that the dead should live on in our memory," we are still thinking of the idea in terms of a diminution or an effigy. We admit that the object has disappeared, but that there remains a likeness which it is in our power to keep, as a daily woman "keeps" a flat or a set of furniture. It is all too evident that this manner of keeping can have no ontological value whatsoever. But it is altogether different in the case where fidelity is creative in the sense which I have tried to define. A presence is a reality; it is a kind of influx; it depends upon us to be permeable to this influx, but not, to tell the truth, to call it forth. Creative fidelity consists in maintaining ourselves actively in a permeable state; and there is a mysterious interchange between this free act and the gift granted in response to it.

An objection which is the converse of the preceding one may be expected at this point. I will be told: "All right. You have now ceased to decorate a psychological platitude with metaphysical ornaments, but only to make a gratuitous assertion which is unproved and which is beyond all possible experimental proof; this was inevitable as soon as you replaced the ambiguous and neutral term 'presence' by the much more compromising term 'influx.'"

To reply to this objection, we must refer again to what I have already said of mystery and of recollection. Indeed, it is only on the meta-problematical level that the notion of influx can possibly be accepted. If it were taken in its objective sense, as an accretion of strength, we would indeed be faced with a thesis, not of metaphysics, but of physics, which would be open to every possible objection. When I say that a being is granted to me as a presence or as a being (it comes to the same, for he is not a being for me unless he is a presence), this means that I am unable to treat him as if he were merely placed in front of me; between him and me there arises a relationship which, in a sense, surpasses my awareness of him; he is not only before me, he is also within me—or, rather, these categories are transcended, they have no longer any meaning. The word influx conveys, though in a manner which is far too physical and spacial, the kind of interior accretion, of accretion from within, which comes into being as soon as presence is effective. Great and almost invincible is the temptation to think that such effective presence can be only that of an object; but if we believed this we would fall back to the level of the problematical and remain on the hither-side of mystery; and against this belief fidelity raises up its voice: "Even if I cannot see you, if I cannot touch you, I feel that you are with me; it would be a denial of you not to be assured of this." *With* me: note the metaphysical value of this word, so rarely recognised by philosophers, which corresponds neither to a relationship of inherence or immanence nor to a relationship of exteriority. It is of the essence of genuine *coesse*—I must use the Latin word—that is to say, of genuine intimacy, to lend itself to the decomposition to which it is subjected by critical thought; but we already know that there exists another kind of thought, a thought which bears upon that thought itself, and is related to a bottled up yet efficacious underlying intuition, of which it suffers the attraction.

It must be added (and this brings us to the verge of another sphere) that the value of such intimacy, particularly in regard to the relation between the living and the dead, will be the higher and the more assured the more this intimacy is grounded in the realm of total spiritual availability *(disponibilité)*—that is to say, of pure charity; and I shall note in passing that an ascending dialectic of creative fidelity corresponds to the dialectic of hope to which I have already referred.

The notion of availability is no less important for our subject than that of presence, with which it is bound up.

It is an undeniable fact, though it is hard to describe in intelligible terms, that there are some people who reveal themselves as "present"—that is to say, at our disposal—when we are in pain or in need to confide in someone, while there are other people who do not give us this feeling, however great is their goodwill. It should be noted at once that the distinction between presence and absence is not at all the same as that between attention and distraction. The most attentive and the most conscientious listener may give me the impression of not being present; he gives me nothing, he cannot make room for me in himself, whatever the material favours which he is prepared to grant me. The truth is that there is a way of listening which is a way of refusing, of refusing *oneself;* the material gift, the visible action, do not necessarily witness to presence. We must not speak of proof in this connection; the word would be out of place. Presence is something which reveals itself immediately and unmistakably in a look, a smile, an intonation or a handshake.

It will perhaps make it clearer if I say that the person who is at my disposal is the one who is capable of being with me with the whole of himself when I am in need; while the one who is not at my disposal seems merely to offer me a temporary loan raised on his resources. For the one I am a presence; for the other I am an object. Presence involves a reciprocity which is excluded from any relation of subject to object or of subject to subject-object. A concrete analysis of unavailability *(indisponibilité)* is no less necessary for our purpose than that of betrayal, denial or despair.

Unavailability is invariably rooted in some measure of alienation. Say, for instance, that I am told of some misfortune with which I am asked to sympathise: I understand what I am told: I admit in theory that the sufferers deserve my sympathy; I see that it is a case where it would be logical and just for me to respond with sympathy; I even offer my sympathy, but only with my mind; because, when all is said and done, I am obliged to admit that I feel absolutely nothing. Indeed, I am sorry that this should be so; the contradiction between the indifference which I feel in fact and the sympathy which I know I ought to feel is humiliating and annoying; it diminishes me in my own eyes. But it is no use; what remains in me is the rather embarrassing awareness that, after all, these are people I do not know—if one had to be touched by every human misfortune life would not be possible, it would indeed be too short. The moment I think: After all, this is only a case, No. 75,627, it is no good, I can feel nothing.

But the characteristic of the soul which is present and at the disposal of others is that it cannot think in terms of *cases;* in its eyes there are *no cases at all.*

And yet it is clear that the normal development of a human being implies an increasingly precise and, as it were, automatic division between what concerns him and what does not, between things for which he is responsible and those for which he is not. Each one of us becomes the centre of a sort of mental space arranged in concentric zones of decreasing interest and participation. It is as though each one of us secreted a kind of shell which gradually hardened and imprisoned him; and this sclerosis is bound up with the hardening of the categories in accordance with which we conceive and evaluate the world.

Fortunately, it can happen to anyone to make an encounter which breaks down the framework of this egocentric topography; I know by my own experience how, from a stranger met by chance, there may come an irresistible appeal which overturns the habitual perspectives just as a gust of wind might tumble down the panels of a stage set— what had seemed near becomes infinitely remote and what had seemed distant seems to be close. Such cracks are repaired almost at once. But it is an experience which leaves us with a bitter taste, an impression of sadness and almost of anguish; yet I think it is beneficial, for it shows us as in a flash all that is contingent and—yes—artificial in the crystallised pattern of our personal system.

But it is, above all, the sanctity realised in certain beings which reveals to us that what we call the normal order is, from a higher point of view, from the standpoint of a soul rooted in ontological mystery, merely the subversion of an order which is its opposite. In this connection, the study of sanctity with all its concrete attributes seems to me to offer an immense speculative value; indeed, I am not far from saying that it is the true introduction to ontology.

Once again a comparison with the soul which is not at the disposal of others will throw light on our subject.

To be incapable of presence is to be in some manner not only occupied but encumbered with one's own self. I have said in some manner; the immediate object of the preoccupation may be one of any number; I may be preoccupied with my health, my fortune, or even with *my inward perfection.* This shows that to be occupied with oneself is not so much to be occupied with *a particular object* as to be occupied in a *particular manner.* It must be noted that the contrary of this state is not a state of emptiness or indifference. The real contrast is rather between the being who is opaque and the being who is transparent. But this inward opacity remains to be analysed. I believe that it consists in a kind of obduracy or fixation; and I wonder if, by generalising and adapting certain psychoanalytical data, we would not find that it is the fixation in a given zone or in a given key of a certain disquiet which, in itself, is something quite different. But what is remarkable is that the disquiet persists within this fixation and gives it that character of constriction which I mentioned in connection with the degradation of the will. There is every reason to believe that this indefinite disquiet should be identified with the anguish of temporality and with that aspiration of man not towards, but *by* death, which is at the heart of pessimism.

Pessimism is rooted in the same soil as the inability to be at the disposal of others. If the latter grows in us as we grow old, it is only too often because, as we draw near to what we regard as the term of our life, anxiety grows in us almost to the point of choking us; to protect itself, it sets up an increasingly heavy, exacting and, I would add, vulnerable mechanism of self-defence. The capacity to hope diminishes in proportion as the soul becomes increasingly chained to its experience and to the categories which arise from it, and as it is given over more completely and more desperately to the world of the problematical.

Here at last can be brought together the various motifs and thematic elements which I have had to bring out one by one. In contrast to the captive soul we have described, the soul which is at the disposal of others is consecrated and inwardly dedicated; it is protected against suicide and despair, which are interrelated and alike, because it knows that it is not its own, and that the most legitimate use it can make of its freedom is precisely to recognise that it does not belong to itself; this recognition is the starting point of its activity and creativeness.

The difficulties of a philosophy of this sort must not be disguised. It is inevitably faced by a disquietening alternative: Either it will try to solve these difficulties—to give all the answers; in that case it will fall into the excesses of a dogmatism which ignores its vital principles and, I would add, into those of a sacrilegious theodicy, or else it will allow these difficulties to subsist, labelling them as mysteries.

Between these two I believe that there exists a middle way—a narrow, difficult and dangerous path which I have tried to discover. But, like Carl Jaspers in his Philosophy of Existence, I can only proceed in this kind of country by calling out to other travellers. If, as it occasionally happened, certain minds respond—not the generality, but this being and that other—then there is a way. But, as I believe Plato perceived with incomparable clarity, it is a way which is undiscoverable except through love, to which alone it is visible, and this brings us to what is perhaps the deepest characteristic of that realm of the metaproblematical of which I have tried to explore certain regions.

A serious objection remains to be mentioned. It will perhaps be said: All that you have said implies an unformulated reference to the data of Christianity and can only be understood in the light of these data. Thus we understand what you mean by presence if we think of the Eucharist and what you mean by creative fidelity if we think of the Church. But what can be the value of such a philosophy for those who are a-Christian—for those who ignore Christianity or who do not accept it? I would answer: it is quite possible that the existence of the fundamental Christian data may be necessary *in fact* to enable the mind to conceive some of the notions which I have attempted to analyse; but these notions cannot be said to depend on the data of Christianity, and *they do not presuppose it.* On the other hand, should I be told that the intellect must leave out of a count anything which is not a universal data of thinking as such, I would say that this claim is exaggerated and in the last analysis, illusory. Now, as at any other time, the philosopher is placed in a given historical situation from which he is most unlikely to abstract himself completely; he would deceive himself if he thought that he could create a complete void both within and around himself. Now this historical situation implies as one of its essential data the existence of the Christian fact—quite independently of whether the Christian religion is accepted and its fundamental assertions are regarded as true or false. What appears to me evident is that we cannot reason to-day as though there were not behind us centuries of Christianity, just as, in the domain of the theory of knowledge, we cannot pretend that there have not been centuries of positive science. But neither the existence of Christianity nor that of positive science plays in this connection more than the role of a fertilising principle. It favours the development of certain ideas which we might not have conceived without it. This development may take place in what I would call para-Christian zones; for myself, I have experienced it more than twenty years before I had the remotest thought of becoming a Catholic.

Speaking more particularly to Catholics, I should like to note that from my own standpoint the distinction between the natural and the supernatural must be rigorously maintained. It will perhaps be objected that there is a danger that the word "mystery" might confuse this very issue.

I would reply that there is no question of confusing those mysteries which are enveloped in human experience as such with those mysteries which are revealed, such as the Incarnation or Redemption, and to which no effort of thought bearing on experience can enable us to attain.

It will be asked: why then do you use the same word for two such distinct notions? But I would point out that no revelation is, after all, conceivable unless it is addressed to a being who is *involved—committed*—in the sense which I have tried to define—that is to say, to a being who participates in a reality which is non-problematical and which provides him with his foundation as subject. Supernatural life *must,* when all is said and done, find a hold in the natural—which is not to say that it is the flowering of the natural. On the contrary it seems to me that any study of the notion of *created Nature,* which is fundamental for the Christian, leads to the conclusion that there is in the depth of Nature, as of reason which is governed by it, a fundamental principle of inadequacy to itself which is, as it were, a restless anticipation of a different order.

To sum up my position on this difficult and important point, I would say that the recognition of the ontological mystery, in which I perceive as it were the central redoubt of metaphysics, is, no doubt, only possible through a sort of radiation which proceeds from revelation itself and which is perfectly well able to affect souls who are strangers to all positive religion of whatever kind; that this recognition, which takes place through certain higher modes of human experience, in no way involves the adherence to any given religion; but it enables those who have attained to it to perceive the possibility of a revelation in a way which is not open to those who have never ventured beyond the frontiers of the realm of the problematical and who have therefore never reached the point from which the mystery of being can be seen and recognised. Thus a philosophy of this sort is carried by an irresistible movement towards the light which it perceives from afar and of which it suffers the secret attraction.